BIOGRAPHY OF
RAJA RAM MOHAN ROY

D.C. Vyas

CYBER TECH PUBLICATIONS
4264/3, Ansari Road, Daryaganj, New Delhi-110002 (India)
Ph.: 011-23244078, 011-43559448 Fax: 011-23280028
E-Mail: cyberpublicationsdelhi@yahoo.com
Website: www.cybertechpublications.com

BIOGRAPHY OF RAJA RAM MOHAN ROY

D.C. Vyas

First Edition 2010

Published by :

G.S. Rawat for **Cyber Tech Publications**
4264/3, Ansari Road, Daryaganj, New Delhi-110002 (India)
Ph.: 011-23244078, 011-43559448 Fax: 011-23280028
E-Mail: cyberpublicationsdelhi@yahoo.com
Website: www.cybertechpublications.com

Printed at: Asian Offset Printers, Delhi-53

Preface

Raja Ram Mohan Roy was born on May 22, 1772 in village Radhanagar in the District of Murshidabad in Bengal. His father Ramkanto Roy, was a Vaishnavite, while his mother, Tarini, was from a Shakta background. Raja Ram Mohun Roy was sent to Patna for higher studies. By the age of fifteen, Raja Rammohun Roy had learnt Bangla, Persian, Arabic and Sanskrit. Raja Ram Mohan Roy was against idol worship and orthodox Hindu rituals. He stood firmly against all sort of social bigotry, conservatism and superstitions. But his father was an orthodox Hindu Brahmin. This led to differences between Raja Ram Mohan Roy and his father. Following differences he left the house. He wandered around Himalayas and went to Tibet. He traveled widely before returning home. After his return Raja Ram Mohan Roy's family married him in the hope that he would change. But this did not have any effect on him. Raja Ram Mohan Roy went to Varanasi and studied the Vedas, the Upanishads and Hindu philosophy deeply. When his father died in 1803 he returned to Murshidabad. He then worked as a moneylender in Calcutta, and from 1809 to 1814, he served in the Revenue Department of the East India Company.

In 1814, Raja Ram Mohan Roy formed Atmiya Sabha. Atmiya Sabha tried to initiate social and religious reforms in the society. Raja Ram Mohan Roy campaigned for rights for women, including the right for widows to remarry, and the right for women to hold property. He actively opposed Sati system and the practice of polygamy. He also supported education, particularly education of women. He believed that English-language education was superior to the traditional Indian education system, and he opposed the use of government funds to support schools teaching Sanskrit. In 1822, he founded a school based on English education. In 1828, Raja Ram Mohan Roy founded the 'Brahma Samaj'. Through 'Brahma Samaj, he wanted to expose the religious hypocrisies and check the growing influence of Christianity on the Hindu society. Raja Ram Mohan Roy's efforts bore fruit when in 1929, the Sati system was abolished. In 1831 Ram Mohan Roy traveled to the United Kingdom as an ambassador of the Mughal emperor to plead for his pension and allowances. Raja Ram Mohan Roy passed away on September 27, 1833 at Stapleton near Bristol due to meningitis. This book is intended to focus on his life and works.

—*Author*

CONTENTS

1

Introduction

Ram Mohan was born in a Brahmin family of *Radhanagar* village in the *Hoogly* district of *West Bengal* on 22nd May 1772 (there's some uncertainty as to the exact date; the epitaph noted the year of birth as 1774). His father Ramakanta Roy's family belonged to the *Vaisnava* (who worship Lord Vishnu-the Preserver; followers of *Sricaitanya Maha Prabhu)* a liberal sect that flourished in Bengal and South India. His mother Tarini Devi's orthodox priestly family (Bhattacharyas of Chatra) on the other hand belonged to the *Shakta* sect (worshippers of Goddess Kali-the Shakti-the Mother Energy of the universe).

In the 16th Century, the Koli-Avatar (Kalyug incarnate of God), Lord Sricaitanya renunciated the caste and proclaimed supremacy of God and universal brotherhood. Followers of this proletariet religion are known as Vaishnavas. Despite being Vaishnav descendants, the Roy family was very conservative. The Shaktas hardly ever see things the same way as the Vaishnavas do; they appear to be even more conservative.

In a 18th century Bengali non-urban family setting, where active religious conflicts were bound to arise between the shakta (maternal side) and vaisnava (paternal side) rituals, it is not hard to imagine that some degree of uncertainty and unease would exist in younger minds as to why there were such apparent differences within the one and the same religion. Ram Mohan too must have been at a loss to not find a real handle on questions as to why there are so many gods and goddesses, why so many sects, why so much confusion and why such a large variety of rites and practices to reach the same goal-attaining Moksha (nirvana).

Ram Mohan learned Bengali and Sanskrit to start with; Ramakanta Roy then sent young Ram Mohan (merely 12 years old at the time) to Patna to learn Persian and Arabic languages at a Islamic institution in the hope that it would assist the young man to secure a better occupation in one of Mughal high offices, even though the British victory at *Battle of Plassey* in 1757 was gradually undermining the foundation of the Mughal empire. The youngman quickly learned these languages and became well-versed in Koranic teachings. The logical organisation of Koran and its monotheistic interpretations-in contrast with the overwhelming breadth and diversity of Hindu literature-appealed to the young mind. The veil of mist lifted from before his eyes. His ever-inquisitive free-thinking mind wanted to know more about other religions and philosophies. He fell out with his parents for leaving home on more than one occasion without their consent. One of these excursions took young Ram Mohan to Tibet where he gained insight into the Buddhist philosophy and religion. His unceasing questions, inquisitions and critical analyses of rational principles from dogmas annoyed his Llama teachers.

His utter disregard for what can be described as the normal *parental expectation* displeased his father no end who finally forced him out of the family home. His unabating criticisms of Hindu rituals, superstitious beliefs on the one hand and open support for monotheistic principles of Koran, Bible and Tripitak, on the other, later (after his father's death) led him to the Court of Law when his mother and sister unsuccessfully tried to disinherit him on grounds of apostasy.

The Man Who Found Unity in God

Ram Mohan moved to Kolkata in 1897 and started a minor lending business to earn a modest living for a while. Shortly before his father's death in 1803 Ram Mohan moved North to Mushidabad with a job with the *East India Company*. In 1805 he published *Tuhfat-ul-Muwahhidin* (A Gift to Monotheism)-written in *Persian* with an introduction in *Arabic* in which he preached *unity of God*. This publication antagonised a section of the muslim community.

In 1809 he was appointed a Reveue Officer in the *Company* and was posted in Rangpur. Here he vigorously continued his Vedic and Tantrik studies and held regular evening discussions with like-minded Hindu, Muslim and Jain friends. During this period he also spent time honing his English language skills with private study and with the help of an English friend (John Digby-Collector of Rangpur). He followed English and European political trends with keen interest and closely absorbed the cause and implications of the French Revolution for India. Later he learnt Greek, Hebrew and Latin to quench his thirst for knowledge of peoples and their religions. He thoroughly mastered the scriptures, doctrines and genesis of the Jewish religion and Christianity.

During the course of his researches into Sanskrit literature Ram Mohan was impressed by the purity of the monotheistic doctrines imbued in the Upanishads, which were in sharp contrast with the decadent idolatrous and superstitous Hindu rituals. In 1815 Roy founded the *Atmiya Sabha* (friendly society) comprising like-minded Indian liberals-like Prince Dwarkanath Tagore, Prasanna Kumar Tagore, Kali Nath and Baikuntha Nath Munshi, Raja Kali Shankar Ghoshal. The Shabha was also frequented by William Carey's missionaries of Serampore who needed his help in translating the New Testament to Bengali. While he was attracted by the monotheistic aspects of Christianity, he seriously questioned the misguided Christian doctrine of Trinity on grounds of idolatry. He criticised that such doctrines are nothing short of direct parrallels of Hindu beliefs and practices. He clashed with other missionary members of the translation team and a vigorous debate followed. Ram Mohan's *The Precepts of Jesus* (1820) was the product of this debate. Roy, with his extensive knowledge and understanding of the Gospels, smashed the claimed supremacy of the holy trinity doctrine with the same arguments and disdains that the missionaries used to criticise Indian idolatrous practices as a load of rubbish. Ram Mohan's doctrine of unity of Godhead was an object of criticism from all corners of the orthodoxy-hysterical Brahmins, fundamental muslims, European missionaries, theocrats and political masters alike. Some at the higher echelons of the missionary churches in England were incensed by comments made in *The Precepts of Jesus* by a *heathen*. Not being able to defend against Roy's watertight logic, they instead patronised and attacked Roy himself. How come a non-believer, a creature who does not possess the mental faculties to comprehend the grand purpose and design of the doctrine of Trinity dare to pass such a callous judgement on their superior faith and their prophet! For fear of retribution from the rulers, friends advised Roy to exercise caution in future. But Roy was determined. He satirised his response in the *Padari Sishya Sambad* (in Bengali 1823).

Ram Mohan's point was crystal clear: one doesn't need a prophet (Jesus) to preserve Christianity. One doesn't need to attribute divinity to Jesus to believe in the Christian God. One doesn't need a son to vouch for the existence of the Father. He argued that Trinity = idolatry. A distinct stream of Christian thinkers, who established the Unitarian Church, needed no convincing.

They found a resourceful ally in Ram Mohan. In August 1828 Ram Mohan inaugurated his *Brahma Sabha*, which formed into a church in 1830 (Church of Brahma). The followers, among whom Debendranath Tagore, Keshab Chandra Sen, Pratap Chandra Mazumdar, Raj Narayan Bose etc. of this rejuvinated Hindu Church, known as the Brahma Samaj, played a major role in reforming and modernising the Indian society.

The Man Who Fought Superstitions

Ram Mohan's attack on the Hindu religious idolatry, rituals, caste system and the criminal 'Suttie'(-daho) system of burning alive of widows in the funeral pyre of their husbands (a practice which has evolved motivated more by petty property greed of the surviving relatives than by the need for spiritual salvation) has been not only a bold and forthright attempt at the reform of Hindu societies, but a death blow to ignorance, superstitions and dogmas of his ancestors. Ram Mohan was aghast with these practices. He witnessed the burning of his own sister-in-law (brother Jogmohun's wife was killed in the suttie practice by his own family and he had no power to stop it). His active movement against these senseless practices dissatisfied in particular the 'upper classes of the society' (the *kulins*)-those who seemed to have benefited the most at the expense of the deprived mass. Each practice of a society always has two parties-the beneficiary and the victim.

While the suttie practice was abolished in 1829 (as a result of Ram Mohan's earnest pleading with and direct assurance to William Bentinck that it is not sanctioned by any Hindu scriptures), similar practices against the less priviledged of the society persist. While the incidences (to a lesser extent, their impact too) are somewhat in decline, India still suffers from the indignation of the remnants of caste discrimination, polygamy, child marriage and ban on widow marriage (still a social stigma-even though allowed under the law since a quarter century after Roy's death); despite Ram Mohan's or Iswarchandra Vidyasagar's active educational drives and moral persuasions of the ignorant mass and the priviledged few. Old habits-the white-anting of the Indian life-die hard. Particularly, if one may benefit from their existence.

Pioneer of Indian Education

Ram Mohan was the first Indian who realised that the only way India can rid itself of ignorance and superstions of the dark ages is by educating its mass by modern European method *i.e.*, by teaching language, science and philosophy.

He knew India had to retain its rich heritage from the past, but she also required the best of modern European thoughts and practices to step into the future. He established a number of schools to popularise the modern system of education. He supported David Hare in his educational drive for native Indians. Roy was instrumental in establishing the Hindu College, which was to be later known as the Presidency College.

Pioneer of Bengali Prose and Indian Press

Roy retired from the Company service in 1814 and published his first book of prose called *Vedantasar* in 1815. A well deserved break with the tradition was established in Bengali prose style. The influence of Sanskrit, Arabic and Persian words was minimised. Ram Mohan, for his time, was a fiercely independent journalist. In 1821 he published his first Bengali Newspaper-Sambad Kaumudi. In a speech in the Kolkata Press Club, the Prime Minister of India, Manmohan Singh, regarded Ram Mohan as "the father of the Indian press and of Bengal renaissance". PM stated that: "He published newspapers in Bengali and Persian languages and remained at the forefront of the struggle for a free press. Raja Ram Mohan Roy brilliantly expounded the importance of the freedom of the press as early as in 1823."

PM quoted from Ram Mohan's own thoughts on freedom of press: "..... a free press has never yet caused a revolution in any part of the world .... whereas, where no freedom of the press existed and grievances consequently remained unrepresented, innumerable revolutions have taken place in all parts of the globe."

He went on to recollect the history: "When restraints were imposed on the press in Calcutta, Raja Ram Mohan Roy submitted a memorandum to the British Government lamenting the decision of the Government. He drew the Government's attention to the useful role of the press in these words:" '........ever since the art of printing has become generally known among the Natives of Calcutta numerous Publications have been circulated in the Bengalee Language which by introducing free discussion among the Natives and inducing them to reflect and inquire after knowledge, have already served greatly to improve their minds and ameliorate their condition'.

In the space of 15 years, from 1815 to 1830, Ram Mohan wrote thirty books in Bengali. According to Soumendranath Tagore, "the excellence that the Bengali prose [later] achieved in literary form under Bankim Chandra and Rabindranath owes its beginning to the

Bengali prose developed by Ram Mohan". The major publications during this period includes the following-not all those mentioned here are in Bengali:

- Vedantasara 1815,
- *Translation of an Abridgment of the Vedant 1816,*
- Ishopanishad 1816,
- Kathopanishad 1817,
- *A Conference between an Advocate for, and an Opponent of the Practice of Burning Widows Alive* (Bengali and English) 1818,
- Munduk Upanishad 1819,
- *A Defence of Hindu Theism 1820,*
- *A Second Defence of the Monotheistical System of the Veds* 1820,
- *A Second Conference,* 1820 (the case for women's rights),
- The Precepts of Jesus-Guide to Peace and Happiness 1820,
- *Sambad Kaumudi*-a Bengali newspaper 1821,
- *Mirat-ul-Akbar*-Persian journal 1822,
- *Padari Sisya Sambad* (Bengali satire) 1823,
- Bengali Grammar 1826,
- Brahmapasona 1828,
- Brahmasangeet 1829 and
- The Universal Religion 1829

Ram Mohan composed a large number of Bengali songs (hymns) called Brahma sangeet that are still popular in Brahma Churches.

Travel to England and France

Ram Mohan was awarded the 'Raja' title by Delhi's titular king. In 1829 he travelled to England to meet the East India Company bosses and the British Parliament. He was received by the local Unitarian ministers with great adulation. He met with King William IV. He went to France in 1833 and was received by King Louise-Phillippe. Incidentally, the French Revolution left a lasting impact on Roy's thought. Back from Paris to Bristol, where Roy lived with a family of local Unitarian Church minister friend, Raja Ram Mohan died on September 27th. 1833. He was buried locally there. A decade later his mortal remains were taken to Arno's Vales cemetery and were buried there with a memorial built by Prince Dwarkanath Tagore.

The Prophet of the New Age

Given the economic, social, religious and political context in which Raja Ram Mohan Roy grew up in India, there is no measuring rod with which one can measure and understand the depth of contribution made by this phenomenal character to his society. Radhakrishnan, a well known academic who became President of India, like so many others, called him the father of modern India.

Rabindranth Tagore in a speech on Ram Mohan Roy Centenary said this in the opening: "Ram Mohan Roy inaugurated the Modern Age in India. He was born at a time when our country having lost its link with the inmost truths of its being, struggled under a crushing load of unreason, in abject slavery to circumstance. In social usage, in politics, in the realm of religion and art, we had entered the zone of uncreative habit, of decadent tradition and ceased to exercise our humanity. In this dark gloom of India's degeneration Ram Mohan rose up, a luminous star in the firmament of India's history, with prophetic purity of vision and unconquerable heroism of soul. He shed radiance all over the land; he rescued us from the penury of self-oblivion. Through the dynamic power of his personality, his uncompromising freedom of the spirit, he vitalized our national being with the urgency of creative endeavour, and launched it into the arduous adventure of realisation. He is the great path-maker of this century who has removed ponderous obstacles that impeded our progress at every step, initiated us into the present Era of world-wide cooperation of humanity."

According to another Indian hero, Netaji Subhash Bose "Raja Ram Mohan Roy therefore stands out against the dawn of the new awakening in India as the prophet of the new age." Raja Ram Mohan Roy has come to be called the 'Maker of Modern India'. Without giving up what was good and noble in the past, he laid the foundations for a great future. He put an end to the horrible custom of burning the living wife with the dead husband. He was a great scholar and an independent thinker. He advocated the study of English, Science, Western Medicine and Technology. He spent his money on a college to promote these studies.

During the 1965 Indo-Pak War, the tiny 'Gnat' manufactured by the 'Hindustan Aeronautics Ltd.' chased away the powerful bombers supplied by the United States of America to Pakistan.

Sri C.V. Raman won the Noble Prize for Physics. Indian scientists, technologists and teachers are working in different parts of the world.

We have the 'Hindustan Machine Tools Ltd.', which manufactures machines which make machines.

When we think of such facts, we feel overjoyed. We feel confident that we shall equal Western nations in the 20th century. But suppose we knew nothing of modern science, medicine and engineering?

How difficult it would be for us to compete with countries like America, Russia, Japan and Germany!

Suppose we had to depend upon foreigners to teach subjects like English, Physics, Chemistry, Biology and Engineering-all subjects, except Samskrita (Sanskrit) and Kannada in our colleges! How much more difficult it would have been for us!

About 150 years ago, only Sanskrit and Persian were taught in our schools. There were very few to tell us anything about Western Science. But even they were in English. And our people did not know English.

It was the great Raja Ram Mohan Roy, who realized that India would be a backward country, if her people did not learn English, Mathematics and Science. He spent his own money and started a college to teach English and Science. That is why he is called the 'Maker of Modern India'. He had a high regard for India and Hinduism and was proud of them.

Birth and Boyhood

It was the last part of the 18th century. Foreigners had invaded India again and again and India has suffered at their hands for centuries. The rule of the Muslims, which had lasted 800 years, was coming to an end. India was filled with poverty and ignorance. The English who came to India for trade gradually conquered kingdoms. Many Indians did not understand their own great religion and culture. There were many castes and creeds. The glorious tradition of Vedic times was like a mirror covered with dust. All round, there was the darkness of ignorance. It was at such a time that Raja Ram Mohan Roy was born.

Radhanagar is a village in the District of Murshidabad in Bengal; Ram Mohan was born in this village on the 22nd of May 1772. His father was Ramakanto Roy, an orthodox Brahmin. Ram Mohan's parents were devoted to God. They had great faith in their religion. They performed strictly the duties set down by their religion.

Ram Mohan was very much devoted to Lord Vishnu. Everyday he would not put down the 'Bhagavantha' without completing the reading of Valmiki Ramayana. But when he came to know that his mother also was fasting, he had his food for her sake. In his 14th year he was about to become a monk. But his mother came in his way.

Education

Persian was the language of the government during the Muslim rule. Knowledge of Arabic and Persian was necessary to get employment or to correspond with the government. Ram Mohan had been educated in Sanskrit, Bengali, Arabic and Persian in his own village. Though Ramakanto was very orthodox, he wanted that his son should have higher education. For this purpose, he sent him to Patna in his ninth year. The boy was very intelligent. He studied Arabic and Persian under famous Muslim scholars in Patna. Aristotle and Euclid were two great thinkers who lived in Greece, hundreds of years ago. Ram Mohan read their works in Arabic. By studying their books, Ram Mohan developed the ability to think for himself.

Many people in India who believed in God worshipped pictures and idols of God. Ram Mohan wondered if God hand any form. He was not interested in idol-worship and in festivals at home. He opposed idol-worship. But his father, who was a very firm believer in idol-worship, felt he was doing wrong. He advised him. The son did not change his mind. Owing to differences between Ram Mohan and his parents, he left the house.

Travels

Ram Mohan was sensible, though young. The boy who left his house did not wander aimlessly. He joined a group of monks. They wandered about the foot of the Himalayas, and went to Tibet. The Tibetans were Buddhists. They used to worship their teacher. Ram Mohan understood the principles of Buddhism. He condemned the worship of the teacher. He condemned the worship of the teacher. Therefore, the teacher and his disciples grew angry. There was even a plot to kill this bold boy. But the women there took pity on him and saved his life. They cleverly managed to send him back to India.

Sanskrit Education

The parents lovingly received their son who had gone away. But even now, the father and son could not agree on many matters. Ramakanto celebrated his son's marriage, hoping that he would change. But the son did not change. Ram Mohan went to Benaras and studied the Vedas, the Upanishads and Hindu philosophy deeply. When his father died in 1803 he returned to Murshidabad.

Ram Mohan and Religion

His differences with his father regarding idol-worship and the manner in which he conducted himself in Tibet show clearly one thing. Ram Mohan was a man who thought for him. In the Vedas and the Upanishads we see great freedom of thought. Ram Mohan admired this spirit of freedom. He proclaimed that simple living and high thinking should be a man's motto in life. And he lived accordingly. Once a man brought a conch for sale. He wanted a price of Rs 500. He said: "This conch can give anything a man wants. He can get all prosperity by possessing it." Kalinath, a friend of Ram Mohan, wanted to by it. He asked Ram Mohan for his opinion. Ram Mohan laughed and said, "If this conch can give all the wealth of the world, it must be Goddess Lakshmi herself. I can't understand why this poor fellow wishes to sell Goddess Lakshmi!" As soon as the man heard this, he disappeared.

At Rangpur

Ram Mohan joined service in the Revenue Department of the East India Company. He was an assistant to Mr. John Digby, an English officer, from 1809-14 at Rangpur. Digby appreciated his efficiency. Though he held a high post on a and some salary and had property in his village, he did not seek a life of luxury.

Ram Mohan was six feet tall. He had a well-built body and a handsome and bright face. He was a highly cultured man. He had an exceptional personality.

Ram Mohan began the study of English in his 22nd year. He used to read books. He also used to read English newspapers received by Digby from England. Therefore, he knew much that many Indians knew nothing about. He knew about the French Revolution (1789 to 1795) which had just then ended. He saw that the stock of knowledge was growing rapidly in Europe. He knew what the people and the Scholars of Europe felt about the ideals of Liberty, Equality and Democracy. Digby used to have visitors from several foreign countries. Ram Mohan mixed with them freely and learnt how to converse fluently and how to write good English. He developed an elegant and forceful English style.

Ram Mohan loved knowledge. How much knowledge he amassed! With the help of Jain scholars, he studied books on Jainism. From Muslim scholars, he learnt Sufism. He was already well versed in the Vedas. He used to arrange meetings of learned men in his house and exchange ideas. This widened his knowledge.

Ram Mohan spent his leisure in learning new subjects and doing social service. He translated the Upanishads and other sacred books into English and Bengali and got them printed. He wished to go abroad and learn more. But his own relatives filed a suit in the court. This came in the way of his visit to other countries. Digby, who had gained the confidence of Ram Mohan, returned to England in 1814. Ram Mohan returned to England in 1814. Ram Mohan resigned his post and settled in Calcutta. He devoted the rest of his life to public service. That India should prosper was Ram Mohan's ardent desire. But the people had to be cured of ignorance, they needed education. He dedicated himself to this task.

A mighty task calls for earnest mighty preparation, does it not? Ram Mohan prepared himself in every way to undertake this big task. He had understood the essence of all religious books. He had first to remove the dirt of superstitions and bad customs, which had dimmed the brightness of Indian culture. Then he had to learn how the educational system had developed in other countries, the ways of life there and what efforts were made to put an end to poverty. What was good in other countries had to be learnt and to be followed here. In this way Ram Mohan began the work of reformation.

But he did not believe that all old customs in India should be given up and that Indians should blindly imitate the foreigners. He did not condemn all the religious customs; but he said that they should use their discretion in following them. Many times people do wrong things without knowing what has been said in the scriptures. They can read these holy books if they are available in the language of the people. When other people say 'This is what the scriptures say, that is what the scriptures say', people can find out for themselves what these books say. The holy books of the Hindus were in Sanskrit. Ram Mohan translated them into Bengali. In his preface, he said, 'We should understand correctly what is said in our religious books and what is relevant to our times.' Ram Mohan was a firm believer in truth. He would admit his faults. He used to quote the words of Vashishta: Words of wisdom should be accepted even if they come from a child; but even if Lord Brahma utters unwise words, they should be ignored as a blade of straw

'Atmiya Sabha'

The marriage of girls five or six years old. Burning the wife with her dead husband whether she is willing or not. Meaningless observance of festivals and worshipping for show. The worship of several gods and ranking gods as high and low. Ram Mohan was sick of these practices. He had a high regard for Hinduism. But he felt that the Hindus had yet to understand their religion correctly. There should be equality between men and women. People should give up superstitious beliefs. Many of Ram Mohan's friends accepted his line of thinking. An association of such close friends was formed. It was called 'Atmiya Sabha' (The Society of Friends). Religious discussion took place there. The members had to give up idol-worship. They had to spread the Society's views on religion among the people. Many scholars opposed Ram Mohan. Ram Mohan wrote articles in reply. The people read them and understood what was said in the sacred books

Regard for Hinduism

Some Christian priests were overjoyed at Ram Mohan's interest in and enthusiasm for Christian doctrines. They suggested that he should become a Christian. These priests did not understand the mind of Ram Mohan, who was a staunch believer in Hinduism. He had great respect for the Vedas and the Upanishads, which he had studied deeply. Some men spoke lightly of the Vedas and the Upanishads. Ram Mohan gave them a very clear answer: "There is only one God in the universe. He has no form and qualities, which men can describe. He is full of joy. Every living being has an element of God. These noble ideas sparkle in the Upanishads. Moreover, these books encourage people to think for themselves, they strike out new paths. They do not chain man's intelligence." Just as he condemned the bad customs of the Hindus he condemned the superstitions of the followers of other religions.

Education for the Progress of the County

If we are to be happy we must have good crops. For this purpose, we must learn how to use good manure and machinery.

We must build dams and dig canals. We must have good roads, bridges, hospitals and factories to manufacture medicines. Thus, the list of the 'musts' is very long. To fulfil all our needs, we need education, don't we? We need persons well versed in the Arts and the Sciences. We should learn how knowledge is expanding in foreign countries.

Today, if a county is to prosper, it is not enough if it merely recalls its ancient history and culture. Without forgetting them, the country should develop the knowledge and strength suited to the world of today. Of course, there were schools in Ram Mohan's age also. But they used to teach Arabic and Persian needed for the work of the government. There are people who use languages like Bengali, Marati, Kannada and Telugu, aren't there? These languages also should grow. There was no scope for this. The methods of teaching were also old-fashioned. Much emphasis was laid upon memorization. If children did not memorize, they were punished cruelly. The subjects taught in the schools were very few. Mathematics, History, Geography, Physics and Botany were not at all taught. Some people were running English Schools. Even there, the System of education was not satisfactory. English words were taught to children. Those who had memorized them felt proud that they had learnt much.

Ram Mohan came to Calcutta in 1815. He formed an association of English and Hindu scholars. He started a college also and arranged for the teaching of modern subjects like Science, Political Science, Mathematics, and English. One of the members of the association was rich and educated man called Radhakanto Dev. He had some followers from the beginning. He did not like Ram Mohan. He obstinately said that he would not help the association, if Ram Mohan were a member. To Ram Mohan, the prosperity of the association was more important than his status. So, he did not become a member of the association, though he himself had started it. During 1816-17, Ram Mohan started an English College with his own money. Today it is difficult even to believe that he spent so much money for the spread of education. He understood the condition of the country; he saw that the students should learn the

English language and scientific subjects. But in his college, besides Sanskrit also were taught.

Ram Mohan criticized the government's policy of opening only Sanskrit schools. 'Because of this, Indians would have no contact with Western civilization. They would lag behind without studying modern subjects like Mathematics, Geography and Latin were held in high esteem in Europe. But, are the students in England learning only Latin, Greek and the Bible? If Science and Mathematics are necessary for us?' He argued that the government should examine this point. Government accepted this idea of Ram Mohan and implemented it after his death.

Service to Literature

Ram Mohan was the first to give importance to the development of the mother tongue. His 'Gaudiya Vyakaran' in Bengali is the best of his prose works. His Bengali was terse, simple and elegant. By translating the scriptures of the Hindus into Bengali he gave Bengali a new dignity. Rabindranath Tagore and Bankimchandra followed in his footsteps. Ram Mohan wrote lyrics also.

With the Poor

When Ram Mohan was in Calcutta, he used to go for walks all alone at night. He wished to find out for himself the difficulties of the poor. It was very cold in a slum. Mosquitoes swarmed. People were sweating profusely. There was stinking smell from the dirt all around. Dirty water was flowing near by. The labourers were returning home after the day's work.

A man was following them.

"Brothers!" he said.

The labourers turned back in wonder.

"How many people live here?" he continued. The wonder of the labourers increased.

Who was this man? Why had he come there? "How much do you work in the days" How many families are here?" So question followed question. The labourers said, "Why does he want to know all these things? He may be mad. He may be an idle fool." They said to Ram Mohan, "Have we nothing else to do? Let us go home."

Ram Mohan bore their mockery and contempt. He followed them. He found out much about their way of life.

'Suttee System' Or 'Sahagamana'

Ram Mohan's brother Jagmohan died. His wife Alakamanjari had to observe 'Sahagamana' (that is, she was to be burnt alive with the dead body). All arrangements were made for cremation. All the relatives gathered. Alakamanjari put on a laced-sari and there was 'Kumkum' on her forehead. (A mark of Kumkum' or vermilion on the forehead is considered sacred by a Hindu wife; it is an indication that her husband is alive.) Her hair was dishevelled. Fear was written upon her face. The corpse was brought to the cremation ground. Ram Mohan begged his sister-in-law not to observe 'Suttee'. Relatives objected to Ram Mohan's words. They bound her to the corpse and placed her on the funeral pyre with the corpse. The pyre was set on fire.

Alakamanjari screamed and cried in fear, but she was not set free. Poor woman! She was burnt to ashes along with her husband. All the relatives praised her shouting 'Maha Sati! Maha Sati!' (a great wife) and went back.

This heart-rending sight of his sister-in-law's 'Suttee' made a deep impression on Ram Mohan's mind. Then and there he took a vow to put an end to this dreadful. Custom. Some people believed that the scriptures said that the wife should die along with her husband. Ram Mohan referred to all the sacred books. But, nowhere was it laid down that the wife should perform 'Suttee'. This custom had come into practice in some age. Some people who knew it was wrong did not have the courage to condiment. The brave Ram Mohan took up this difficult task.

But his task was not easy. Lakhs of people had faith in Suttee system. Many people opposed Ram Mohan and abused him. Some even tried to murder him. But Ram Mohan did not flinch. Even the people of the West, who saw all this wondered, when even the government was afraid to interfere in this matter, Ram Mohan risked his life and fought against this evil practice. In the end, he won and the government made 'Suttee' a crime. Along with fight for the abolition of 'Suttee', Ram Mohan started a revolution for women's education and women's right to property. He showed that woman enjoyed equal freedom with man according to Hinduism.

Love of Independence

Ram Mohan was an exceptional patriot and lover of freedom. 'I do not think I shall be fortunate enough to see freedom reign supreme all over the world', so he used to lament. Like Tilak, Ram Mohan believed that Liberty was every man's birthright.

Ram Mohan was intensely patriotic, but he was generous and broad-minded. In 1823, the Spanish colonies in South America became independent. He invited his friends to a party to celebrate this joyous event. A friend of his asked him, "Why are you so elated if people in South America become independent?" Ram Mohan said, "What! They may be in South America, but are they not our brothers? Their language and religion may be different. Should we not sympathize with them in their troubles?"

Have you Heard of 'The League of Nations'?

The First World War was fought from 1914 to 1918. The object of starting the League of Nations in 1920 was to see that another such war did not break out. Any dispute was to be settled by peaceful methods. (As this did not function effectively, the United Nations Organization was set up in 1945.)

A hundred years before the League of Nations was started, Ram Mohan had said that such an organization was necessary. If there is difference of opinion. If there is difference of opinion between two persons, they do not fight; they go to a court and accept its decision. If there is difference of opinion between two countries, their dispute must be settled without a fight. An organization is necessary to see that all nations cooperate with and help each other

The First Editor

As soon as we get up in the morning, we eagerly wait for the newspaper. No sooner is the paper delivered than every one wants to read it.

Times were when the number of newspapers was very small. And even those few were in English. There was not a single newspaper in any Indian language!

It was Ram Mohan Roy who first published a newspaper in an Indian language.

Newspapers are absolutely necessary to reform the people. It is possible to make thousands of people understand many things in their own language. Ram Mohan made the newspaper the means of bringing home his views to many people.

'Atmiya Sabha' used to publish a weekly called 'Vangal Gazette'. Besides, Ram Mohan was himself bringing out a newspaper in Persian called 'Miratul-Akhbar' (the Mirror of News) and a Bengali weekly called 'Sambad Kaumudi' (the Moon of Intelligence).

In those days, items of news and articles had to be approved by the government before being published. So, there was no freedom of the press.

Ram Mohan protested against this control. He argued that newspapers should be free and that the truth should not be suppressed simply because the government did not like it. Newspapers should have the right to uphold the truth. It needed much courage to speak out like this 150 years ago, when India was under the British rule. The press secured freedom by the constant efforts of Ram Mohan.

In his articles in the papers, Ram Mohan explained his views and replied to his opponents. He made his words very carefully. He made his comments with tolerance and without wounding anybody's feelings. He thus set a good example to later editors of newspapers.

For Justice and Equality

In those days, courts conducted trials by jury. Some persons were invited to attend the proceedings of the court. At the end, these persons gave the judges their opinions regarding the case. These men were called 'the Jury'. Indians were invited only to lower courts. But Englishmen were invited to higher courts.

Ram Mohan wrote to the government against this practice; he argued that it was an insult to Indians. Finally, the government ended this discrimination.

We now hear the slogan, "Land to the tiller," don't we?

In those days, the landlords had much freedom and authority. Some used to exploit the farmers. There was no limit to their luxury, pomp and arrogance. The farmers had to give almost all the produce to them in the shape of rent. The poor farmers shed tears of blood. Ram Mohan, who had seen all this exploitation, had said, even so long ago, that the land should belong to the tiller.

Brahma Samaj

Ram Mohan and his followers used to attend prayers in the church of a Christian sect. Chanrashekar Dev, a disciple of Ram Mohan, and others wondered why they should not have a prayer Hall of their own. Ram Mohan approved this idea. They hired a building belonging to a man called Ram Kamal Basu and opened a Prayer Hall called 'Brahma Samaj'. The members used to meet every Saturday. Vedic hymns and hymns from the Upanishads were chanted by scholars. Religious discussions were held. Ram Mohan recited the religious poems composed by him. Christian and Muslim boys sang songs in English and Persian. Many Hindus and foreigners used to attend these meetings.

'There is only one God. None equals Him. He has no end. He is present in all living beings'-this was the faith of the Brahma's. This was the message of Ram Mohan. The Brahma Samaj did not recognize differences of caste, creed, race or nationality. It emphasized the idea of universal brotherhood.

Ram Mohan in England

It is wrong to cross the ocean and go to the other countries! Such a view appears laughable today. But, a hundred and fifty year ago, it was believed that it was wrong and irreligious for a Hindus to cross the seas.

Ram Mohan was one of the first Indians who rejected this idea and went to England. The allowances granted by the British to the Mughal King of Delhi, Akbar the Second was very small. He had to submit a representation to the King of England to increase it. The Mughal King decided to send Ram Mohan to England at his expense. Before he left for England, the King gave him the title of 'Raja'. The second reason for Raja Ram Mohan Roy's visit to England was to plead for the abolition of 'Suttee' before the Parliament.

Many people objected to Ram Mohan's visit to England. Some British officers also opposed his going to England. But his fame had already reached England. When Ram Mohan landed at Liverpool, the leading citizens were there to welcome him. The famous historian William Rathbone who was laid up with paralysis sent his son. He fulfilled his last desire by inviting him to his house and by talking to him. Several associations honoured him. He visited France also. Everywhere scholars appreciated his learning.

Though the allowances of the King was not finally settled, it was decided that he could be given three lakhs rupees annually. Ram Mohan's efforts for the abolition of 'Sahagamana' were also successful. On the day when the Bill was passed by the Parliament, the joy of Ram Mohan knew no bounds.

Ram Mohan was very rich. He was a great man who spent his money for other people and for his country. In Calcutta, even foreigners borrowed money from him in times of need. Such a rich man was reduced in England to total dependence upon others, even for food. His health broke down. The main reason for his financial difficulties was that the firm in which he had invested his capital became insolvent.

Out of spite, some people filed a suit against Ram Mohan and his son accusing them of misusing money. Ram Mohan had to spend money like water to prove that he was not guilty. Though he got justice, he lost his entire honour and status in England. Even the financial help from his son stopped. Moreover, one or two persons in England cheated him. He became worried. He fell ill and became bedridden. Some people, who had respect for him looked after him, like relatives. Reputed doctors treated him. But his health did not improve.

Ram Mohan passed away on 27th of September 1833.

A friend of Ram Mohan visited England in 1843. He removed the coffin of Ram Mohan from Stapleton Grove to Arno's Vale, the commentary on the outskirts of Bristol, and buried it there. A memorial in Indian style was raised over his tomb. It is a hundred and forty years since Ram Mohan died. But his memory is still green in the minds of Indians. He was an intellectual who tried to lead India to modernity. He taught the Hindus to give up meaningless beliefs and customs. He was the lamp that led Hindus to the essence of Hinduism. His memory itself guides us to a noble life.

Raja Ram Mohan Roy

Most people remember Raja Ram Mohan Roy as the man who fought to abolish Sati (the practice of a wife immolating herself on her husband's funeral pyre) and also founded the Brahmo Samaj. But his contribution was a great deal more than that. Roy was born in Radhanagar village in Bengal's Hooghly district on May 22, 1772, to conservative Bengali Brahmin parents. Not much has been chronicled about his early life but what is known is that he had an eclectic education that sowed the seeds for his founding a universal religion, the Brahmo Samaj.

Roy did his elementary education in the village school in Bengali, his mother tongue. At the age of 12, Roy went to a seat of Muslim studies in Patna where he mastered Persian and Arabic. His knowledge of Arabic enabled him to read the Koran in the original, as well as the works of Sufi saints. He also devoured Arabic translations of the works of Aristotle and Plato. When he was 16, Roy clashed with his orthodox father on the issue of idol worship and left home. To acquaint himself with the Buddhist religion, he travelled across northern India and Tibet for the next three years. His questioning mind objected to the deification of the Buddha and this did not go down well with some of the lamas. He then visited Varanasi where he learnt Sanskrit and studied ancient Hindu scriptures.

In 1803, he secured a job with the East India Company and in 1809, he was posted to Rangpur. From the Marwaris of Rangpur, he learnt about Jainism and studied the Jain texts. Roy was drawn to certain aspects of Christianity that led some of the followers of the religion to suggest that he convert; but he politely declined.

Roy's understanding of the different religions of the world helped him to compare them with Vedantic philosophy and glean the best from each religion. Sufi mysticism had a great influence on Roy. He loved to repeat three of their maxims: "Man is the slave of benefits"; "The enjoyment of the worlds rests on these two points-kindness to friends and civility to enemies"; and "The way of serving God is to do good to man".

To pursue his interests, Roy resigned from the East India Company a few years later and came to Calcutta in 1815. Dissatisfied with the system of education and the rote method of teaching English, he formed an association of English and Hindu scholars. He also invested his own money in the starting of a school where he introduced subjects like science, mathematics, political science and English. Roy felt that an understanding of these "modern" subjects would give Indians a better standing in the world of the day. Though initially antagonistic towards British rule in India, Roy later began to feel that the country would benefit in terms of education and by exposure to the good points of Christianity. For this he was called a stooge of the British.

Along with a group of like-minded people, Roy founded the Atmiya Sabha in 1815. The group held weekly meetings at his house; texts from the Vedas were recited and theistic hymns were sung. Roy was drawn to the Unitarian form of Christianity that resulted in him supporting a Unitarian Mission to be set up in Calcutta in 1824.

Roy's efforts to abolish the practice of Sati were largely driven by his concern for the moral dimensions of religion. It was the sight of the burning of his brother's widow on her husband's funeral pyre and his inability to save her that spurred Ram Mohan into action.

He delved into the scriptures in great detail and proved that the practice of Sati could not gain moksha (salvation) for the husband as each man was responsible for his own destiny. He also realized that very often it was greedy relatives interested in the property of the dead husband who were behind promoting the practice.

His relentless efforts in the form of petitions, writings and the organizing of vigilance committees paid off when the William Bentinck administration passed a law in 1829 banning the practice of Sati. Roy also succeeded in starting a revolution for women's education and women's right to property. By delving into Hindu scriptures, he showed that women enjoyed equal freedom with men.

Among Roy's other firsts was the publishing of a newspaper in an Indian language. The Atmiya Sabha brought out a weekly called the 'Bangal Gazette'. He also published a newspaper in Persian called 'Miratul-Akhbar' and a Bengali weekly called 'Sambad Kaumudi'. Roy placed a great deal of importance on the development of his mother tongue. His 'Gaudiya Vyakaran' in Bengali is rated highly among his writings in prose.

The founding of the Brahmo Samaj was among Roy's most important contributions. Beginning in 1828 as a small group, the Samaj played a major role in Renaissance Bengal of the 19th century by attracting luminaries like Keshub Chandra Sen and Rabindranath Tagore and other members of the Tagore family. The objectives of the Samaj were to follow a theistic form of Hinduism combining the best of what Roy inculcated through his exposure to other religions. Even today, in Brahmo prayer halls all over the country, people meet once a week, most often on Sundays, and worship the one God or Brahma. At these gatherings, discourses are offered, Vedic texts recited and hymns sung. Present-day followers try to inculcate his words: "Testing, questing, never resting, With open mind and open heart."

Roy felt strongly for the downtrodden and his belief in the universal brotherhood of man led him to support many causes and reform movements. A 100 years before the establishment of the League of Nations, Roy expressed the need for a similar institution. He said that just as two individuals resorted to a court of law to settle major disputes, there should be an organization that could help to settle differences between two countries.

Roy made his first and only trip to England in November 1830 where he lived until his life was tragically cut short on September 27, 1833 after a brief illness.

In today's world of turmoil where religious dogma results in hatred, violence and alienation, Roy's universal approach to religion has much to offer.

ASSOCIATES OF MOHAN ROY

David Hare (Philanthropist)

Early Life: David Hare was born in Scotland in 1775. He came to India in 1800 to make a fortune as a watch maker. However, while he prospered in his business his mind was distracted by the deplorable conditions of the native population and unlike most of the other people who returned back to their native land after gathering a fortune to live a life in peace and prosperity, he decided to stay back in the country and devote himself entirely to the cause of its uplift. However, he was no missionary, seeking to convert others to his religion. He lived his own life and allowed others to live their own, only helping to improve their condition.

Contribution: He felt that the need of the country was English education. He used to discuss the topic with many of his customers, who came to buy watches in his shop. Raja Ram Mohan Roy went to Kolkata in 1814 and within a short time, they became friends. In 1816, he went on his own and attended a session of the Raja's Atmiya Sabha. Both of them discussed at length the proposal to establish an English school at Kolkata. He later discussed the matter with Sir Hyde East, Chief Justice of the Supreme Court. That led to the foundation of Hindu College, later renamed Presidency College, Kolkata, on 20th January, 1817.

Thereafter, David Hare established the School Book Society. It took the initiative to print and publish text books in English and Bengali. This society contributed substantially to the flowering of the Bengal Renaissance.

On 1st September 1818, he established the School Society. He and Radhakanta Deb were secretaries of the society. He worked tirelessly to establish some schools to teach in English and Bengali, according to new methods of teaching, at such places as Thanthania, Kalitala and Arpuly. Everyday, he visited the schools and Hindu College and met almost every student. So great was his attachment and commitment to these students that it acted as a great inspiration of many of them. Some of the greatest names in subsequent years were all his students. It was much later that Alexander Duff or Henry Louis Vivian Derozio came on the scene and influenced the course of events.

Later Life: In later life, he did not find time to devote to his watch business and so he sold it to a friend named Grey and spent some of the money to buy a small house for himself and the rest for the development of the schools. After a long life of activity he fell ill. He was attacked by cholera. One of his students, Dr. Prasanna Kumar Mitra, tried his best but all efforts failed and David Hare died on 1st June 1842. As news spread around the city, a pall of gloom spread over the city. The Christian missionaries refused to allot him land in their cemeteries, as they thought that he was a non-believer. He was buried in what was then the compound of Hare School-Presidency College that he had donated. The tomb, marked with a bust statue, currently falls within the College Square (recently renamed Vidyasagar Udyan) swimming pool, opposite to Hare School.

According to Shivanath Shastri, "As his body was brought out of Mr. Gray's house, thousands of people, some in vehicles, others on foot, followed it. The scene that was witnessed by Kolkata on that day will not be witnessed again. Right from Bowbazar crossing

to Madhab Dutta's bazaar, the entire road was flooded with people."
The road where he lived, is called Hare Street, just off Binoy-Badal-
Dinesh Bagh (earlier Dalhousie Square). A life-size statue (pictured)
was built with public donations and placed in the compound of
Hare School.

Hare School: Hare School is one of the oldest existing schools
in Kolkata, and one of the best schools in India, currently teaching
grades 1 to 12 under the West Bengal Board of Secondary Education
and the West Bengal Council of Higher Secondary Education. The
boys-only school was established by the Scottish watchmaker David
Hare with the help of legendary social reformer Ram Mohan Roy.
The actual establishment date is difficult to ascertain and not
universally agreed upon, but the official year is 1818. The school is
an important landmark in the history of western education in India
under the British raj. It is currently situated opposite the Presidency
College, Kolkata, College Square and Hindu School, Kolkata and
next to the University of Calcutta.

History: After establishing the Calcutta School Book Society
and the Hindu College, Kolkata (now Presidency College) in 1817
and the Calcutta School Society in 1818, David Hare established the
school exactly opposite Hindu College in the heart of College Street
(Kolkata). After its initial beginnings as Arpuli Pathshala and later
as Kalutola Branch School, it came to be known as Hare School in
1867.

Campus: The combined campus of the Hare School and
Presidency College is one of the largest in Kolkata. The ownership
of the campus is a contentious issue, leading to frequent conflicts
about which parts of the ground the students can access, whether
they can play in the College's field and whether they can use the gates
of the college. This situation was escalated some time ago after a
widely-publicised incident of eve-teasing in the college campus,
though restrictions have again been brought down to a normal level.

The white school building is of Victorian architecture, having
rooms with very high ceilings, very high doors and no windows. A

third floor was later constructed on top of the original two story building that maintains the architectural style. More recently another adjacent, smaller building has been constructed in a modern architectural style, much to the displeasure of the students. Initially the school had two very large playgrounds, but later the larger of these was given to Presidency College, though it continues to be used casually by students of the school

RAMTANU LAHIRI

Ramtanu Lahiri (1813-1898) was a leading Derozian, a renowned teacher and a social reformer. Peary Chand Mitra wrote about him, "There are few persons in whom the milk of kindness flows so abundantly. He was never wanting in appreciation of what was right, and in his sympathy with the advanced principles." Shivanath Shastri's Ramtanu Lahiri O Tatkalin Bangasamaj, published in 1903, was not only his biography but also an overview of Bengali society of the era, "a remarkable social document on the period of the Bengal Renaissance." It is still widely read and used as reference material for the period. An English version A History of Renaissance in Bengal-Ramtanu Lahiri: Brahman and Reformer, edited by Sir Roper Lethbridge, was published in London in 1907.

Early Life

Ramtanu Lahiri was son of Ramakrishna Lahiri. They belonged to a deeply religious family attached to the dewans of the Nadia Raj. Some of them were also employed as dewans or occupied other high positions in the Raj. At that time, Krishnanagar was amongst the more enlightened towns of Bengal, and Kolkata had just started growing. His father, Ramakrishna Lahiri, was a person of limited means, earning a living in the service of the landed aristocracy and from some property he owned.

As per the traditions of the age, Ramtanu Lahiri attended the local pathsala and to land learnt Arabic, Persian and some English. The environment of song, dance and drinks, in the palace, was not considered ideal for a child to grow up. His elder brother, Keshab

Chandra Lahiri, took him to Kolkata at the age of 12. He taught him at home but desired to place the young boy in David Hare's school.

In those days, there was such a mad rush for learning English and the opportunities were so limited that young boys used to run alongside David Hare's palanquin, pleading "Me poor boy, have pity on me, me take in your school." The number of aspirants were so many that David Hare could hardly do anything much.

Keshab Chandra Lahiri managed to line up Gour Mohan Vidyalankar, a person close to David Hare, to plead with him for the admission of Ramtanu Lahiri. He did accordingly and took the young boy to David Hare, but he refused to oblige. Then, Vidyalankar advised Ramtanu to run along David Hare's palanquin, along with the other boys.

The youngster did so for around two months, sometimes even without having any food in the morning. Ultimately, he won over David Hare with his determination. Ramtanu Lahiri was admitted as a free student in the school established by the School Society. The school later became famous as Hare School, and was known as Colutola Branch School for some time.

Young Ramtanu did not have a place to stay in Kolkata. His elder brother mostly lived in Krishnanagar. He crowded in with other boys in Vidyalankar's house for some time and later found a place in a relative's house. In 1828, Ramtanu Lahiri passed Entrance with flying colours, winning a grand scholarship of Rs. 14 per month, good enough in those days to manage a living in Kolkata. He joined Hindu College.

College Days

The most renowned name of Ramtanu Lahiri's college days was Derozio. He used to publish poems and essays in Dr. Grant's India Gazette. Then aged only nineteen years, he joined Hindu College as a teacher in 1828. Within a short period, Derozio became immensely popular amongst the students. They mobbed him in college and he invited them to their home. On one occasion, Ramtanu

Lahiri went with some others to Derozio's house. They were offered
tea but Ramtanu Lahiri would not have it. It was against the traditions
of the day to have food or drinks in the house of an alien.

Not only Derozio's erudition and scholarship, but his liberal
ways also had an immense impact on the students. For the first time,
they were learning to question things. When Ramtanu Lahiri was in
the third class (second year, as per today's concept), the followers
of Derozio published a monthly magazine named Athenium. One
of the students, Madhab Chandra Mallick, wrote in it, "If there is
anything we hate from the bottom of our heart, it is Hinduism."
Madhab Chandra Mallick was a friend of Ramtanu Lahiri and was
later posted as a deputy collector in Krishnanagar.

The student-society was overwhelmed by Derozio. Shivanath
Shastri quotes extensively from his biographer, Thomas Edwards:
"Derozio acquired such an ascendancy over the minds of his pupils
that they would not move even in their private concerns without
his counsel and advice. On the other hand, he fostered their taste
in literature; taught the evil effects of idolatry and superstition and
so far formed their moral conceptions and feelings, as to place them
completely above the antiquated ideas and aspirations of the age.
Such was the force of his instructions, that the conduct of the
students outside the College was most exemplary and gained them
the applause of the outside world, not only in literary or a scientific
point of view, but what was of still greater importance, they were
all considered men of truth."

In third class, Ramtanu Lahiri won a scholarship of Rs. 16 per
month. He brought two of his brothers for education in Kolkata.
That was not enough money for three persons to survive on. They
had two square meals only and skipped refreshments in between.
They went to school bare foot and did the cooking and all household
work on their own.

Once when Ramtanu Lahiri was ill, David Hare came and
treated him in his house in a dingy lane. Hare used to keep track
of all his students. Those were also the days when Kolkata society

was in turbulence about the formation of the Brahma Sabha by Raja Ram Mohan Roy in 1828. It was an age of change. The practice of suttee was banned in 1829. That led to enormous debates and petitions for and against it. In 1831, Derozio was forced to resign from Hindu College and he died soon afterwards at the tender age of only 22 years, but what a brilliant array of students he left behind: Krishna Mohan Banerjee, Ram Gopal Ghosh, Rasik Krishna Mallick, Sib Chandra Deb, Hara Chandra Ghosh, Peary Chand Mitra, Radhanath Sikdar and Ramtanu Lahiri, to name a few, all fired with the zeal to serve and change the county. In 1832, Krishna Mohan Banerjee, one of the Derozians converted to Christianity. From 1833 onwards, Indians were allowed to be deputy collectors and deputy magistrates, and some of the Derozians benefited because of the relaxation.

First Job

Ramtanu Lahiri passed out in 1833 and joined Hindu College as a teacher. It may be recalled that the system of graduation had not been introduced till then. With a salary of Rs. 30 per month he started living a life surrounded by relatives, many of whom came to Kolkata for education or other work.

Ramtanu Lahiri had already come under the influence of David Hare and Henry Vivian Derozio. Now it was his turn to be influenced by Thomas Babington Macaulay. Initially the English had sponsored classical education in India, based on Arabic, Persian and Sanskrit, but as new ideas came from England, it was felt essential to introduce Indians to western education, particularly the sciences. There were strong protagonists on both sides. Indeed, the setting up of Hindu College in 1817 was a big step forward in the direction of western education.

Former students of Hindu College were strongly in favour of Thomas Babington Macaulay's move for western education. They even went to the extent of supporting his theory, expounded in 1835, "I am quite ready to take oriental learning at the valuation of orientalists themselves. I have never found one among them, who could deny that a single shelf of a good European library was worth the whole native literature of India and Arabia." That was an age when India's past was still to be fully realised.

Entire society was then in turmoil and Ramtanu Lahiri was going through all that. However, certain events in his personal life affected him seriously. First was the death of two of his brothers, one younger and the other elder. His elder brother had by then risen to the position of a sheristadar, a remarkable achievement in those days. The death of his elder brother brought on the entire responsibility of the family on to his shoulders. Second, two of his wives had died and he married a third time. Third, the death of David Hare in 1842. It was a tremendous shock for Ramtanu Lahiri. He revered him as his own father. Throughout his life, he never failed to gather his friends and pay respect to him at his grave on his death anniversary every year.

Outside Kolkata

Krishnanagar College was opened in 1846. Capt. D.L. Richardson was appointed principal and Ramtanu Lahiri was appointed the second teacher on a monthly salary of Rs. 100. As a teacher, Ramtanu Lahiri had picked up the qualities of Derozio. He could light up within his students the urge to acquire knowledge. While teaching he was always engrossed in the subject, trying to explain things in the widest possible manner. He used to mix freely with the students beyond the classroom and often took part in games with them.

In 1844, Maharaja Srish Chandra Roy had initiated steps for setting up a Brahmo Samaj at Krishnanagar. By the time, Ramtanu Lahiri went to Krishnanagar, it had already attracted both converts and strong opponents in the orthodox community. At that time a great debate was raging in the Brahmo Samaj as to whether to accept the infallibility of the Vedas or not. Tattwabodhini Patrika had also engaged in a bitter debate with the Christian missionaries and had launched a tirade against Christianity. While Ramtanu Lahiri was in general agreement with the Brahmo principles, he had some strong reservations on certain points.

In a letter to Rajnarayan Basu he wrote: "I cannot think much of the Vedantic movements here or elsewhere. The followers of Vedanta temporize. They do not believe that the religion is from God, but will not say so to their countrymen, who believe otherwise. Now, in my humble opinion, we should never preach doctrines as true, in which we have no faith ourselves. I know that the subversion of idolatry is a consummation devoutly to be wished for, but I do not desire it by employing wrong means. I do not allow the principle that means justify the end. Let us follow the right path assured that it will ultimately promote the welfare of mankind. It will never do otherwise.

I wish to request the secretary of the Tottobodhini Sabha to discontinue sending me the Society's paper (Patrika), as a person cannot subscribe to it, who is not a member of the Society... I fear also that there is a spirit of hostility entertained by the Society against Christianity which is not creditable. Our desire should be to see truth triumph. Let the votaries of all religions appeal to the reason of their fellow-creatures and let him who has truth on his side prevail."

He did not join the Brahmo Samaj then but inspired the youth of Krishnanagar along the path of modernity. Some of his students later emerged as leaders of the new movement. One of them was Dinanath Mazumdar, a renowned Brahmo preacher. It was only when things improved in the Brahmo Samaj that Ramtanu Lahiri joined it.

Ramtanu Lahiri was possibly the first person in that society to discard his sacred thread. He is believed to have done it at Bardhaman in 1851. This daring act of his led to a huge uproar in orthodox society and he was socially boycotted for a long time. That, however, did not daunt him. Another movement that rocked society of the time was the debate for remarriage of widows first raised by Ramgopal Ghosh and other Derozians in the Bengal Spectator from 1842 onwards, but it was possible that Pandit Iswar Chandra Vidyasagar was behind the scene.

While Ramtanu Lahiri was moving from one place to another on transfer-Bardhaman, Uttarpara, Baraset, Rasapagla, Barisal-new developments were taking place in Kolkata. John Elliot Drinkwater Bethune established his girls' school in 1849. Ramtanu Lahiri and other Derozians extended warm support to the enlightened journalism of Harish Chandra Mukherjee.

Retired Life

Ramtanu Lahiri returned to Krishnanagar College before retirement. Alfred Smith, principal of Krishnanagar College, wrote on his application for pension, "In parting with Baboo Ram Tanoo Lahiri I may be allowed to say that Government will lose the services of an educational officer, than whom no officer has discharged his public duties with greater fidelity, zeal and devotion, or has laboured more assiduously and successfully for the moral elevation of his pupils." On retirement, Ramtanu Lahiri settled down in Krishnanagar but it could not be for long. He lived in Gobardanga for some time as guardian of the zemindar's sons. When Keshub Chunder Sen established the Bharat Ashram in 1872, he moved in along with his family. He presided over the first day meeting of the All-India National Conference in Kolkata in 1883.

With several deaths in the family, Ramtanu Lahiri was somewhat heart broken. When he died, people of Kolkata gathered in large numbers to bid farewell to a saintly man.

A few lines from Max Muller will summarise his achievements: "The Brahminical thread which was retained by the members of the Brahma Samaj as late as 1861, was openly discarded by him as early as 1851. And we must remember that in those days such open apostasy was almost a question of life and death, and that Ram Mohan Roy was in danger of assassination in the very streets of Calcutta. It is true that European officials respected and supported Ramtonoo, but among his own countrymen he was despised and shunned. However, he continued his career, undisturbed by friend and foe... Later in life he was attracted to the new Brahmo Samaj and became a close friend of Keshub Chunder Sen... While cultivating his little garden he was found lost in devotion at the sight of full-blown rose and while singing a hymn in adoration of God, his whole countenance seemed to beam with heavenly light... When his end approached, his old friend Debendranath Tagore went to take leave of him, and when he left, he cried, 'Now that the gates of heaven are open to you, and the Gods are waiting with their outstretched arms to receive you to the glorious region.'"

DEBENDRANATH TAGORE

Debendranath Tagore (May 15, 1817-January 19, 1905) was an Indian Bengali philosopher from current-day West Bengal, in India. He was born in Calcutta, India. His father, Dwarkanath Tagore, was a rich and famous Bengali landlord.

Debendranath was an active Brahmo, and was against sati, idol worship and the concept of multiple gods. The Brahmo Samaj was formed from Debendranath's Tattvabodhini Sabha and the Brahmo Sabha, ten years after the death of the latter's founder, Raja Ram Mohan Roy. The Brahmo Sabha had fallen away from its original practices put forth in its trust deed, such as the renunciation of lauade ll idols; however, Tagore brought back the importance of this deed. However, when the Vedanta of Ram Mohan Roy was attacked by a Presbyterian minister, Duff, and the scientific deist Dutt, Tagore abandoned it in favour of direct contact with the divine. His experiences were fleeting contact, and this love in separation, known in Hindu poetry as mullai, caused him to strive to regain the bliss of that contact. When Keshub Chunder Sen left the Adi Samaj, it caused considerable pain to him and he withdrew from public activity for quite some time.

Debendranath's spiritual prowess was of the highest order, even while he maintained his worldly affairs-not renouncing his material possessions as some Hindu traditions prescribed but rather continuing to enjoy them in a spirit of detachment. He received approbation from no less a spiritual master than Sri Ramakrishna who compared him to the Puranic king Janaka, father of Sita, the heroine of the epic Ramayana, extolled in the scriptures as an ideal man who perfectly synthesized material and spiritual accomplishments. His considerable material property included several estates spread over the districts of Bengal; most famously, the later acquisition Shantiniketan estate near Bolpur in the Birbhum district where his youngest son, the Nobel prizewinning poet Rabindranath Tagore set up his school and later, the [[Visva-Bharati University. What is remarkable in this achievement is that he excelled his father, who received the title Prince from the British colonial government owing to his large fortune and yet retained his dignity before them, famously wearing an all-white outfit bereft of all jewellery in a party attended by the Queen, with only his shoes studded with two diamonds bettering the Koh-i-noor in the Queen's crown.

This was a gesture symbolising the mastery of wealth, as opposed to its slavish pursuit. Debendranath was a master of the Upanishads and played no small role in the education and cultivation of faculties of his sons. Dwijendranath (1840-1926) was a great scholar, poet and music composer. He initiated shorthand and musical notations in Bengali. He wrote extensively and translated Kalidas's Meghdoot into Bengali.

Satyendranath (1842-1923) was the first Indian to join the Indian Civil Service. At the same time he was a great scholar with a large reservoir of creative talents. Jyotirindranath (1849-1925) was a scholar, artist, music composer and theatre personality. Rabindranath (1861-1941) was his youngest son. His other sons Hemendranath (1844-1884), Birendranath (1845-1915) and Somendranath did not achieve that great fame but everybody was filled with creative talents. His daughters were Soudamini, Sukumari, Saratkumari, Swarnakumari (1855-1932) and Barnakumari.

Soudamini was one of the first students of Bethune School and a gifted writer. Swarnakumari was a gifted writer, editor, song-composer and social worker. All of them were famous for their beauty and education. His part in creating the legacy of Thakurbari-the House of Tagore-in the cultural heritage of Bengal, centred in Kolkata, was not negligible. It was largely through the influence of the Tagore family, following that of the writer Bankim Chandra Chatterjee, that Bengal took a leading role on the cultural front as well as on the nationalistic one, in the Renaissance in India during the nineteenth century.

The house of the Tagore family in Jorasanko, popular as Jorasanko Thakur Bari in Northwestern Kolkata, was later converted into a campus of the Rabindra Bharati University, eponymously named after Rabindranath. Shivanath Shastri has paid glowing tributes to Debndranath Tagore in History of the Brahmo Samaj:

Maharshi Devendranath Tagore was one of the greatest religious geniuses this country ever produced. He was truly a successor of the great rishis of old. His nature was essentially spiritual. ... He was a devout follower of the Upanishadic rishis, but was no pantheist on that account. Devendranath in spite of his real sainthood never put on the grab or habits of sadhu or saint. His piety was natural, habitual and modest. He hated or shunned all display of saintliness....::He was a true and living embodiment of that teaching of the Gita where it is said: "A truly wise man is never buffeted by his trials and tribulations, does not covet pleasure, and is free from attachment, fear and anger; the same is a muni." Maharshi Devendranath was a true muni in that respect. He calmly bore all; even the greatest grieves of life. After having done his duty, he quietly rested, regardless of consequences.:: Though personally not much in favour of the idea of female emancipation, he was one of the first men in Bengal to open the door of higher education to women. Valuing conscience in himself, he valued it in all about him. Religious life was growth to him; not an intellectual assent but a spiritual influence that pervaded and permeated life; consequently, he had not much sympathy with merely reformatory proceedings.:: From the west he took only two ideas: first, the idea of fidelity to God; secondly the idea of public worship; in all other things he was oriental. His idea was to plant the Samaj in India, as the Hindu mode of realising universal theism, leaving the other races to realise that universal faith according to their traditional methods.

INSTITUTIONS ASSOCIATED WITH MOHAN ROY

Fort William College

Fort William College (also called the College of Fort William) was an academy and learning centre of Oriental studies established by Lord Wellesley, then Governor-General of British India. It was founded on July 10, 1800 within the Fort William complex in Calcutta. Thousands of books have been translated from Sanskrit, Arabic, Persian, Bengali, Hindi and Urdu at this institution.

The College: The College of Fort William emerged as both a centre of research and a publication unit, a cradle of creativity as well as scholarship. Planned originally to train probationer British civilians in the languages and cultures of the subjugated country, the college rendered services tantamount to those of a university in promoting modern Indian literatures, Bengali in particular... Under the leadership of William Carey, the College could also claim credit for drawing together Sanskrit pandits and Perso-Arabic munshis to reshape Bengali prose... The variety of the College's publication also deserve note. From colloquies and popular stories, chronicles and legends, to definitive editions of literary texts.

Majumdar, Swapan: Fort William College aimed at training British officials in Indian languages and in the process it fostered the development of languages such as Bengali and Hindi. The period is of historical importance. In 1815, Ram Mohan Roy settled in Kolkata. It is considered by many historians to be starting point of the Bengal renaissance. The establishment of The Calcutta Madrassa in 1781, the Asiatic Society in 1784 and the Fort William College in 1800, completed the first phase of Kolkata's emergence as an intellectual centre.

Teaching of Asian languages dominated: Arabic, Hindustani, Persian, Sanskrit, Bengali; and later Marathi and even Chinese were added. Each department of the college was staffed by notable scholars. The Persian department was headed by Neile B. Edmonstone, Persian translator to the government. His assistant teacher was John H. Harington, a judge of Sadar Diwani Adalat and

Francis Gladwin, a soldier diplomat. For Arabic studies, there was Lt. John Baillie, a noted Arabist. The Hindustani language department was entrusted to John Borthwick Gilchrist, an Indologist of great repute. H.T. Colebroooke, the famous orientalist, was head of the Sanskrit department. William Carey, a non-civilian missionary and a specialist in many Indian languages, was selected to head the department of vernacular languages. While notable scholars were identified and appointed for different languages, there was no suitable person in Kolkata who could be appointed to teach Bengali. In those days the Brahmin scholars learnt only Sanskrit, considered to be the language of the gods, and did not study Bengali. The authorities decided to appoint Carey, who was with the Baptist Mission in Serampore. He, in turn, appointed Mrityunjoy Vidyalankar as head pandit, Ramnath Bachaspati as second pandit and Ramram Bose as one of the assistant pandits. Along with teaching, translations were organized. The college employed more than one hundred local linguists. At that time there were no textbooks available in Bengali. On 23 April 1789, Calcutta Gazette published the humble request of several Natives of Bengal for a Bengali grammar and dictionary.

Location: It was located at the corner of Council House Street. The house was subsequently occupied by Messrs. Mackenzie Lyall & Co., and known as The Exchange. Still later, it housed the offices of Bengal Nagpur Railway. In those days, it was at one corner of the parade ground, now known as the Maidan. The Raj Bhavan (then known as Government House) was opened a little later.

Library: For teaching purposes the College of Fort William accumulated a library of old manuscripts (from all over South Asia) and added multiple copies of its own imprints. The list of books recommended later for preservation includes many books of historical value. Subsequently, when the college was wound up, it gave away the magnificent collection in the library to the newly formed Calcutta Public Library, now the National Library.

Hurdles: The court of directors of the British East India Company were never in favour of a training college in Kolkata and as such there always was a fund crunch for running the college.

Subsequently a separate college for the purpose, The East India Company College at Haileybury (England), was established in 1807. However Fort William College continued to be a centre of learning languages.

With the British settling down in the seat of power, their requirements changed. Bentinck announced his educational policy of public instruction in English in 1835, mostly to cater to the growing needs of administration and commerce. He clipped the wings of Fort William College and the Dalhousie administration formally dissolved the institution in 1854.

HINDU SCHOOL, KOLKATA

Hindu School is a school in Kolkata (Calcutta). It is located on College Street, in the vicinity of Hare School, College Square, Presidency College and Calcutta University. Hindu College, allegedly the school's predecessor, was established in 1817 by Raja Ram Mohan Roy, David Hare (philanthropist), Radhakanta Deb and other notable educationists of that time. In 1855, the pathsala part of Hindu College became Hindu School and the other part (mahapathshala) became Presidency College, Kolkata. The date of establishment of the Hindu College, 1817, is considered the official establishment date of both Hindu school and Presidency College, Kolkata. The school is one of the oldest existing schools in Calcutta and India. Currently the school has grade 1 to 12 and the medium of instruction is Bengali. Students apeear for 10+(Madhyamik) examination under West Bengal Board of Secondary Education and 12+(Higher Secondary Examination) examination under West Bengal Council of Higher Secondary Education. Grade 11 and 12 have three streams,-science, arts and commerce. It is a boys-only school with an approximate strength of 1100 students.

Overview

Prior to the advent of the British in India, the indigenous primary schools of Bengal taught very little beyond Bangla, simple Arithmetic and Sanskrit. The tols (local small schools run by individuals) imparted lessons in advanced Sanskrit, grammar and literature, theology, logic and metaphysics. This was not enough to satisfy the aspiration of the enlightened Indians like Raja Ram Mohan Roy, who felt that the process would only 'load the minds of youths with grammatical niceties and metaphysical distinctions' without having any practical use. The necessity of learning English was also keenly felt by people who had to carry on a constant interaction with the British businessmen. A few schools were set up with the purpose of providing rudimentary education in the English language to native Indians. Hindu School was one of them.

History

Early nineteenth century had witnessed an intellectual awakening in Bengal Society. The luminous ray of modern knowledge, education and thought procedure, influenced by European culture and impacted by British rule, had affected the contemporary life very materially. The various protest movements, formation of societies and associations, religious reform movements, coming of new styles in Bengali literature, political consciousness, and other emergent socio-political phenomena have been argued to be the positive symptoms of this Renaissance. Although it immediately affected a small portion of the upper stratum of Bengal Hindu society only, it eventually spread to Muslims (rather partially) through the Aligarh movement and others as well as to other parts of the subcontinent before the century ended. One of the prominent outcome of this Renaissance was change in the curriculum taught in the schools and establishment of new schools imparting modern and practical education. The idea of establishing an English school was already there. David Hare's plan of English education in India received general approbation and Dewan Baidya Nath Mukherjee was deputed to collect the subscriptions. Sir Edward Hyde East, Chief Justice of the Calcutta Supreme Court was invited to chair the committee and Joseph Baretto became the Treasurer. The committee succeeded in raising Rupees 1,13,179.00, the principal donors being the Maharajah of Burdwan (Tejchand Bahadur) and Gopee Mohun Thakur, each contributing Rupees 10,000. On the opening day there were 20 pupils on the rolls but within the next three months the number swelled to 69. At a later date the pathshala got separated as Hindu School.

Chronology

- January 20, 1817-Hindu College is established
- 1855-The pathshala part became Hindu School, and the other part (mahapathshala) became Presidency College, Kolkata.
- 1992-175th Anniversary observed

SCOTTISH CHURCH COLLEGE, CALCUTTA

The Scottish Church College, which is located at 1 & 3 Urquhart Square, Calcutta 700006 is the oldest continuing Missionary administered liberal arts and sciences college in India. It is affiliated with the West Bengal Board of Secondary Education (for the Scottish Church Collegiate School), the West Bengal Council of Higher Secondary Education, and the University of Calcutta for the awarding of baccalaureate, post baccalaureate and undergraduate degrees. It is well-known for its beautiful campus, renowned faculty, robust intellectual milieu and its English Palladian architecture. Its students and alumni call themselves "Caledonians" in the name of the college festival, "Caledonia". The collegian motto is "Nec Tamen Consumebatur", which means "Burning, but yet not consumed".

Founder

The inception of what is now known as the Scottish Church College is intertwined with the life of Dr. Alexander Duff, D. D. LLD. (1806-1878), the first overseas missionary of the Church of Scotland, to India. Initially known as the General Assembly's Institution, it was founded on the 13th of July 1830.

Alexander Duff was born in Moulin, Perthshire, the very heart of Scotland, on 15th April 1806. From the country school, he passed on to the University of St. Andrews, where, after getting his degree, he ended a brilliant career. Subsequently, he undertook his evangelical mission to India. After an adventurous voyage during which he was twice shipwrecked, he arrived in Calcutta on 27th May 1830.

Rev. Alexander Duff opened his institution in Feringhi Kamal Bose's house, located in upper Chitpore Road, near Jorasanko. In 1836 the institution was moved to Gorachand Bysack's house at Garanhatta. Mr. MacFarlon, the Chief-Magistrate of Calcutta, laid the foundation stone on 23rd February 1837. Mr. John Gray, elected by Messrs. Burn & Co. and superintended by Captain John Thomson of the Honourable East India Company designed the building. The construction of the building was completed in 1839.

Historical Significance

In the early 1800s, the General Assembly of the Church of Scotland sent Reverend Alexander Duff, a young and dedicated missionary, to Kolkata to set up an English-medium institution. Though Bengalis had shown some interest in the spread of Western education from the beginning of the 19th century, both the local church and government officers were skeptical about the high-caste Bengali's response to the idea of an English-medium institution. Raja Ram Mohan Roy helped by organizing the venue and bringing in the first batch of students. He also assured the guardians that reading the Bible did not necessarily imply religious conversion.

Although his ultimate aim was the spread of English education, Duff was aware that without a good command on one's native language, it was impossible to master a foreign language. Hence in his General Assembly's Institution (as later in his Free Church Institution), the teaching and learning of the Bengali language and literature was given high priority. Duff was keen on sports and had accumulated different kinds of sports-related equipment for use in his institution. When he introduced political economy as a subject in the curricula, the Church strongly criticized him.

In 1840, Duff returned to India. At the Disruption of 1843, Duff sided with the Free Church. He gave up the college buildings, with all their effects and with unabated courage, set to establish a new institution, which came to be known as the Free Church Institution. He had the support of Sir James Outram and Sir Henry Lawrence, and the encouragement of seeing a new band of converts, including several young men born of high caste. In 1844, governor-general Viscount Hardinge opened government appointments to all who had studied in institutions similar to Duff's institution. In the same year, Duff co-founded the Calcutta Review, of which he served as editor from 1845 to 1849. These two institutions founded by Duff, *i.e.*, the General Assembly's Institution and the Free Church Institution would be merged later to form the Scottish Churches College. After the unification of the Church of Scotland in 1929, the institution would be known as Scottish Church College.

Along with Raja Ram Mohan Roy, the father of modern India, Dr. Duff played a significant role in supporting Lord Macaulay in drafting his famous Minute for the introduction of English education in India. Successive eminent missionary scholars from Scotland, *viz.* Dr. Ogilvie, Dr. Hastie, Dr. Macdonald, Dr. Stephen, Dr. Watt, Dr. Urquhart and others contributed to the spread of the liberal Western education. Along with other educational institutions like Serampore College, Hindu College, the Scottish Churches College played a pivotal role in ushering the spirit of intellectual enquiry and a general acceptance of the ideals of the European Enlightenment, among Bengalis, in what came to be regarded as the Young Bengal Movement and later, the Bengal Renaissance.

Duff's contemporaries included such luminaries as Reverend Mackay, Reverend Ewart and Reverend Thomas Smith. Till the early 20th century the norm was to bring teachers from Scotland (like William Spence Urquhart, Leslie Stephen, H.M. Percival, Ian Fairweather etc.) but eminent Indian scholars were also engaged as teachers by the college authorities. Scholars like Surendranath Banerjea, Kalicharan Bandyopadhyay, Jnan Chandra Ghosh, Gouri Shankar Dey, Adhar Chandra Mukhopadhyay Sushil Chandra Dutta, Mohimohan Basu, Sudhir Kumar Dasgupta, Nirmal Chandra Bhattacharya, Bholanath Mukhopadhyay and Kalidas Nag had all contributed hugely to enhance the academic standards of the college.

Dr. Duff played a leading part in founding the University of Calcutta in 1857, he was associated with the Agro-horticultural Society and the establishment of a medical college, the first in India. He also aimed at breaking down caste-barriers by founding several girls schools. The Scottish Church College played a pioneering role in women's education as well as co-education in the country. Female students comprise half the present roll strength of the college. With the added interest of the missionaries in educational work and social welfare, the college stands as a monument to Indo-Scottish co-operation. The aims and principles of the College are essentially those of its founder namely, the formation of character through education based on Christian teaching.

Current Status

Until 1953, the administrative control over the college was exercised by the Foreign Mission Committee of the Church of Scotland. This was exercised by jointly by a local council consisting of representatives of the Church of Scotland and the United Church of Northern India. Later the Foreign Mission Committee of Church of Scotland relinquished its authority to the United Church of Northern India, and in 1970, the United Church of Northern India joined the Church of North India as a constituent body. This made the Church of North India the de facto and de jure successor (to the Church of Scotland) in running the administration of the college. As the college was founded on Christian (Protestant and Presbyterian) foundations, it derives its legal authority and status as a religious minority institution as defined by the scope of Article 30 of the Constitution of India.

CITY SERVICE HONOURS HUMANITARIAN

Representatives from the Indian High Commission have attended a special ceremony in Bristol.

They came to Arnos Vale cemetery in Brislington to mark the anniversary of the death of the Indian leader and humanitarian, Rajah Ram Mohan Roy.

Bristol's Lord Mayor joined the Deputy High Commissioner to lay flowers at his tomb while Hindu, Muslim and Sikh women sang Sanskrit prayers of thanks.

Rajah Ram Mohan Roy died in Bristol and was buried at Arnos Vale in 1833.

A statue which stands on College Green, was given by India to Bristol to remember the life of the Rajah, who died in the city on 27 September 1833.

£50k restoration for Indian tomb

The Bristol grave of a social, religious and educational Indian reformer is to be restored with £50,000 raised by the Mayor of Kolkata.

Ram Mohan Roy, 61, died of a fever while visiting the city in 1833 and was buried in Arnos Vale cemetery.

Carla Contractor, a local historian who has campaigned to have the tomb restored, welcomed the news.

"The dome is leaking, the pillars and sandstone tomb are crumbling, but finally now it will be done," she said.

A Learned Indian in Search of Religion: A Discourse, Occasioned by the Death of the Rajah, Ram Mohan Roy

"They shall come from the east, and from the west, and from the north, and from the south, and shall sit down in the kingdom of God." LUKE xiii.29.

A DISCOURSE, &c. PSALM LXXXVI. 8, 9, 10.

"Among the gods there is none like unto thee, O Lord! Neither are there any works like unto thy works. All nations whom thou hast made shall come and worship before thee, O Lord; and shall glorify thy name-for thou are great, and doest wondrous things: thou are God alone."

  . Yes-Jehovah is God alone, and all attempts to raise up any god beside God the Father, are as impotent as would be the attempt to sap the foundation of the earth, or pluck the sun from his orbit. His works, through all their boundless variety and amplitude, declare him, by the unity of their design, to be ONE. The voice of Revelation, through all the rich diversity of her communications, declares him to be ONE. The great legislator of the JEWS, their kings, their prophets, the inspired apostles; the blessed Saviour himself, he who was filled with the Spirit of the Most High-all declare him to be ONE.-This is the conclusion at which the wisest and best of men, in all ages and countries, who have faithfully followed the twin lights of nature and revelation, have arrived.

The light of nature and the light of revelation, flow in parallel lines from the same great fountain of everlasting truth. The latter shines with a brighter and more intense ray than the former-but they never cross each others path, nor stream in opposite directions; nay, they may be said to blend and mingle together, as the rays of heat, and of colour, in the solar beam, to produce one white and brilliant illumination. The God of nature is God of revelation; and it is impossible, that by the voice of the one, he can contradict what he has uttered by the voice of the other. What nature has spoken, revelation has repeated in more audible sounds. The aspirations of nature in the soul of man, after a holier, happier state of being, are re-echoed by revelation; and nature's "longings after immortality," are cherished and exalted into a lively faith in the resurrection from the dead, by that "gospel, which hath brought life and immortality to light."

Though few things, in the usual course of events, are more hopeless than conversion to belief in one God, of the man who has been taught to believe in many; though the religious principles first implanted in the mind, especially those which are irrational and mysterious, are too tenacious of their hold, to be easily eradicated-yet instances are not wanting of men of superior minds, who have boldly laid the axe to the root of their early prejudices, extirpated them with an unsparing hand, and planted in their place the scions of knowledge and truth. Some who have been brought up in a belief of the monstrous fiction of heathen mythology, have been led by the strength of their own mental powers, properly exercised, to embrace a belief in one God, the Father and Creator of all.

Suppose a heathen of good natural understanding, which has been improved by culture, an honest inquirer, well versed in the science and literature of his country, painfully sensible of the falsehood and demoralizing tendency of its popular creed, yet aware of the importance of some system of faith and worship, to human virtue and happiness, were to commence his search of a religion, to which he could trust as to an unerring guide, where, let us ask, should he begin, and where terminate his pursuit? By religion, let us suppose him to understand, not an engine of the state, not an idol of priestcraft, nor an assemblage of abstruse and mystical notions, a thing of scenic exhibition and ceremony, of genuflexions, apostrophes and unmeaning sounds--but that sublime science which imparts a knowledge of God and his attributes, of man and his duty, his happiness, his chief good, and the means of promoting his best interests in time and in eternity.

Suppose our enquirer were assured that he should find the object of his search in the books of the Old and New Testament, but that as there are many forms of religion, all pretending to be taken from those sacred books, he should exercise his own understanding, and judge for himself, being influenced solely by a desire of ascertaining clearly what they reveal. We shall also suppose that previous to his entrance on this task, he has duly considered what is meant by revelation-that he understands by it a special communication of God, in all respects worthy of an infinitely wise, and good being-that its object is to inform mankind of some momentous truths, which are not clearly discoverable by the light of nature-that it should be conveyed in perspicacious language, and not in such obscure terms, as to require another revelation to explain them, for in this case it would be useless, and a third revelation might become necessary for the interpretation of the second. And since language, in the lapse of time, becomes partly obsolete, since words lose their primitive meaning, and acquire a new one, and since a revelation intended for universal adoption, must suffer some changes by translation from one language to another, he will see the necessity of judging of revelation, not so much by particular words, phrases, or detached sentences, as by the general tenor and spirit of the whole. He will consider the style of oriental composition, its magniloquence, its hyperboles, its poetry-with the history, manners, customs, laws, institutions, the peculiar modes of thought ans expression of the people to whom the communication was addressed.

Hence he will be guarded against the danger of giving a literal meaning to figures of speech, or of supposing that doctrines of vital importance will depend on the interpretation of an ambiguous text, much less on a particular idiom, or the presence or absence of some monosyllabic particle, while long chapters are devoted to subjects of comparatively small interest. Revelation being intended as a guide to the right knowledge of what we ought both to believe and practice-for the poor, and the ignorant, as well as for the rich and the learned; he should not imagine that it would require the aid of metaphysics, or the erudition of the schools, to render its saving truths intelligible even to the humblest capacity; not that it should shrink from minute analysis, or refuse to be tried by the most searching rules of criticism, for those truths which rise prominent to the view, and first arrest attention, are rooted in its profoundest depths; while they attract the broad gaze of the clown, they challenge the microscopic examination of the philosopher. We shall further suppose our inquirer to come to the study of his Bible, in happy ignorance of the various subjects of controversy, which have so often agitated the Christian world, or, at least, without having any bias to the tenets of one sect, rather than of another-and that without any aid or embarrassment from creeds, articles of faith, tradition, comments, glosses, expositions, he was to form his own code of religious doctrine, what, according to our knowledge of the Sacred Scriptures, and the best judgement we are capable of forming, would be the leading principles of that code?

With respect to the beings and perfections of God, the first object of inquiry in the study of religion, he would learn from the Sacred Scriptures, that there is one self-existent, supreme, eternal, almighty, omniscient, omnipresent Being, the Creator of heaven and earth, and of all things visible and invisible. But of the physical or metaphysical nature of God, of his substance or essence, he could learn nothing, for Scripture reveals nothing, except what may be contained in the expression of our Saviour, "God is a Spirit," a spirit, *i.e.* one spirit, observe, by which we understand that God is a simple intelligence-meaning by simple the opposite of complex, uncompounded, or not composed of parts, more than he is influenced by passions, or corporeal affections.

Our inquirer, having been a Polytheist, or a believer in many gods, would be particularly struck by the frequency and earnestness with which Scripture asserts the unity of Jehovah, by its denouncement of polytheism-by its utter contempt-its stern abhorrent rejection of all the gods or idols of the heathen-and by its repeated assertions that Jehovah endures no rival; that he has no equal-no partner-that beside him there is no god-that he is God alone-that he reigns absolute, independent-that all other intelligences, from the lowest to the highest, from men to angels, cherubim and seraphim, are the creatures of his hands-that he bade them be and they were-that he formed them by his breath-that he "forms the light and creates the darkness; that he makes peace and creates evil: I, saith Jehovah, do all these things."

Of the moral nature of God, a subject still more important than his physical nature, and because more important, our inquirer would learn much that would gratify his own moral sense, and fill his heart with love and veneration. He would learn from the inspired word, that God is the Father of the Universe, that he delights in the paternal character, and rules his intelligent creatures, all of whom are equally his offspring, as a wise, just, impartial and beneficent father-that he "is good to all, and that his tender mercies are over all his works,"-that God is love-slow to anger, compassionate, abounding in goodness, and causing all things, even sufferings and afflictions, to cooperate for the permanent good of those who endure them with patient and pious resignation. He would find that God is represented in his word, as providing not only for the animal wants of his creatures, "sending them rain from heaven, with fruitful seasons, and filling their hearts with food and gladness,"-but for their moral, intellectual, and spiritual wants-conducting the operations of his providence, in reference to those wants, by the ministry of intelligent agents-that he "spake unto the fathers by the Prophets in time past,-and in these last days hath spoken unto us by his Son."

In the New Testament he would find a revelation of the divine will communicated to mankind by one, bearing the high title of the well-beloved Son of God-one superior to all the preceding prophets and messengers of the Most High-invested with greater power, adorned with greater virtue, accomplishing a more arduous task, promoting more extensive good. He would find the special objects of the Saviour's mission to be these, to inculcate the belief, the worship, and the love of one God, the Father;-to confirm the moral law-to give it greater extent, to lend it new sanctions and arm it with more powerful authority,-to preach forgiveness on condition of repentance-to convince man of his accountability-to reveal a future state in which God will judge all men according to their deeds, and proving its reality by his own resuscitation from the dead. He would find the Apostles, the first Christian Missionaries, insisting on the same topics, executing the commands of their divine master, proving that he is "THE CHRIST," preaching on "righteousness, temperance and judgement to come," and inviting all, both Heathen and Jew, bond and free, to receive the offered grace and live.

Thus would he find that of which he was in search-a religion addressed to the intellectual, the moral, the spiritual nature of man-a religion adequate to his wants, his hopes, his wishes-in all respects worthy of the Father of mercies to reveal-accordant to the religion of nature, though still superior to its purest and most sublime dictates-a religion based not on conjecture or opinion, on dark reasoning, or metaphysical subtleties, on the arbitrary decrees of ecclesiastical councils, or the imperial mandate of a purple tyrant, but on the fixed and immoveable foundation of fact-facts proved and authenticated by a host of witnesses of unimpeachable veracity. He would not indeed, find a systematic body of divinity, nor regularly digested code of Ethics, deduced from reasoning on the constitution of man, such as may be found in schools of philosophy; but a series of miscellaneous instructions, bearing on them the seal and superscription of heaven, addressed to the mind and heart, appealing to the parental, the filial, the conjugal, the brotherly affections, and so admirably calculated to promote the great objects for which the Saviour lived, and taught, and suffered, and died, and rose again-the moral improvement, the spiritual life, the everlasting salvation of man, as to leave no room for doubt in minds properly susceptible of moral and religious impressions, that all come from God.

Nothing, I should think, would strike the mind of a candid inquirer who had a just perception of the beauty of virtue, more forcibly than the morality of the Gospel. When he compared it with that of any human system, of Mohammed, of Confucius, of the Indian Brahmins, of Socrates, who was pronounced by the oracle to be the wisest of men; he would see and acknowledge it to be infinitely superior in purity, in extent, in motives, in sanctions; so adapted to exalt, to dignify, to adorn the nature of man-to advance the great ends of his existence-to conduct him still forward and forward in the way leading to perfection, that he must at last conclude with Locke, that "it has God for its author, salvation for its end, and truth without any mixture of error, for its matter?"

He would be particularly struck with that great rule so much admired, so much neglected, of which the Saviour declares that it is the Law and the Prophets-a rule so simple, so comprehensive, so universally applicable to the whole conduct of social life. Much would he rejoice in a religion which speaks of "glory to God in the highest; on the earth, peace; good will to men"-which enjoins us to make God our great example in the practice of mercy and forgiveness-in doing good even to the unthankful-not to be overcome of evil, nor swayed from our benevolence even by the ingratitude and wickedness of its object-which breathes philanthropy throughout, and exalts charity as the greatest and best of the Christian graces. Much too would he admire those sentiments of self-respect which the gospel enjoins us to cherish-to be pure in heart-and to consider our bodies as the temple of God, into which nothing unholy should find admission. Delighted would he be to contemplate the moral glory of God in the face of Christ Jesus-to see those virtues which were enjoined by the heaven-commissioned teacher, investing him, as with a robe of light, forming the essential of his character-speaking in his words, working in his actions.

In him he would contemplate a bright a beautiful personification of philanthropy, of purity, of truth, the living reality of the just man imagined and depicted by Plato,* a model of moral perfection, of which the world exhibits no second example,-just without the reputation of justice-righteous and holy, though called a friend of publicans and sinners,-bearing the most relentless persecution with a benevolence never to be overcome, in pursuance of his great scheme for man's moral and spiritual redemption, and at last sealing his testimony to the truth by his blood. And if our inquirer followed the Saviour to the cross, and to the tomb, with emotions of sympathy and veneration, with what delight and amazement would he hail his resurrection and ascension-and in them, with joy behold the type and the pledge of his own? Hence new motives and incentives to pursue the Christian life with constancy and perseverance-and to love and honour Jesus as the author and finisher of a more pure, holy and sublime faith then is to be found in any other religion which the world has ever witnessed.

Such is a rapid sketch, a hasty outline-easy however to be completed and filled up-of the doctrines which an honest inquirer would discover by his own perusal of the Scriptures; and if he believed all this, and endeavoured to form his life by the precepts and example of our Lord, ought we to deem his creed deficient, or should we deny to him to the title of Christian, though he failed to discover the peculiar doctrines by which some Churches choose to be distinguished? Assuredly there are many tenets deemed of primary importance by some denominations of Christians, which by the utmost diligence of research, he could not find.

All Protestants will agree that he would explore the Scriptures in vain for the charter conferring infallibility, or the right of supremacy on the visible head of any particular Church. They would all concur is declaring, that it is equally vain to seek in them for the doctrine of Transubstantiation-prayer to the Virgin Mary, Penance, Auricular Confession, Extreme Unction, and masses for the souls of the departed. But what if he should be unable to discover some of their own favourite articles? What if not one of those popish doctrines, appears to him a title more irrational and unscriptural than those of Original Sin, Infinite Satisfaction, Vicarious Punishment, Vicarious Righteousness, Election and Reprobation, and the Three in One? To many who are as sound believers in Christianity, and as much under its sacred influences, as the most orthodox man upon earth, none of those doctrines seems to have any legitimate claim to belief, resting as they do on tradition, or the flimsy authority of mystified and mystifying ecclesiastics, but destitute of any solid foundation in the records of evangelic truth.

The case, I can well imagine, would be altogether different with a man who should come to the perusal of the sacred volume with a previously adopted creed, and with all the influence of first impressions continually interfering, and counteracting the plain and obvious meaning of Scripture. Such a man engages in the study not for information, but proof; not to discover what is actually taught, but what support he can find for his peculiar notions. He will mould the Scriptures to his creed, and not his creed to the Scriptures. Hence so many shocking perversions of their meaning, so much twisting and screwing to adjust them to particular formulas; their beauty marred, their wisdom turned to folly, their power over the heart and affections abused to serve the interests of a blind superstition.

Though he cannot readily find that which he seeks, yet giving implicit credence to the assertion, that such and such doctrines may be collected from holy writ, he becomes a collector; delights in that "index learning, which turns no student pale;" sweeps through the leaves of his Concordance; gathers texts upon texts from every book in the Bible, which have the least reference to the subject, and which, though they have no manner of connexion, nor even a similar sense, yet having a similar sound, answer his object equally well. In proportion to his imagined success in his task, or his real want of it, he will laud his skill, or tax his stupidity; the latter seldom happens, for nothing is more easy, if the mind be properly predisposed, than to find a whole system of divinity in half a dozen texts.

He soon falls into the belief, that in certain expressions more is meant than meets the ear-that learned theologians understand and can explain them best-that there are mystical and cabalistic meanings, known only to adepts, and therefore he must become an adept. Shall he trust to his own judgement? Shall he dare to differ from great and learned authorities? To his plain sense the Scriptures may say one thing, but the adepts, who can extract the pure theological gold from baser matter, say another. They possess the infallible touchstone, by which they can distinguish the genuine ore from the counterfeit, and shall he question the rectitude of their decision?-What! oppose his modern home-spun sense, to their ancient and refined traditionary lore!

Thus he reasons, and thus instead of exercising his own powers of thought, and following the Scripture precepts to "prove all things" and "in understanding to be a man," he proves nothing, but surrenders his free-born mind to be harnessed and yoked, to be whipped and spurred. If he has already been taught to believe in the "real presence," he will remain quite satisfied that this is the doctrine taught in the words "this is my body." And if he has already acquiesced in the assertion, that three may be one, and one three, what proof that the Son is the Father, should he demand beyond the declaration, "I and my Father are one?" In defiance of all reason and sense, and the demonstrative evidence of parallel texts, that unity of purpose, and not unity of essence, can be meant, he adheres, with desperate fidelity, to the orthodox interpretation, and yet if he had not before heard of that doctrine, most assuredly he could never have found it in the Bible.

We shall be told by some of the advocates of human formulas of faith, that the doctrines contained in them, though not directly taught in any chapter, or paragraph of the sacred text, may be inferred from a number of texts properly strung together! Yes-this is exactly the mode in which so many foolish and extravagant notions have been deduced from holy writ. But inferences are not revelations-and it amazes me to think, how any man assuming to be an honest teacher of Christianity, and an expounder of the gospel, would so dishonour his own judgement, and tamper with his conscience, as to take inferences in place of positive announcements. Can any man be fully persuaded in his own mind, that he is justifiable in supposing that a question of such magnitude, as whether there be only one God, or three, is left to depend on an inference? Were the Trinity a doctrine of revelation, revelation would teach it-yes, would teach it to the poor, to children, to babes-and not leave it to be discovered by an intricate process of investigation, which, after all, could never lead to conviction, many of the best reasoners who ever formed a syllogism.

On the other hand, there are numerous instances of persons coming to the study of the Bible with all their early prepossessions matured in favour of a creed called orthodox, who, notwithstanding, have been obliged to abandon it, as not only untenable by the Scriptures, but in direct contradiction to their plainest statements. They have been forced, by the irresistible power of truth, to give up, one after another, every text which they thought favourable to their cause, till not an iota was left for its support, and the whole system has crumbled into fragments, like the enchanted castle of some wicked wizard of romance, at the sound of a true knight's horn, and vanished away, leaving "not a wreck behind."

The simple and sublime doctrine of the Unitarian Christian, "To us there is one God, the Father," is not an inference, but a positive declaration of Holy writ.

The passages by which it is corroborated are so numerous, so explicit, and so strong, that [it] is impossible to controvert or explain them away, by all the sophistry and chicanery of theological schools; though it must be admitted that many churches by maintaining what they term a Trinity in Unity and Unity in Trinity destroy the beauty, the simplicity, and the power of the Christian doctrine, contradict the Scriptures in which they find no similar expressions, nor similar ideas-raise fatal obstacles to the progress of Christianity, and in the opinion of the most intelligent Heathens, Jews, and Christians, bring themselves the imputation of polytheism and idolatry.

The justice of the preceding reflections, occasioned by the death of the Rajah, Ram Mohan Roy, is proved and illustrated by his history-to a review of which, in connexion with some of his opinions on one of the most interesting questions which has ever engrossed the thoughts of the learned, let me now solicit attention. This is a subject which has occupied, and is now occupying, the minds of many of our brethren in England and Scotland. The Rajah was a Christian of such intrinsic worth, he was so distinguished by his talents, his learning, his virtues-by the unprecedented example of an Indian Brahmin becoming a genuine Christian,-that he was an object of universal interest; and we need not wonder at the panegyrics heaped on his name, or the profound regret which has attended his departure. I lament that it is not in my power to speak from personal knowledge of this great and good man-but I have heard much of him from friends who frequently enjoyed his society and conversation both in Calcutta and London; and their report has been uniformly such as to amply justify all that warmth of eulogy which has been pronounced on him by the public Press. The preface to his works republished in London 1824, from the Calcutta edition, contains much interesting matter concerning him. It was composed by Dr. Thomas Rees, Secretary to the British and Foreign Unitarian Society, and as the work has become scarce, being now out of print, and known only to a small number of those whom I address, I shall give copious extracts from it, accompanied with a few of the reflections which the subject may suggest.

"Ram Mohan Roy was born about the year 1780, at Bordouan, in the province of Bengal. The first elements of his education he received under his paternal roof, where he also acquired a knowledge of the Persian language. He was afterwards sent to Patna, to learn Arabic; and here, through the medium of Arabic translations of Aristotle and Euclid, he studied Logic and Mathematics. When he had completed these studies, he went to Calcutta, to learn Sanskrit, the sacred language of the Hindu Scriptures; the knowledge of

which was indispensible to his caste and profession as a Brahmin."
"It was about the year 1804 or 1805, he became possessed by the
death of his father, and of an elder and younger brother, of the
whole family property, which is understood to have been very
considerable. He now quieted Bordouan, and fixed his residence at
Mourshedabad, where his ancestors has chiefly lived. Shortly after
his settlement at this place, his commenced his literary career, by
the publication of a work in the Persian language with a preface in
Arabic, which he entitled, 'Against the Idolatry of all Religions.' The
freedom with which he animadverted on their respective systems,
gave great umbrage both to the Mohammedans and Hindus, and
created him so many enemies, that he found it necessary to remove
to Calcutta, where he again took up his residence in the year 1814.

"Two years previously to this period he had begun to study the
English language, but he did not then apply to it with ardour or
success. Being some years subsequently appointed Dewan, or chief
native officer in the collection of the revenues, and the duties of
his office affording him frequent opportunities of mixing with
English Society, he applied to it with increased attention, and very
soon qualified himself to speak and write it with considerable facility,
correctness and elegance. He afterwards studied the Latin, Greek,
and Hebrew Languages; of his proficiency in the two last he has
given very decisive evidence in the tracts which are here published."

Here let me observe, his early studies were an admirable
preparative for the part, he was afterwards to take in religious
controversy. His logic and mathematics taught him to reason well,
to draw right conclusions from their premises, and detect the sophistry
of his opponents; while by his knowledge both of ancient and
modern languages, he was eminently qualified to discharge the office
of a Biblical critic; and when he entered the polemic arena, to
manifest a decided superiority, not only in the part which he espoused
in the grand question, but in the minutiae of verbal criticism.

"From his first work 'Against the Idolatry of all Religions,' it
is evident that he had been led at an early period of life to regard
with disapprobation the monstrous and debasing system of idolatry

which was embraced by his countrymen. Hence he became anxious
to reform their creed and their practice, and determined to devote
his talents and his fortune to this important and honourable
undertaking." "My constant reflections," he writes in the preface to
one of his works, "on the inconvenient or rather injurious rites
introduced by the peculiar practice of Hindu idolatry, which more
than any other Pagan worship destroys the texture of society; together
with compassion for my countrymen, have compelled me to use
every possible effort to awaken them from their dream of error; and
by making them acquainted with the Scriptures, enable them to
contemplate with true devotion, the unity and omnipresence of
nature's God. By taking the path which conscience and sincerity
direct, I, born a Brahmin, have exposed myself to the complainings
and reproaches even of some of my relations whose prejudices are
strong, and whose temporal advantage depends upon the present
system. But these, however accumulated, I can tranquilly bear, trusting
that a day will arrive when my humble endeavours will be viewed
with justice-perhaps acknowledged with gratitude. At any rate
whatever man may say. I cannot be deprived of this consolation:
my motives are acceptable to that Being who beholds in secret and
compensates openly."

That these sentiments, and many others of a similar kind which
it would be tedious to quote on the present occasion, are worthy
of a mind imbued with the spirit of Christianity, bigotry itself must
be constrained to admit. Fearless of consequences and listening only
to the call of duty, he bore his testimony to a momentous truth-
and suffered the alienation of friends and the persecution of enemies,
with the piety of a saint, and the courage of a martyr.

"The liberal views, and the devout and amiable spirit which are
displayed in these extracts, and are indeed discernible in the whole
of the author's writings, may be well thought to have disposed his
to a candid examination of the Christian Revelation. From the
perusal of the New Testament in his 'long and uninterrupted
researches into religious truth' he found, he asserts 'the doctrines
of Christianity more conducive to moral principles and better adapted

for the use of rational beings, than any other which had come to his knowledge.'

The doctrine of the Trinity, however, which appeared to his mind quite as objectionable as the Polytheism of the Hindus, presented an insuperable obstacle to his conversion to Christianity, as he found it professed by those with whom he conversed. But as the system so fully approved itself in other respects, to his reason and his piety, his candour would not, on account of this single difficulty, allow him at once to reject it as false. As the most likely method of acquiring a correct knowledge of its doctrines, he determined upon a careful perusal of the Jewish and Christian Scriptures in their original languages. From this undertaking he arose with a firm persuasion, that the doctrine of the Trinity was not inculcated in them, and that the Christian religion was true and divine."

Great and important conclusion! the doctrine of the Trinity is not inculcated in them-and yet the Christian Religion is true and divine! That the learned Brahmin should come to this conclusion. Excites as little surprise as to be told that he preferred the monotheism of Mohammed to the tritheism of the Hindus. "He had early observed the diversities of opinion, existing among the idolators; and that while some exalted Brahma, the Creator; others gave the ascendancy to Vishnu, the Preserver; and others again to Shiva, the Destroyer." When he came to examine the creeds of Christians, he must have been struck by a similar diversity of character in the persons of their Trinity, and by the different degrees of respect or fear in which each is held by different denominations.

The first person is, to many, an object of awful apprehension; the second of supreme love and veneration; while the third is overlooked or disregarded, except when occasionally required to complete the triad. If in the second person he should trace any similitude to Vishnu, the Preserver, he would see the counterpart of Shiva, the Destroyer, in the first, especially as he is depicted in certain books of Calvinistic Divinity, and in the well known popular hymn of Watts which describes him as seated on a "burning throne," besprinkled with blood."

"Having now become upon deliberate and rational conviction a Christian, he hastened to communicate to his countrymen such a view of the religion of the New Testament as he thought best adapted to impress them with a feeling of its excellence, and to imbue them with its pure and amiable spirit. For this purpose he compiled the work entitled, 'The precepts of Jesus the guide to peace and happiness.' To this work, which consists entirely of extracts from the moral discourses of our Lord, he prefixed an 'Introduction,' in which he stated his reasons for omitting the doctrines and the historical and miraculous relations which accompany them in the writings of the Evangelists. Soon after the publication of this tract, there appeared in the 'Friend of India,' a periodical work under the direction of the Baptist Missionaries, an article animadverting upon it, which was signed 'a Christian Missionary,' but was written by the Rev. Mr. Schmidt. To this paper Dr. Marshman, the editor of the magazine, appended some 'Observations' of his own, in which he styled the Compiler of the 'Precepts' an 'intelligent Heathen, whose mind is as yet completely opposed to the grand design of the Saviour's becoming incarnate.'"

"Opposed to the grand design of the Saviour's becoming incarnate!" What could the "respected Editor," mean by this? Verily, he evinces himself to be altogether ignorant of the "grand design" of Christianity; while the Compiler of the "Precepts" not only proved that he understood it well, but took the most essential mode by which it could be promoted. Opposed to the grand design! No, its great opponent was the "respected Editor" himself, who by the mysterious dogmas of his unscriptural creed, provoked the ridicule and bitter sarcasm of every intelligent Hindu and Mussalman whom he tried to convert, and raised prejudiced against Christianity which were not to be overcome. The Rajah understood the "grand design" of Christ, better than all the Missionaries, and did more for its service than ever their joint labours will achieve, until they alter their system, and commence the work of conversion by those very "precepts," which they hold so cheap, and of which they understand so little, but which are indeed the guide, and the only true guide to peace and happiness.

"These 'Observations,' produced a second pamphlet, entitled 'An Appeal to the Christian Public in defence of the Precepts of Jesus, by a friend to truth.' The writer is now known to have been Ram Mohan Roy himself. He complains in strong terms, of the application to him of the term Heathen as 'a violation of truth, charity and liberality;' (as he well might) and also controverts some of Dr. Marshman's objections to his compilation and to his reasonings in the introduction. In a subsequent number of 'The Friend of India,' Dr. Marshman inserted a brief reply to this Appeal, 'in which he still denied to the author the title of Christian, disclaiming, however, all intentions of using the term Heathen in an invidious sense.'

"In consequence of some farther observations of Dr. Marshman, Ram Mohan Roy published 'A Second Appeal to the Christian Public.' To this Dr. Marshman printed an elaborate answer in the 4th No. of the Quarterly Series of 'The Friend of India.' In the month of January, 1823, the author of the 'Precepts of Jesus' appeared before the public in a third and 'Final Appeal' in defence of that work, and in reply to the last answer of Dr. Marshman. Dr. Marshman's friends having collected and printed in England, his papers in this controversy, it was thought by many to be demanded by truth and justice that Ram Mohan Roy's pamphlet should be given to the British public to enable them to form an accurate judgement of the merits of both the parties in support of their respective tenets. As there appeared no prospect of the work being undertaken by any bookseller, the Unitarian Society were induced to become the publishers."

You will find the preceding statement corroborated, with much additional interesting matter, in a paper which appeared recently in the Bristol Gazette, and which has been reprinted in some of our journals. To that account, give me leave to refer you, as it would be utterly incompatible with the limits, and with the object of this discourse, to enter more minutely into the history of the excellent Rajah. This must be the task of some industrious and well qualified biographer. Suffice it therefore to say, that influenced by a desire to promote his philanthropic views for the benefit of India, by his personal influence with the British legislature, he arrived at Liverpool in the month of April, 1831-preceded by a character which excited a deep interest in the public mind, and rendered him an object of marked regard.

He received numerous congratulatory addresses on his arrival in the British Metropolis-addresses, which to him must have been peculiarly gratifying, as evincing that the cause to which he was attached, and which he had laboured so zealously to promote, had numerous respectable supporters in England. He received addresses also from Ireland, particularly from Belfast, and Cork-and a Gentleman of this city, was commissioned by the Irish Unitarian Society, to invite him to a public entertainment. It was accordingly his intention to pay this country a visit. He seemed to take a deep interest in the affairs of Ireland, and I can state on the unquestionable authority of a friend, who was frequently in his society in London, that in the course of a month after his arrival, he had acquired such an intimate knowledge of its statistics, politics, and religion, as might almost justify the belief that he had long been directing his exclusive attention to those subjects of inquiry. He paid a visit to France, and was well received in the French court. He also intended to cross the Atlantic, and greet his Unitarian Brethren, in the land of Channing and of Ware. In London he attended the Unitarian chapel, and was twice present at the anniversary of the Unitarian Society; "but it was his system to avoid so far identifying himself with any religious body, as to make himself answerable for their acts, and opinions; and he also wished to hear preachers of other denominations, who had acquired a just celebrity. He appears to have most frequented the Church of the Rev. Dr. Kenny, (St. Saviour's, Southwark,) who peculiarly interested him by the Christian spirit, and influence of his discourses.

In Bristol he attended worship at the Unitarian Chapel, Lewin's Mead, (of Dr. Carpenter, who wrote the able answer to Dr. Magee's book on the atonement;) and there he had directed his son statedly to attend." At Stapleton Grove, where his son had been passing his vacation, and where the Rajah intended to pass a few weeks, he was seized with a fever, which, notwithstanding the best medical aid that could be procured, proved fatal, and he breathed his last on Friday morning, September 27th. "His son, Rajah Ram Roy, and two Hindu servants, with several attached friends, who had watched over him from the first day of his illness, were with him when he expired. He conversed very little during his illness, and was observed to be often engaging in prayer. He told his son, and those around him, that he should not recover." But he was prepared for the event, and could look on death, not as the king of terrors, but as the angel of God's kind providence, come to release him from earth, and transport him to heaven. Happily he was permitted to die in peace, commanding his spirit to God, undisturbed by the cant of fanatics, and by those frightful images, which they delight to conjure up around the bed of the dying.

In reference to his interment, the following notice appeared in a Bristol paper. "Interment of The Late Rajah, Ram Mohan Roy. The remains of this eminent individual will not be deposited in any of the usual receptacles of the dead. It has always been an object of great importance in the view of the Rajah, to convince his countrymen that the relinquishment of idol worship, and the abolition of their superstitions and cruel rites, might be effected without deviating from the principles of their ancient faith, or incurring the loss of Brahminical caste,-thus wisely preparing the way for the introduction of Christianity among them. It has, therefore, been deemed expedient by the friends who have long been concerned in the management of his affairs, as well as by his son, that his body should not be interred in any of our usual cemeteries. There is also room to apprehend that his enemies in India might avail themselves of the fact of his being buried with Christians, or with Christian rites, to renew their unsuccessful endeavours to deprive him of caste, and embarrass his children in their succession to his property. Under these peculiar circumstances they have availed themselves of the permission given to deposit the honoured remains within the walls of Stapleton Grove, there to await any further decision of his family respecting them; fulfilling, by thus interring them alone, and in an appropriate spot, the desire often expressed by the Rajah-'Where he died he be interred, privately and in silence.'"

The Rajah was a Brahmin by birth, and he died retaining his distinction. "After his death, the thread of his caste was seen round him passing over his left shoulder, and under is right." Wherefore, may someone ask, when he became a Christian, did he not renounce caste, and all Brahminical connexion? The reason is given in the foregoing quotation-because he was a Christian, and wished his countrymen to embrace Christianity. Had he lost caste, his influence would have been gone; and it was no more incompatible with his Christianity to retain caste, than with the apostle Paul's, after his conversion, to conform to some parts of the Jewish ritual; and, if necessary, a greater example might be adduced in our Saviour, who, though his religion was to supercede Judaism, continued as a Jew, to "fulfil all righteousness."

The Rajah is described as "a remarkably stout, well-formed man, nearly six feet in height, with a handsome and expressive countenance." His manners were engaging to all, and to females in particular, were marked by a suavity, a courtesy and a refinement expressive of the benevolence of his heart-a circumstance the more striking in a native of the East, where females are not usually regarded with the same distinction as in the more cultivated nations of Europe. If in any thing his virtues, by excess, might seem verging to a fault, it was in too great a facility of concession to the opinions of those with whom he conversed, proceeding from reluctance to disturb their self-complacency. In an article on Ram Mohum, in the Asiatic Journal for Nov. 1833, it is stated that

"In the East, there are modes of conveying a civil negative by an affirmative.-He was indeed by no means deficient in the firmness requisite to deal with an adversary who defied him to the arena of argument, in which his great resources of memory and observation, his vigour and quickness of mind, his logical acuteness with no small share of wit, commonly brought him off victorious."

His Bristol biographer says: "That disposition to acquiescence, which eastern politeness requires, and which his own kindness of heart contributed to strengthen, was known to place him in circumstances, and lead him to expressions, which made his sincerity questioned. But, where he was best and fully known, the simplicity, candour, explicitness, and openness of his mind, were striking and acknowledged; and from these, together with his profound acquirements, his extensive information, his quick discrimination of character, his delicacy and honourable sentiments, his benevolent hopes and purposes for human welfare, his benignant concern for the comfort and happiness of all around him, his affectionateness and humility of disposition, his gentleness and quick sensibility, there was a charm in his presence and conversation which made one feel love for him as well as high respect. It was impossible to be much with him in the narrow circle of private life, without entertaining attachment to him; or without feelings approaching to reverence, for the greatness of his endowments, the high excellencies of his character, for the purity and refinement of his sentiments, and for the earnest and elevated piety of his spirit. Those who had the best opportunities of knowing him, say that the perusal of the Scriptures was his constant practice; and that his devotion was habitual-manifested by stated prayer, and by a frequent absorbedness of soul, the external expression of which left no room for doubt as to the direction and object of it."

To this I can add from other sources, that his morals were characterized by spotless purity and innocence, insomuch that he has been seen, by the expression of his countenance, to manifest the deepest horror, on discovering that certain persons into whose society he was thrown, were tainted by the commission of some offences against Christian morality, which among the general mass of Christians, are regarded as venial, or involving but a very small degree of criminality.

Of the character of the excellent Rajah, intellectual, moral, religious, there seems to be only one opinion among all those whose opinion merit consideration. As for what may be thought or said of him by those, and such no doubt there are, who because he could not embrace their peculiar doctrines, would still denominate him a heathen, it is unworthy of a moment's notice. Would that but one little shred of his Christianity were shared among them, it would make them better Christians, than ever they are likely to become with their ignorant, and malevolent bigotry! We have the testimony, not only of friends to his religious views, but of some who were opposed to them, that he was pious, and good, and learned, and wise, and patriotic, and generous, and disinterested. In fact, I cannot at this moment, recollect the name of any individual, since the days of the apostles, that has so preeminent a claim to the title of Christian. D'Acosta, the editor of a journal at Calcutta-the Abbe Gregoire "through whom he became extensively known, and highly appreciated in France"-Lieut. Col. Fitzclarence, now the Earl of Munster, who knew him well-all speak in terms of high panegyric, of his talents, his learning, his intellectual and moral endowments, his logical powers of reasoning, his philanthropy, disinterestedness, and pecuniary sacrifices in the cause of virtue and truth.

The Editor of the Indian Gazette, a journal devoted to the constituted authorities, speaking of the controversy arising out of "The Precepts of Jesus," says that "whatever other effects it may have caused, it still further exhibited the acuteness of his mind, the logical power of his intellect, and the unrivalled good temper, with which he could argue,-it roused up a most gigantic combatant in the theological field; a combatant, who we are constrained to say, has not yet met with his match here!" Think of this being affirmed within hearing of Dr. Marshman, by the Editor of "a journal devoted to the constituted authorities!" Verily the truth is great, and it must prevail. Yes, and the antagonist of the Rajah knew this, and they dreaded this, and they acted over again, as nearly as they could, the part of the enemies of Christianity to its first promulgators. They did not, indeed, expel him from their synagogue, but they called him reproachful names, and would have imposed silence on him, and prevented him from speaking to the world, through the press, that great organ of the world's regeneration. His first and second Appeal had been printed at the Baptist Missionary press-but when they found him proving himself to be a champion invincible and triumphant, with a mean and dastardly dread of the result, they refused him the farther use of their printing materials. But he was not this to be baffled. With a zeal and perseverance worthy of all praise, and at considerable expense, he purchased types, employed printers, and commenced an independent printing office, for his "Final Appeal."

The accession of such a convert as the Rajah to the truth of Christianity, should, we might suppose, be hailed with exultation by all its friends, and especially by those employed in Missionary labours, though his opinions did not altogether harmonize with theirs. But no, such is the spirit of bigotry-such the effect of entertaining narrow views of Christianity, and making it consist, not in "meat and drink" indeed, but in something still worse, in the belief of doctrines, which shock reason, and impeach the justice and mercy of the Father of all-that it would rather such converts as he, had remained still immersed in the idolatries, and abominations, from which he had escaped! That a Brahmin of such high character, so distinguished for strong intellectual powers-for superior mental cultivation-for such patient and persevering industry in the study of languages to aid him in the search after truth-that such a man should strip off the prejudices of education, should renounce the popular superstitions of his country, under the severe penalty of incurring the hostility of his relatives and friends, and at the no small risk of losing his paternal property, and most dreadful of all, of losing caste-which, as you well know, is the Hindu, a grievance more terrible than excommunication in the Roman Catholic Church-that such a man, under such circumstances, should come forward to avow his belief in Christianity at all, ought surely to be a subject of rejoicing to every one who feels a real interest in the extension of the Saviour's kingdom. By what authority, or on what grounds, did Marshman, or any of his fraternity, refuse the name of Christian to the Rajah?

To what standard different from that erected by the apostles, do they presume to ask conformity? When Philip baptized the Ethiolpian officer of the court of Candace, did he require a profession of belief in any such tenets, as those held by Marshman? When that officer seeing water by the way side, said, "What doth hinder me to be baptized?" Philip replied, "If thou believest with all thine heart, thou mayest." And he answered and said, "I believe that Jesus Christ is the Son of God." This was deemed quite enough, by an inspired apostle. "He accordingly commanded the chariot to stand still, and the went down both into the water-and he baptized him," Acts viii. 36, 38. That simple confession, I repeat, was sufficient for an apostle to admit an Ethiopian to the rights and privileges of Christianity. Wherefore should the terms of admission to the same privileges, be more restricted to an Indian Brahmin-a Brahmin too, whose knowledge of the gospel, and whose pretensions to the Christian name, it may be fairly presumed, were far superior to those of the Ethiopian, and infinitely beyond those of his Trinitarian opponents?

But such is ever the ignorant and intolerant presumption of bigots, with their tests, and their "shibboleths," and their assumed infallibility! They "take away the key of knowledge: they enter not in themselves, and them that were entering they hinder." Well did the Rajah shew that they deviated widely from the example of him whom they called Master-by reminding them of Christ's rebuke of John for a similar act of uncharitableness. "We forbad him," said the disciple, "because he followeth not us." "Forbid him not," said Jesus, "for he that is not against us, is on our part." Mark ix. 40. "The compiler of the precepts, having obviously in view, at least one object in common with the Reviewer and Editor, that of procuring respect for the precepts of Christ, might have reasonably expected more charity from professed teachers of his doctrines." Thus thought and thus wrote the learned convert. But he had yet to learn "what spirit they were of," and in how little estimation they held any precept in comparison of profession of faith in some of their own stupid dogmas. It is a small compliment to the Rajah to say, the he not only knew the genius and spirit of Christianity, but that he practised its duties, and rendered far more essential service to its cause, than any, or all of those whose sophistry he Scriptural arguments, in the fair field of controversy, crushed and annihilated.

In selecting and publishing the ''Precepts of Jesus,'' he manifested his knowledge of human nature, and particularly the nature and disposition of his own countrymen, and thus also he manifested no small degree of wisdom in preparing the way for the admission of every other part of Christianity. Yes-he acted wisely in not shocking the prejudices of his countrymen-in not proposing to them any doctrine which they were not qualified to receive, not doubting but that the most simple and intelligible points being once admitted, those which are abstruse or difficult, would in due time be admitted also. He gave them such milk, as Paul gave his infant converts, and not strong meat, which they were unable to digest. These are wise principles, which, I rejoice to say, are received and acted on by the Board of Education, in this Island-and acted on most successfully, though opposed in every variety of form, which can be assumed by misrepresentation, falsehood, and the agonized hypocrisy of a crest-fallen, disappointed, and now expiring faction.

The Saviour himself acted on this principle. Mark, the evangelist, informs us, that "he spake the word unto the people, as they were able to hear it." iv. 33. And in John xvi. 12, he says, "I have many things to say unto you, but ye cannot bear them now." The soil must be prepared, or the seed will be scattered in vain, and the husbandman's labour will perish.

The Rajah saw the folly of proposing for the adoption of his countrymen, those tenets which have been a subject of perpetual dispute among Christians. What possible advantage could the Hindu derive from those favourite questions of divines, the very terms of which, admit no definite or intelligible meaning? As for Trinities, and incarnations, he had enough of them in the religion of his own country, and was not likely to favour the importation of articles with which the market was already overstocked.

"For these reasons," says the Rajah, "I decline entering into any discussion on these point, and confine my attention, at present, to the task of laying before my fellow creatures the words of Christ, with a translation from the English into Sungskrit and the language of Bengal. I feel persuaded that by separating from the other matters contained in the New Testament, the moral precepts found in that book, these will be more likely to produce the desirable effect of improving the hearts and minds of men of different persuasions and degrees of understanding. Moral doctrines tending evidently to the maintenance of the peace and harmony of mankind at large, are beyond the reach of metaphysical perversion, and intelligible alike to the learned and to the unlearned. This simple code of religion and morality is so admirably calculated to elevate men's ideas to high and liberal notions of one GOD, who has equally subjected all living creatures, without distinction of caste, rank, or wealth, to change, disappointment, pain and death, and has equally admitted all to be partakers of the bountiful mercies which he has lavished over nature, and is also so well fitted to regulate the conduct of the human race in the discharge of their various duties to GOD, to themselves, and to society, that I cannot but hope the best effects from its promulgation in the present form." Introduction, pp. xxvii. xxviii.

Thus did the Indian Rajah teach the Christian Missionaries a most useful lesson, by which they must profit, unless they are incapable of learning, and steeled against conviction, He taught them that Christianity is not a crude concoction of human opinions- a compilation of creeds and articles, gathered our of the records of the dark ages-a book of conundrums, enigmas, and contradictions; but a practical rule of life, which can be felt and understood. He told them that the great barriers to the Christian religion, are the irrational and unscriptural doctrines advocated by its Missionaries; and that if they hope for success, they must change their plan, and have recourse to reason and common sense.-It is devoutly to be wished that some of our popular declaimers at home, would condescend to take a lesson from the Rajah, and if they really feel

the desire which they profess to promote Christianity, sometimes
expatiate on the words of Christ, and give the people a little practical
instruction, in place of the vapoury rodomontade, with which they
make their pulpits twang.

The learned Indian went, like the well known "Irish Gentleman,"
in search of religion; but how different was the result! The one
sought it in the dark and ponderous tomes of the Fathers-in the
mouldy records of general councils-in monkish legends, and the
collectanea of Priestcraft:-the other, in the page of nature and the
volume of revelation. The one depended on human authority, the
other on the oracles of the living God. The one followed the
"faithless phantom" of tradition-the other fixed his gaze on the "sun
of righteousness." The "Irish Gentleman" went, as he was led,
hoodwinked, up the theological stream, where it ran dark and feculent,
and never reached the fountain head. The Indian sprang boldly
forward, in defiance of the clamours of bigotry, and drank the living
waters as they flowed from the stricken rock.

The former found a religion which invested the mortal head
of her Church with infallibility-a man with the attributes of God-
exacted blind submission to ecclesiastical authority, with prostration
of the understanding, with distrust of the evidence of the senses;
and taught Transubstantiation, the Trinity, and the worship of Mary
the mother of God! The latter found a religion which takes her
stand, not on the decrees of councils which are often contradictory,
on the opinions of men which are always uncertain, but on the word
of God, which is the "same yesterday, today, and for ever;" on those
positive announcements of holy writ, which no artifice can disguise,
nor any sophistry explain away:-a religion which he recognized as
the offspring of heaven, which taught him, as we have seen, that
God is love-that man is accountable, that to obey God and keep
his commandments is the duty, the happiness, the chief end of man;
a religion which enlightens the mind and purifies the heart, elevates
the thoughts from earth to heaven, and while it stimulates to run
the high career of virtue, opens to the enraptured gaze bright visions
of bliss and glory; blooming as Paradise, durable as eternity.

Such was the learned Indian's high veneration for the sacred Scriptures, that he refused to receive any doctrine, as a doctrine of religion, which they have not revealed. He gave the decrees of Councils and Fathers to the winds, and taking the word of God as his only true guide and instructor, asserted with it, the divine unity, in opposition to all Tritheism and Polytheism.

"It is my reverence for Christianity" says he, in his Second Appeal (p. 304) "and for the author of this religion, that has induced me to endeavour to vindicate it from the charge of Polytheism, as far as my limited capacity and knowledge extend. It is indeed mortifying to my feelings, to find a religion that from its sublime doctrines and pure morality should be respected above all other systems, reduced almost to a level with Hindu theology, merely by human creeds and prejudices; and from this cause brought to a comparison with the Paganism of ancient Greece, which while it included a plurality of Gods, yet maintained that [...] 'God is one,' and that their numerous divine persons were all comprehended in that one Deity."

"Having derived my own opinions on this subject entirely from the Scriptures themselves, I may perhaps be excused for the confidence with which I maintain them against those of so great a majority, who appeal to the same authority for their; inasmuch as I attribute the different views, not to any inferiority of judgement compared with my own limited ability, but to the powerful effect of early religious impressions; for when these are deep, reason is seldom allowed its natural scope in examining them to the bottom. Were it a practice among Christians to study first the books of the Old Testament as found arranged in order, and to acquire a knowledge of the true force of scriptural phrases and expressions, without attending to interpretations given by any sect; and then to study the New Testament, comparing the one with the other, Christianity would not any longer be liable to be encroached on by human opinions." (304, 305)

Again his observes in his Final Appeal, "The doctrine of the Trinity appears to me so obviously unscriptural, that I am pretty sure, from my own experience and that of others, that no one possessed of merely common sense, will fail to find its unscripturality, after a methodical study of the Old and New Testaments, unless previously impressed in the early part of his life with creeds and forms of speech preparing the way to that doctrine."

The Rajah attributes that prevalence of belief in the Trinity, which exists in Christendom, to the same causes as those which perpetuate and establish Hinduism in the East,-the force of early impressions.

"The minds of youths, and even infants, being once thoroughly impressed with the name of the Trinity in Unity and Unity in Trinity, long before they can think for themselves, must be always inclined, even after their reason has become matured, to interpret the sacred books, even those texts which are evidently inconsistent with this doctrine, in a manner favourable to their prepossessed opinion, whether their study be continued for three, or thirty, or thrice thirty years. Could Hinduism continue after the present generation, or bear the studious examination of a single year, if the belief of their idols being endued with animation, were not carefully impressed upon the young before they come to years of understanding?" (355.)

Having in another place noticed some facts in Muslim, and shewn how some nominal converts to Christianity, came to pass a decree, constituting Christ one of the persons of the Godhead, he says,

"These facts coincide entirely with my own firm persuasion of the impossibility, that a doctrine so inconsistent with the evidence of the senses as that of the three persons in one being, should ever gain the sincere assent of any one, into whose mind it has not been instilled in early education. Early impressions alone can induce a Christian to believe that three are one and one is three; just as by the same means a Hindu is made to believe that millions are one, and one is millions; and to imagine that an inanimate idol is a living substance, and capable of assuming various forms. As I have sought to attain the truths of Christianity from the words of the author of this religion, and from the undisputed instructions of his holy apostles, and not from a parent or tutor, I cannot help refusing my assent to any doctrine which I do not find scriptural."

Noble, magnanimous declaration! Would that those who pride themselves on their exclusive right to the name of Christian, were to profit by this example!

Well did the Rajah understand from his own observation and experience, the strongly marked and almost indelible colour of first impressions.

"The vessel, well

With liquor seasoned, long retains the smell."

He knew, as Wordsworth expresses it, that "The child is the father to the man," or, as Dryden amplifies the thought.

"By education most have been misled;

So they believe because they were so bred;

The Priest continues what the Nurse began,

And thus the child imposes on the man."

But early impressions are not the only source of an erroneous belief. A "golden image" erected by royal hands, and surrounded with "all kinds of music," will never lack worshippers. There are other Goddesses beside the great Diana, who have their Demetrius to excite an uproar against the friends of genuine Christianity. Wherever there are fashion and popularity, and the smiles of the fair, with their silver shrines, and academical honours, and Church preferments, and places of dignity and emolument; all inviting to the adoption and profession of error; error will assuredly be adopted and professed. Naked truth, though beautiful and captivating to the heart and mind of those who dare to love her for herself alone, will have small chance of being chosen by the selfish and dastardly time-serving idolater of the world, in preference to falsehood, in all her distortion and monstrosity, if clad in ermine and brocade, and rolled in a coach and six. But were truth and error to come fairly into the arena with no extraneous appendages, we should see the former claiming the victory amidst universal acclamations, without even the appearance of a skirmish. This, however, would be a small triumph. She must and she will, one day, prevail over all prejudice, prepossession, worldly interest, intolerance, bigotry, superstition, and idolatry. For Christ "must reign, till he hath put all enemies under his feet." "Then cometh the end, when he shall have delivered up the kingdom of God, even the Father;" "that God may be all in all."

Having, during the progress of this discourse, been under the painful necessity of animadverting on the illiberality of some of the Rajah's opponents, it is with no small satisfaction that I turn to the agreeable task of shewing, that his character and views were highly appreciated, not only by that denomination of Christians, who claim him as their own, but by liberal and enlightened members of other denomination. A striking instance of this occurs in the dedication to him of a Sermon, entitled, "Charity, the greatest of the Christian graces," by the Rev. Richard Warner, Rector of Great Chalfield, Wilts. (1832.) The Letter dedicatory runs thus:

"Rajah!

"Allow me to introduce the following Sermon to the notice of the Public, under the auspices of your 'respected and respectable name.'

"The epithets are appropriate: not so much on account of the condition, fortune, or talent, (distinguished as they may be) of the person to whom they are applied; as for the deep interest which he takes in the happiness of his fellow creatures; and for the labours in which he exercises himself, for the diffusion of the LIGHT OF CHRISTIANITY, and the promotion of EVANGELICAL LOVE, among an hundred millions of his countrymen; immersed in spiritual darkness, or drunken with intolerant superstition!

"Rajah! never shall I forget the long and profoundly interesting conversation, which passed between us a few days ago, on subjects the most important to the comfort and peace of mankind here, and their felicity hereafter-nor will the noble declaration fade from my recollection-that-'you were not only ready to sacrifice station, property, and even life itself, to the advancement of a religion, which (in its genuine purity and simplicity) proved its descent from the GOD OF LOVE, by its direct tendency to render mankind happy, in both a present and a future world-but that you should consider the abstaining from such a course, as the non-performance of one of the HIGHEST DUTIES, imposed upon rational, social, and accountable man!

"Rajah! 'a door' of the most extensive usefulness is 'opened' to you by DIVINE PROVIDENCE, macte virtute esto. Go on as you have begun! and may God prosper you benevolent endeavours to spread through the fairest, but most benighted portion of the earth's surface, the KNOWLEDGE OF CHRIST and the PRACTICE OF CHRISTIAN CHARITY!

"I am, Rajah,

"Your friend and brother in Christ,

"Richard Warner."

This, I doubt not, you will affirm to be a truly Christian letter, as worthy of its writer as of him to whom it is addressed. Such sentiments, from a Rector of the Church of England, is a sign of the approach of favourable times, of "times of restitution" to the knowledge and the worship of the only living and true God. On the sure word of prophecy we found our belief, that the time is approaching when "all nations whom Jehovah hath made, shall come and worship before thee, O Lord, and shall glorify thy name. For thou art great, and doest wondrous things; thou art God alone." "They shall come from the east, and from the west, and from the north, and from the south, and shall sit down in the kingdom of God." We may wish to see that day at hand, and we should do all in our power to expedite its approach. But let us remember that great mental changes are seldom instantaneous. Religious as well as political revolutions are the work of time; and though, in this country, many strenuous efforts have been made to impede the progress of improvement, and though the spirit of Antichrist has wrought with great industry, and not without some success, among the little Popes and Cardinals of the Synod of Ulster, there are still some minds in that reverend assembly, which are ashamed of their degradation, and impatient of the muzzle and the yoke which were strapped upon them during a reign of terror. Let us hope and pray that they will assume courage, to come out of the house of bondage, and vindicate their rights as Christian men.

Every where else the human mind is advancing:-will they alone continue retrograde? Every where else the principles of religious liberty, of which "the Reformers" had very imperfect notions, are now beginning to be well understood. It is not yet three centuries since Servetus was burned for holding Arian tenets. This day is exactly the 280th anniversary, since that atrocity was perpetrated by the "reformer," as he is called, of Geneva-but of whom the arch deformer of Christianity, would be a more appropriate title. How much has knowledge advanced since that time; and how much has the power of persecution been curtailed? Instead of kindling Smithfield fires, she can only threaten another fire, over which she has, happily, still less controul; and she must now be contented with such weapons as calumny and vituperation, instead of thumb-screws, boots, fair maidens, and other instruments of torture. It was only yesterday, I might almost say, since a statute was repealed, that might have punished by fine and imprisonment, the expression of those great evangelical truths, which you have this day heard advocated-that inflicted on the man who stood in the very pulpit from which you are now addressed, on the learned and virtuous Emlyn,-a sentence which lies a dark and heavy blot, on the religious history of this land.

How would it rejoice his spirit to hear that those great truths for which "he suffered hardships, as a good soldier of Jesus Christ," are now boldly avowed by thousands of the most virtuous and intelligent of our species? Theologians, from attachment to early hereditary notions, and various other causes, may labour as much as they please, to bolster up the doctrine of a Triune God, and an Incarnate God-but all their efforts will prove unavailing. Nature, reason, philosophy, scripture, all protest against the monstrous corruption-and though it may obtain credence in the same way as a belief in Transubstantiation, it is equally unfounded and must come to an end. Whereas belief in the simple unity of the Most High, is by the indomitable power of truth, forcing itself daily on the minds of many whose early prejudices were all opposed to its reception. Before this belief false systems of divinity, whether of Rome, of Geneva, or of England, must fall prostrate, as Dagon before the ark of Jehovah, and leave not a stump behind.

The illustrious Rajah is among the first and choicest fruits of Indian conversion-and his conversion is remarkable in this, that is was effected, in opposition to difficulties and discouragements, which to any mind of ordinary stamp, must have proved insuperable, solely by his superior knowledge of Scripture, combined with an invincible love of truth. It is well known that Mr. William Adam, a Baptist Missionary of Serampore, who endeavoured to make him a convert to orthodoxy, concluded his task by acknowledging himself a convert to the true evangelical opinions of the Rajah! By him has the great, the everlasting truth, "Jehovah our God is one," been proclaimed to the nations of the East.-It has been attested to those of the West by his appearance among them, by his character, by his writings. May his great and good example be followed by thousands and millions of his countrymen-and may we lend our strenuous efforts to promote a cause, which has for its objects the glory of God, the honour of Christ, and the felicity of man. Amen.

Brahma Samaj, a religious association in India which owes its origin to (Raja) Ram Mohan Roy, who began teaching and writing in Calcutta soon after 1800. The name means literally the "Church of the One God," and the word Samaj, like the word Church, bears both a local and a universal, or an individual and a collective meaning. Impressed with the perversions and corruptions of popular Hinduism, Ram Mohan Roy investigated the Hindu Shastras, the Koran and the Bible, repudiated the polytheistic worship of the Shastras as false, and inculcated the reformed principles of monotheism as found in the ancient Upanishads of the Vedas. In 1816 he established a society, consisting only of Hindus, in which texts from the Vedas were recited and theistic hymns chanted. This, however, soon died out through the opposition it received from the

Hindu community. In 1830 he organized the society known as the Brahma Samaj.

The following extract from the trust-deed of the building dedicated to it will show the religious belief and the purposes of its founder. The building was intended to be "a place of public meeting for all sorts and descriptions of people, without distinction, who shall behave and conduct themselves in an orderly, sober, religious and devout manner, for the worship and adoration of the eternal, unsearchable and immutable Being, who is the author and preserver of the universe, but not under and by any other name, designation or title, peculiarly used for and applied to any particular being or beings by any man or set of men whatsoever; and that no graven image, statue or sculpture, carving, painting, picture, portrait or the likeness of anything shall be admitted within the said messuage, building, land, tenements, hereditament and premises; and that no sacrifice, offering or oblation of any kind or thing shall ever be permitted therein; and that no animal or living creature shall within or on the said messuage, &c., be deprived of life either for religious purposes or food, and that no eating or drinking (except such as shall be necessary by any accident for the preservation of life), feasting or rioting be permitted therein or thereon; and that in conducting the said worship or adoration, no object, animate or inanimate, that has been or is or shall hereafter become or be recognized as an object of worship by any man or set of men, shall be reviled or slightingly or contemptuously spoken of or alluded to, either in preaching or in the hymns or other mode of worship that may be delivered or used in the said messuage or building; and that no sermon, preaching, discourse, prayer or hymns be delivered, made or used in such worship, but such as have a tendency to the contemplation of the Author and Preserver of the universe or to the promotion of charity, morality, piety, benevolence, virtue and the strengthening of the bonds of union between men of all religious persuasions and creeds."

The new faith at this period held to the Vedas as its basis. Ram Mohan Roy soon after left India for England, and took up his residence in Bristol, where he died in 1835. The Brahma Samaj maintained a bare existence till 1841, when Babu Debendra Nath Tagore, a member of a famous and wealthy Calcutta family, devoted himself to it. He gave a printingpress to the Samaj, and established a monthly journal called the Tattwabodhini Patrikd, to which the Bengali language now owes much for its strength and elegance. About 1850 some of the followers of the new religion discovered that the greater part of the Vedas is polytheistic, and a schism took place,-the advanced party holding that nature and intuition form the basis of faith. Between 1847 and 1858 branch societies were formed in different parts of India, especially in Bengal, and the new society made rapid progress, for which it was largely indebted to the spread of English education and the work of Christian missionaries. In fact the whole Samaj movement is as distinct a product of the contest of Hinduism with Christianity in the 19th century, as the Panth movement was of its contest with Islam 300 years earlier.

The Brahma creed was definitively formulated as follows:- (1) The book of nature and intuition supplies the basis of religious faith. (2) Although the Brahmas do not consider any book written by man the basis of their religion, yet they do accept with respect and pleasure any religious truth contained in any book. (3) The Brahmas believe that the religious condition of man is progressive, like the other departments of his condition in this world. (4) They believe that the fundamental doctrines of their religion are also the basis of every true religion. (5) They believe in the existence of one Supreme God-a God endowed with a distinct personality, moral attributes worthy of His nature and an intelligence befitting the Governor of the universe, and they worship Him alone. They do not believe in any of His incarnations. (6) They believe in the immortality and progressive state of the soul, and declare that there is a state of conscious existence succeeding life in this world and supplementary to it as respects the action of the universal moral government. (7) They believe that repentance is the only way to salvation. They do not recognize any other mode of reconcilement to the offended but loving Father. (8) They pray for spiritual welfare and believe in the efficacy of such prayers. (9) They believe in the providential care of the divine Father. (10) They avow that love towards Him and the performances of the works which He loves, constitute His worship. (11) They recognize the necessity of public worship, but do not believe that communion with the Father depends upon meeting in any fixed place at any fixed time. They maintain that they can adore Him at any time and at any place, provided that the time and the place are calculated to compose and direct the mind towards Him. (12) They do not believe in pilgrimages and declare that holiness can only be attained by elevating and purifying the mind. (13) They put no faith in rites or ceremonies, nor do they believe in penances as instrumental in obtaining the grace of God. They declare that moral righteousness, the gaining of wisdom, divine contemplation, charity and the cultivation of devotional feelings are their rites and ceremonies.

They further say, govern and regulate your feelings, discharge your duties to God and to man, and you will gain everlasting blessedness; purify your heart, cultivate devotional feelings and you will see Him who is unseen. (14) Theoretically there is no distinction of caste among the Brahmas. They declare that we are all the children of God, and therefore must consider ourselves as brothers and sisters.

For long the Brahmas did not attempt any social reforms. But about 1865 the younger section, headed by Babu Keshub Chunder Sen, who joined the Samaj in 1857, tried to carry their religious theories into practice by demanding the abandonment of the external signs of caste distinction. This, however, the older members opposed, declaring such innovations to be premature. A schism resulted, Keshub Chunder Sen and his followers founding the Progressive Samaj, while the conservative stock remained as the Adi (*i.e.* original) Samaj, their aim being to "fulfil" rather than to abrogate the old religion. The vitality of the movement, however, had left it, and its inconsistencies, combined with the lack of strong leadership, landed it in a position scarcely distinguishable from orthodox Hinduism. Debendra Nath Tagore sought refuge from the difficulty by becoming an ascetic. The "Brahma Samaj of India," as Chunder Sen's party styled itself, made considerable progress extensively and intensively until 1878, when a number of the most prominent adherents, led by Anand Mohan Bose, took umbrage at Chunder Sen's despotic rule and at his disregard of the society's regulations concerning child marriage.

This led to the formation of the Sadharana (Universal) Brahma Samaj, now the most popular and progressive of the three sections of the movement and conspicuous for its work in the cause of literary culture, social reform and female education in India. But even when we add all sections of the Brahma Samaj together, the total number of adherents is only about 4000, mostly found in Calcutta and its neighbourhood. A small community (about 130) in Bombay, known as the Prarthna (Prayer) Samaj, was founded in 1867 through Keshub Chunder's influence; they have a similar creed to that of the Brahma Samaj, but have broken less decisively with orthodox and ceremonial Hinduism.

BRAHMAPUTRA

Ram Mohan Roy (1774-1833), Indian religious reformer, and founder of the Brahma Samaj or Theistic Church, was born at Radhanagar, in the district of Hugli, Bengal, in May 17 74. He was the son of a small landowner, and in his early life acquired a knowledge of Persian, Arabic and Sanskrit, besides his own vernacular, Bengali. At the age of sixteen he first assailed idolatry in his Bengali work, entitled The Idolatrous Religious System of the Hindus. This gave offence to his orthodox father, and Ram Mohan left home and spent some years in travel. At the age of twenty-two he began his study of the English language, and he also acquired a knowledge of other modern and ancient European languages. On the death of his father he obtained an appointment under the British government in 1800, from which he retired in 1814, settled down in Calcutta, and devoted himself to religious reform. He had already inaugurated a circle for discussing the absurdities of idol worship, and published a striking book in Persian called Tuhfat-al-Muwahhiddin (" A Gift to Monotheists"). On his settlement in Calcutta he established a little friendly society (Atmiya Sabha), which met weekly to read the Hindu scriptures and to chant monotheistic hymns. In 1820 he issued a selection from the Christian Gospels entitled The Precepts of Jesus the Guide to Peace and Happiness. He also wrote Bengali works on the Vedanta philosophy, translated some of the Upanishads, entered into controversies with Christian missionaries, and on the 23rd of January 1830 definitely established the Brahma Samaj "for the worship and adoration of the Eternal, Unsearchable, Immutable Being who is the Author and Preserver of the Universe." He gave his support to the governor-general, Lord William Bentinck, for the abolition of the suttee rite, *i.e.* the custom of permitting Hindu widows to burn themselves on the funeral pyre of their husbands. He also worked hard to spread education among his fellow-countrymen, and to improve the quality and the prestige of the native press.

In 1830 the emperor of Delhi bestowed on Ram Mohan the title of raja, and sent him to England as his agent. Raja Ram Mohan Roy gave his evidence before the Select Committee of the House of Commons on the judicial and revenue systems of India. He presented petitions to the House of Commons in support of the abolition of the suttee rite, and had the satisfaction of being present in the House when the appeal against such abolition was rejected on the 11th of July 1832. As the first educated and eminent Indian who had come to England, he received a cordial welcome from learned men; and Bentham addressed him as an "intensely admired and dearly beloved collaborator in the service of mankind." Ram Mohan also visited France and contemplated a voyage to America, but a sudden attack of brain fever led to his death on the 27th of September 1833. He was buried at Bristol, where a tomb was erected by his friend Dwarka Nath Tagore.

2

Role in Bengal Renaissance

BENGAL RENAISSANCE

The Bengal Renaissance refers to a social reform movement during the nineteenth and early twentieth centuries in the region of Bengal in undivided India during the period of British rule. The Bengal renaissance can be said to have started with Raja Ram Mohan Roy (1775-1833) and ended with Rabindranath Tagore (1861-1941), although there have been many stalwarts thereafter embodying particular aspects of the unique intellectual and creative output. Nineteenth century Bengal was a unique blend of religious and social reformers, scholars, literary giants, journalists, patriotic orators and scientists, all merging to form the image of a renaissance, and marked the transition from the 'medieval' to the 'modern'.

Background

During this period, Bengal witnessed an intellectual awakening that is in some way similar to the Renaissance in Europe during the 16th century, although Europeans of that age were not confronted with the challenge and influence of alien colonialism. This movement questioned existing orthodoxies, particularly with respect to women, marriage, the dowry system, the caste system, and religion. One of the earliest social movements that emerged during this time was the Young Bengal movement, that espoused rationalism and atheism as the common denominators of civil conduct among upper caste educated Hindus.

The parallel socio-religious movement, the Brahmo Samaj, developed during this time period and counted many of the leaders of the Bengal Renaissance among its followers. In the earlier years the Brahmo Samaj, like the rest of society, could not however, conceptualize, in that feudal-colonial era, a free India as it was influenced by the European Enlightenment (and its bearers in India, the British Raj) although it traced its intellectual roots to the Upanishads. Their version of Hinduism, or rather Universal Religion (similar to that of Ramakrishna), although devoid of practices like sati and polygamy that had crept into the social aspects of Hindu life, was ultimately a rigid impersonal monotheistic faith, which actually was quite distinct from the pluralistic and multifaceted nature of the way the Hindu religion was practiced. Future leaders like Keshub Chunder Sen were as much devotees of Christ, as they were of Brahma, Krishna or the Buddha. It has been argued by some scholars that the Brahmo Samaj movement never gained the support of the masses and remained restricted to the elite, although Hindu society has accepted most of the social reform programmes of the Brahmo Samaj. It must also be acknowledged that many of the later Brahmos were also leaders of the freedom movement.

The renaissance period after the Indian Rebellion of 1857 saw a magnificent outburst of Bengali literature. While Ram Mohan Roy and Iswar Chandra Vidyasagar were the pioneers, others like Bankim Chandra Chatterjee widened it and built upon it. The first significant nationalist detour to the Bengal Renaissance was given by the brilliant writings of Bankim Chandra Chatterjee. Later writers of the period who introduced broad discussion of social problems and more colloquial forms of Bengali into mainstream literature included the great Saratchandra Chatterjee.

Later, Ramakrishna Paramhansa, a great saint of Bengal, is thought to have realized the mystical truth of all religions, and to have reconciled the conflicting Hindu sects ranging from Shakta tantra, Advaita Vedanta and Vaishnavism, as well as other religions like Christianity and Islam. In fact Ramakrishna made famous the Bengali saying: Jato Mat, Tato Path. (All religions are different paths to the same God). The Vedanta movement prospered principally through his disciple and sage, Swami Vivekananda who on his return from the highly successful Parliament of the World's Religions in Chicago in 1893 and subsequent lecture tour in America, became a revered national idol.

Swami Vivekananda urged Indians to break free from the shackles of colonialism, past and present and reaffirmed service to mankind as the highest truth of the Hindu Vedantic religion. "Service to mankind is service to god" was his motto. He was the first Indian to conceptualize an absolutely free, prosperous and strong India, which while appreciative of its rich cultural past would be vibrant enough to walk confidently into the future. Ramakrishna Mission, the great organization founded by Swami Vivekananda, was totally non-political in nature. It must be stressed that the Ramakrishna Movement founded by Swami Vivekananda carried forward their Master's (Ramakrishna's) message of all religions being true. In essence they were reliving what the Rig Veda--one of the holiest Hindu scriptures--had said ages ago: Ekam Sat, Vipra Bahuda Vadanti (That which is, is. Wise Men speak of it in many ways).

The Ramakrishna Movement is also noted for their unstinting service to mankind--they pioneered schools, colleges and hospitals and put in action the memorable clarion call of their founder Swami Vivekananda--Shiboggnyane Jib Seba (Serve Mankind as you would serve God (Shiva).

The Tagore family, including Rabindranath Tagore, were leaders of this period and had a particular interest in educational reform. Their contribution to the Bengal Renaissance was multi-faceted. Indeed, Tagore's 1901 Bengali novella, Nastanirh was written as a critique of men who professed to follow the ideals of the Renaissance, but failed to do so within their own families. In many ways Rabindranath Tagore's writings (especially poems and songs) can be seen as imbued with the spirit of the Upanishads. His works repeatedly allude to Upanishadic ideas regarding soul, liberation, transmigration and--perhaps most essentially--about a spirit that imbues all creation not unlike the Upanishadic Brahman.

Tagore's English translation of a set of poems titled the Gitanjali won him the Nobel Prize for Literature in 1913. He was the first Bengali, the first Indian as well as the first Asian to win the award. That is only one example but the contribution of the family is enormous.

Comparison with European Renaissance

The word "renaissance" in European history meant "rebirth" and was used in the context of the revival of the Graeco-Roman learning in the fifteenth and sixteenth centuries after the long winter of the dark medieval period. A serious comparison was started by the dramatis personae of the Bengal renaissance like Keshub Chunder Sen, Bipin Chandra Pal and M. N. Roy. For about a century, Bengal's conscious awareness and the changing modern world was more developed and ahead of the rest of India. The role played by Bengal in the modern awakening of India is thus comparable to the position occupied by Italy in the European renaissance. Very much like the Italian renaissance, it was not a mass movement; but instead restricted to the upper classes. Though the Bengal Renaissance was the "culmination of the process of emergence of the cultural characteristics of the Bengali people that had started in the age of Hussein Shah, it remained predominantly Hindu and only partially Muslim." There were some examples of Muslim intellectuals such as Saiyed Amir Ali and Mosharraf Hussain.

Some scholars in Bangladesh, now hold Bengal Renaissance in a different light. As Professor Muin-ud-Din Ahmad Khan of the department of Islamic History and Culture of Chittagong University, observes:

> *During nineteenth century A.D., Bengal produced a galaxy of reform movements among the Hindus as well Muslims... the Islamic reform movements such as Faraizi, Tariquah-i-Muhhamadiyah, and Taaiyni and Ahl-i-Hadith, occupied a conspicuous position amongst them. These Islamic movements were revivalist in character... these Islamic movements were born of the circumstances, which had also given birth to the contemporary Hindu reform movements such as Brahmo Samaj*

and Arya Samaj, which thrived in Bengal side by side with them…
Raja Ram Mohan Roy's movement is generally regarded as 'Renaissance movement'.

It is called by some as 'Hindu Renaissance' and by others as 'Bengali Renaissance' movement. It should nevertheless be observed that compared with the European 'Renaissance model', it was a Renaissance with a difference, especially, deeply inlaid by a revivalist make-up of pristine Hindu or Aryan religious spirit… Raja Ram Mohan Roy's Renaissance aimed at resuscitating the pristine Aryan spirit, 'Unitarianism of God', with the help of modern Western rationalist spirit.

Literature

According to historian Romesh Chunder Dutt: The conquest of Bengal by the English was not only a political revolution, but ushered in a greater revolution in thoughts and ideas, in religion and society… From the stories of gods and goddesses, kings and queens, princes and princesses, we have learnt to descend to the humble walks of life, to sympathise with the common citizen or even common peasant … Every revolution is attended with vigour, and the present one is no exception to the rule. Nowhere in the annals of Bengali literature are so many and so bright names found crowded together in the limited space of one century as those of Ram Mohan Roy, Akshay Kumar Dutt, Isvar Chandra Vidyasagar, Michael Madhusudan Dutt, Hem Chandra Banerjee, Bankim Chandra Chatterjee and Dina Bandhu Mitra. Within the three quarters of the present century, prose, blank verse, historical fiction and drama have been introduced for the first time in the Bengali literature.

Ram Mohan Roy, also written as Ram Mohan Roy, or Raja Ram Mohan Roy, (May 22, 1772-September 27, 1833) was the founder of the Brahmo Samaj, one of the first Indian socio-religious reform movements. His remarkable influence was apparent in the fields of politics, public administration and education as well as religion. He is most known for his efforts to abolish the practice of sati, a Hindu funeral custom in which the widow sacrifices herself on her husband's funeral pyre. It was he who first introduced the word "Hinduism" (or "Hindooism") into the English language in 1816.

In 1828, prior to his departure to England, Ram Mohan founded, with Dwarkanath Tagore, the Brahmo Samaj, which came to be an important spiritual and reformist religious movement that has given birth to a number of stalwarts of the Bengali social and intellectual reforms. For these contributions to society, Raja Ram Mohan Roy is regarded as one of the most important figures in the Bengal Renaissance.

Raja Ram Mohan Roy is Regarded as the Father of the Bengal Renaissance

Early Life and Education: Roy was born in Radhanagore, Bengal, in 1772. His family background displayed an interesting religious diversity. His father Ramkant was a Vaishnavite, while his mother Tarini was from a Shakta background. Ram Mohan learnt successively Bangla, Persian, Arabic and Sanskrit by the age of fifteen.

As a teenager, Roy became dissatisfied with the practices of his family, and travelled widely, before returning to manage his family property. He then worked as a moneylender in Calcutta, and from 1803 to 1814 was employed by the British East India Company.

Reformer: Religious Reformer:

- Roy advocated monotheism, or the worship of one God.
- He denounced rituals, which he deemed meaningless and giving rise to superstitions.
- He published Bengali translations of the Vedas to prove his points.
- In 1814, with the help of young Indians, he set up the Amitya Sabha to propagate rational religious ideas.

Social Reformer:

- Crusaded against social evils like sati and polygamy.
- Demanded property inheritance rights for women.

- In 1828, he set up the Brahmo Sabha to campaign against social evils.

- Due to his efforts, Governor General William Bentinck made sati illegal through an act in 1829.

Educationist:

- Roy believed education to be an implement for social reform.

- In 1817, in collaboration with David Hare and Alexander Duff, he set up the Hindu College at Calcutta.

- In 1830, he helped Alexander Duff in establishing the General Assembly's Institution, by organizing the venue and getting the first batch of students.

- He supported induction of western learning into Indian education.

- He also set up the Vedanta College, offering courses as a synthesis of Western and Indian learning.

- He was a polyglot and was well versed in many world languages.

Journalist:

- Roy published journals in English, Hindi, Persian and Bengali.

- His most popular journal was the Samvad Kaumudi. It covered topics like freedom of press, induction of Indians into higher ranks of service, and separation of the executive and judiciary.

In the social, legal and religious reforms that he advocated, Roy was moved primarily by considerations of humanity. He took pains to show that his aim was not to destroy the best traditions of the country, but merely to brush away some of the impurities that had gathered on them in the days of decadence. He respected the Upanishads and studied the Sutras. He condemned idolatry in the strongest terms. He stated that the best means of achieving bliss was through pure spiritual contemplation and worship of the Supreme Being, and that sacrificial rites were intended only for persons of less subtle intellect.

Roy campaigned for the rights of women, including the right of widows to remarry and the right of women to hold property. As mentioned above, he actively opposed polygamy, a system in which he had grown up. He also supported education, particularly of women. He believed that English-language education was superior to the traditional Indian education system, and he opposed the use of government funds to support schools teaching Sanskrit. In 1822, he founded a school based on English education. To overcome the social and religious evils, as he perceived them, he started a religious group known as the Brahmo Samaj. The Samaj borrowed beliefs and practices from several religions, and was eclectic in its philosophy.

A HISTORY OF LIBERALISM IN INDIA
1757-1947: *The Effect of British Liberal Ideas*

The strengthening of British influence in Bengal with the battle of Plassey in 1757 coincided with significant developments of thought in England (John Locke in the 1680s, Adam Smith with his monumental book in 1776, and Edmund Burke) and in the USA (Thomas Jefferson, John Adams and Alexander Hamilton, among others). The English language came to India in 1603 in Akbar's time but there was then no pressing economic reason for Indian people to learn English. It was only after the consolidation of Bengal by Robert Clive and the extension of the East India Company into the Indian political landscape, that the demand for learning English began to grow.

By 1835, Indians were paying serious money to be taught English, as it gave them job openings in the Company. As Thomas Babington Macaulay noted in his famous Minute: "the natives" had become "desirous to be taught English" and were no longer "desirous to be taught Sanskrit or Arabic". Further, those who wished to, seemed to picked up English very well: "it is unusual to find, even in the literary circles of the Continent, any foreigner who can express himself in English with so much facility and correctness as we find in many Hindus." (see the Minute at).

Those who learnt English quickly became aware of its literature, including the rapid evolution of Western political thought. This greater awareness of the advances in freedom laid the seeds for the demand for self-rule.

While people like Raja Ram Mohan Roy (1772-1833) were beginning to articulate elements of these political arguments, no one was in a position to explore and articulate new insights. However they did catch up with key liberal ideas and began implementing some of these advances thought through their new demands for greater freedom in India. While the West was firmly embedding its new political institutions, or contesting the growing forces of socialism (which had overpowered parts of the feudal and aristocratic West), the Indian intelligentsia was grappling with the challenge of the first major task ahead of it, namely independence. As well as Raja Ram Mohan Roy, other contributors to political thought on freedom in 19th century India included Dadabhai Naoroji (1825-1917), Mahadeo Govind Ranade (1842-1901), Gopal Krishna Gokhale (1866-1915) and Pherozeshah Mehta (1845-1915). Theory led to an independence movement in India. Gandhi demonstrated through a humane, non-violent, and dignified protest, that all humans were equal and should be treated equally, including their being given the opportunity to govern themselves. This was a major advance in the theory and practice of freedom and can be argued to have had a major effect in ending the age of imperialism and the age of racial discrimination.

Nehru, who was very well-educated and fully aware of the history of liberalism, seems to have had surprisingly little faith in an individual's ability to think and take responsibility for himself or herself. Nehru did not emphasise the importance of each individual undertaking self reflection and choosing among ethical alternatives. Possibly, in his view, making these ethical choices was too difficult for the common man. He definitely believed that these choices were best directed through state level dictates laid down by governing elites. Through planning. In any event, he veered toward collectivist and socialist thinking where decision making power is concentrated in the state. Decentralisation, where power and freedom vests with people at the lowest levels, was anathema to Nehru. He stated in his Autobiography: "socialism is... for me not merely an economic doctrine which I favour; it is a vital creed which I hold with all my head and heart." Indian industrialists (with their Bombay Plan) also sided with Nehru on a socialist pattern based on the Russian 5-year plan model.

Despite the environment in which socialist thought was flourishing, India was fortunate to enjoy at least a few liberties even before independence. The advances made in political institutions in England as a result of liberalism were imported and embedded into India over the decades by British rulers. Things like the right of assembly and protest under reasonable circumstances, the right to property, and freedom of expression? with a relatively free press, became a part and parcel of Indian political landscape before independence.

BENGALI PROSE AND RAJA RAM MOHAN ROY

It was through the immense influence of a towering personality like Ram Mohan Roy (1774-1833) that Bengali culture, society, education and literature took a giant step forward. It is an undeniable fact that Ram Mohan Roy had wielded his pen in Bengali Prose with the prime motto of social reformation and purification. He had never intended to create immortal or classical forms of literary extravaganza. But he used the Bengali language, for the first time, as an effective medium of transliteration, discussion and debates. Among his notable transliterations from the ancient Sanskrit texts are-'Bedanta Grantha' (1815), 'Bedanta Sara' (1815), 'The Upanishads' etc. His other commendable works were 'Gauriya-Vyakarana', 'Samvad Kaumudi' etc. The sketchy report attracted little notice. But more than a month later, a well-researched, detailed and strikingly-presented follow-up shook Parliament.

On November 22, the front page of the paper displayed the picture of a blinded man under the heading "Eyes punctured twice to ensure total blindness." The article by Arun Sinha, the Patna Correspondent, drew attention to the atrocity. Bihar Chief Minister

Jagannath Mishra reluctantly ordered an inquiry. Two days later, the matter was raised in Parliament. The weeklies took up the story, and published more close-ups of the blinded prisoners, with gory details of eyeballs being pierced with cycle spokes and acid poured into them. Prime Minister Indira Gandhi said she was sickened and phoned the Chief Minister, who, on November 30 suspended 15 policemen. The expose continued with Indian Express Executive Editor Arun Shourie writing two front-page articles criticising the administrative, police and jail procedures which allowed such atrocities to take place.

The Bhagalpur blindings provide an object lesson in the crucial contribution that sustained journalistic research can make in creating public awareness of human rights, more so in a traditional society in which entrenched abuses are apt to be overlooked. The reporter must be able to place the abuse in its wider legal, social and constitutional context to enable the reader to realise its implications. Stories on human rights must touch the conscience of the reader if they are to arouse rethinking of traditional norms. This requires skill in presentation as well. But the impact can be more lasting and more valuable to society than other newspaper events.

In Bhagalpur, many residents protested against the suspension of the policemen, arguing that such punishment deterred crime more effectively than protracted legal cases. It took a sustained campaign on the rights of prisoners, together with the impact of pictures of the blinded men, to touch the public conscience and expose similar brutal practices elsewhere. In recent years, media has reflected and further strengthened increasing awareness of human rights in many areas in which they were overlooked before. Exploitation and ill-treatment of domestic workers, often children, is still routine in many households. But a series of press reports describing the cruel conditions in which they are often kept has pierced the silence and forced the police to intervene.

Special cells have been set up to deal with violence against and ill-treatment of women following sustained exposure of dowry deaths and other crimes.

Bonded labour-workers and children chained to fields or workplace for their lifetimes to repay old debts-is treated as an offence only after the press joined social activists in exposing the evil. Now the police are active, at least in Delhi. On September 10, 2000, it was reported that the "South District (Delhi) police have rescued 19 children from Bihar who were being used as bonded labourers." They were between six and 12 years of age. But investigations into the trauma of the children and the circumstances in which they were bonded in Bihar are missing.

Few countries, if any, have inherited such a wide-ranging legacy of social, cultural, economic and other restrictions on human rights as India. At the same time, India has given itself a Constitution guaranteeing human rights to an extent unequalled for a country of its size and complexity. But human rights abuses persist; in some areas they have increased. The primary reason lies in widespread ignorance of the rights due to every citizen of the country, even fifty years after the Constitution came into force in 1950. India was a signatory to the Universal Declaration of Human Rights adopted by the United Nations even earlier, in 1948.

India has nurtured a free press since it became independent, except for the brief experience of censorship under the Emergency regulations of 1975-76. This provides an opportunity to create widespread awareness of human rights, a social obligation yet to be adequately fulfilled, as evident from India's low listing in the annual UN Human Development Reports. As a developing country, the range of human rights issues requiring media intervention is particularly wide, with a marked social content. This was recognised by the United Nations in December 1986, when the Universal Declaration was expanded to include Right to Development. Access to education, health services, food, housing, employment and fair distributions of income were mentioned specifically. Measures to ensure that women have an active role in development were stressed.

Few papers have taken up the challenge; it needs study and skill to rouse reader interest in often distant processes of human development. But reports selected by the Press Institute of India for publication in Grassroots, its monthly journal on development reporting, demonstrate that such stories can stand out and have a far more lasting impact than routine news stories, however big their headlines. Kalpana Sharma of The Hindu received a prize for her sensitive treatment of the gradual change in caste relations enabling lower caste girls in a Karnataka village to defy the traditional custom of "sitting in the laps" of upper caste elders, and bring out what this meant for social reform.

Latha Jishnu's account of the transformation of a remote backward village in Madhya Pradesh by a locally conceived literacy programme has helped promote literacy in the region. Other reports make such issues as panchayati raj, exploitation of tribals, preservation of forests and water conservation meaningful for the urban reader.

One of the biggest contributions of the press in recent years is to make the right to information a national issue. The campaign for right to information began five years ago with villagers of south Rajasthan demanding access to official files containing details of money disbursed for local development works. They knew that much of the money was misappropriated, but could not prove it without access to the files. Though opposed by the local bureaucracy, they were able to establish corruption in some cases. Taken up by the press, especially local newspapers, the campaign spread to many parts of the country. At the time of writing, four states have passed their own right to information legislation and the Central Government has introduced a Bill in Parliament.

That the press has a role in promoting awareness of human rights, then described as social reform, was realised long before Independence. In 1823, the noted Bengali author, Raja Ram Mohan Roy, brought out weeklies in three languages to campaign against caste discrimination and sati and for widow remarriage. Social reformers elsewhere followed his example. Nearly a century later, Mahatma Gandhi, the most outstanding exponent of journalism in the service of human rights, entered the field. He focussed on the evil of untouchability but also campaigned for women's rights, basic education, prisoner's rights (long before Bhagalpur), community health, rural employment and other development objectives later adopted by the United Nations.

In 1933, Gandhi brought out the first issue of Harijan, or God's children, his name for untouchable. It marshalled support, including a contribution from Rabindranath Tagore, for the Temple Entry Bill that sought to give untouchables the right to enter temples, the first step in their liberation. That the Bill was defeated in the Central Assembly and officially described as "a serious invasion of private rights" indicates the temper of the times. Largely due to Gandhi's sustained campaign at public meetings and in print, untouchability was abolished and its practice forbidden in 1950 under Article 17 of the Constitution. But, as recounted vividly by the prizewinning journalist P. Sainath in a series of articles in The Hindu, it continues to be practised in many ways. The challenge to eradicate the most deep-rooted denial of human rights in India survives.

FEMALE EDUCATION IN INDIA

(Mary Carpenter addressed the East India Association on her work for the promotion of female education in India. C.Wren Hoskyns, M.P., was in the chair. Carpenter referred to her three journeys to India, taken with the object of showing sympathy with, and learning the wants of female education in India.

Having referred to several native gentlemen who had suffered religious persecution for their efforts to emancipate their ladies from the social customs of India, she detailed the mode which she adopted to bring about to bring about an improved system of instruction by native female teachers, and the valuable assistance which had been rendered by the English ladies.

At present girls were taken from school at eleven years of age, partly because it was not considered proper for them to remain under male teachers after that age. After reviewing the state of female education in Bombay and Madras presidencies, she spoke at length on Calcutta, referring to the efforts of John Drinkwater

Bethune. She said, "I regret to say that I saw in Calcutta extremely little effort for female education among the natives; in fact, I am not aware of any school (at any rate of importance) established by the natives themselves in Calcutta.

Referring to Raja Ram Mohan Roy she said, "He first broke the bonds of superstition; he was persecuted by his family, and exiled from his home; but he succeeded in establishing the worship of the One True God in Calcutta, where he founded and endowed a place of worship for One True God."

She said that she need not enter into an account of that because "the gentleman is present who may be regarded as the head of it, Baboo Keshub Chunder Sen." She added, "In Calcutta, then, among the Brahmos and Theists, I found an advance in many respects beyond what I had seen in other parts of the country."

Dadabhai Naoroji, honorary secretary to the East India Association, spoke at some length in complimentary terms of the good influence which Miss Carpenter had exercised in India. The chairman thanked Miss Carpenter and introduced Baboo Keshub Chunder Sen to the meeting.)

It gives me great pleasure to bear my humble testimony in England, as I have done more than once in India, to the noble work of which Miss Carpenter had done for the promotion of female education in India. The warm and philanthropic interest she has evinced in that work, the readiness with which she risked her life and health and exposed herself to many inconveniences and hardships, entitles her not only to the lasting gratitude of the Indian nation but to the sympathy and respect of all in England who appreciate useful work.

When the first important public female school worthy the name was established by the late Mr. Bethune in the metropolis of India, during the administration of Lord Dalhousie, it evoked a feeling of discontent, throughout the country, and excited great opposition and bitterness; but in spite of a large number of conservative and orthodox men saying, "Thus far shalt thou go, and no farther," the advancing waves of progress went on till at last, not only in the large cities and presidency towns, but even in the small provincial towns and villages, small school after school rose up, and, in the course of a few years, not only were there scores, but hundred of little girls coming day after day in order to receive instruction in vernacular literature, in arithmetic and in writing. In carrying out the work of female education great impediments, some of them of an almost insuperable character, had to be overcome, and many defects had to be rectified.

In a country where little girls became mothers when they would hardly be supposed in civilized countries to have attained the marriageable age, and where they became grandmothers when perhaps they ought to think of marrying; girls could receive education only for three or four years at most in a public school, their education stopping at a time when they ought to begin. This custom of premature marriage was pernicious, not only physically, but intellectually and morally considered; for the work of education was arrested when little girls, having become mothers, began to talk with ridiculous gravity of the duties they owned to their children. It was, therefore, absolutely necessary to supplement this deficient system of education of native girls with zenana instruction.

As soon as that want was felt, many kind-hearted ladies, both in India and in England, took the matter with an amount of earnestness which was very creditable to them. They combined in order to get funds, and sent out trained governesses to visit native ladies in their own houses. Zenana instruction was indispensably necessary for the real welfare of the country. So long as the system of seclusion prevailed, which would prevail for a considerable length of time.

Another want which was deeply felt was the want of female teachers, and just at the time when that want was beginning to be felt, Miss Carpenter arrived in India. Her advent was cordially and enthusiastically hailed by those who were directing their efforts towards the improvement of education of females in India. They knew she would help them, and she did help them. She saw the want with her own eyes. At once she saw that without a large number of well-trained native female teachers it was impossible to make female schools really useful. She, therefore, represented the matter to several distinguished native gentlemen in Calcutta, in Bombay, and in Madras. Many, of course, did not show their appreciation of the usefulness of the scheme. They were backward in the matter; a few, however, stepped forward manfully, and assured her of their warm interest in the scheme, and their readiness to do all in their power to help her.

She was then obliged to lay the matter before the Government. Unfortunately, the Government also had serious misgivings as to the feasibility of the scheme, not that they were unwilling to educate native women, but they felt it might interfere with the prejudices, and shock the feelings of the native population if they went too far in such a delicate matter; and it was not till instructions were sent out by the Secretary of State for India, that the Government began to really in earnest about it. It was then that the Government sanctioned a liberal grant for the purpose of establishing and supporting normal female schools in each of the presidency towns.

In Bengal, hardly anything has yet been done towards the establishment these normal schools. As Miss Carpenter has already very justly said, Bombay is far ahead of Bengal in the matter of female education. I have visited some of the best schools in Bengal and Bombay, and I can say from my own experience that there are a larger number of girls receiving public education in Bombay than in Bengal; but while Bengal has not come up to Bombay as far as regarded extent of education, Bengal is not behind Bombay in the matter of solidarity and depth. Already several books have been published by native ladies of Bengal of a really valuable character; among others a drama, a beautiful story, and some charming verses on the beauties and sublimities of creation. A periodical is also published in Bengal, to which Bengali ladies send very often sent most charming contributions, mostly verses, which native ladies take great delight in composing. Some of the best theistic hymns are from the pen of Brahmo ladies. This shows that native ladies are not slow to learn. The Government having come forward with a liberal grant, it is the duty of the natives of India to cooperate with the Government in a friendly and harmonious manner, in order to give effect to the noble scheme which Miss Carpenter had suggested, and which, through the instrumentality of Government has been realized in at least one of the presidency towns. If full effect can be given to this project, if a sufficient number of schools can be can be brought into existence, not only in the presidency towns, but in the chief provincial cities in the North-West, and in the Punjab, India would be supplied with that which it most wants at the present time.

I hope and trust that the English ladies who are present, would well weigh all that has been said by Miss Carpenter, and that they will be stimulated by her example. I fully agree with Mr. Dadabahai Naoroji that we must not too sanguinely look forward to actual and viable and tangible results, but we must look beneath the surface, in order to see whether or not Miss Carpenter's visit to India has produced a lasting impression on the native public mind, and on the minds of all those who were really interested in the work of female education in India.

(Source: The speech and other details were published with the title Female Education in India in The Brahmo Samaj: Keshub Chunder Sen in England by Brahmo Tract Society, 78 Upper Circular Road, Kolkata in 1915.)

VEDIC PHYSICS : SCIENTIFIC ORIGIN OF HINDUISM

The Vedas can be read at many levels, it is said. Those who have heard the chanting of the Vedas by trained priests will be overwhelmed by the sounds that transport one to a different world. You may not know enough Sanskrit to understand a word but the combination of sounds will make your body a tuning fork resonating to some cosmic sounds. You can read some good translations and find in the Vedas an uplifting philosophy and a beautiful metaphysic. If you have been to a traditional wedding ceremony and heard the

Vedic chants you may thrill to the grandeur and sanctity the Vedas bring to such a ceremony. Some claim that the Vedas include India's pre-history. Some say it contains astronomical codes that enable us to measure anything from the distance to the moon to the movement of stars in the zodiac. However, Dr. Roy says the Rig Veda does not contain history. Nor, he says, is it a treatise on astronomy. It is not merely a praise to the Gods. And surely it is not the emanations of a group of soma-drunk men who wrote the first "magic-realism" novel. What it is, says Dr. Roy of the University of Toronto, is a treatise on cosmology, and it challenges some of the hypotheses that modern physicists have come up with till now about the nature and size of the universe. The Rig Veda is a book of science, and the only reason that we have not been able to understand the science in it is because of the layers of ignorance and misinterpretations that have accumulated over the millennia, says Roy in this intriguing book, *Vedic Physics: Scientific Origin of Hinduism* (1999).

Many during the early 80s' were fascinated with books that tried to explain quantum physics to lay audiences as well as make connections to what seemed to be parallels within eastern mysticism. I was teaching at the Valley School in Bangalore those days and my colleagues and I would read books by Capra, Zukav and others that dealt with quantum physics and eastern mysticism, and our discussions would drag on into the night. After all, in a school that was based on J. Krishnamurti's philosophy most teachers were familiar with Krishnamurti's dialogues with scientists, mathematicians, and psychologists. And there were those innumerable tapes of his discussions with the theoretical physicist David Bohm (author of *Wholeness and the Implicate* Order and some twenty other books on theoretical physics, cognitive science, etc.). Since then there have been other works by Capra, including the movie *Mindwalk* (1995) based on his book *The Turning Point*. Zukav wrote a more critically acclaimed book than Capra, titled *The Dancing Wu-Li Masters*. To this day of course Capra's *The Tao of Physics* enjoys the status of a "modern classic of science". I mention these books because in the past decade or so it seems like the readership for such books is fading. The "establishment" has won, and the experimental physicists and their fellow travellers have been constructing more billion dollar accelerators and cyclotrons, and chortling over the pictures that the Hubble telescope is beaming back to Earth.

Most of us, if not all, in the Krishnamurti schools were more knowledgeable about the books being written by Westerners than of any attempts by Indians at reconciling the findings of modern scientists with the knowledge/information contained in the Vedas. Very few of us were interested in or knew Sanskrit. The physicists and aeronautical engineers amongst us knew their science and technology but cared little to read the Vedas or other Hindu texts. The philosophers amongst us knew little Sanskrit, and less physics. Our knowledge of Hinduism was "second hand". In short, there wasn't a Dr. Roy amongst us. A research scientist at the University of Toronto, Roy, a native of Bihar, did his undergraduate work in metallurgical engineering at IIT, Kanpur, and got his M.S. and Ph.D. from Ohio State University in Materials Science and Engineering. That is his engineering and science background. As he says in the preface to his book, he has combined his early learning and training in Sanskrit with his scientific and engineering vocation.

Most of us who are trained as scientists, or social scientists, or who have grown up in modern, technological societies are skeptics when it comes to accepting the "scientific" worth of ancient texts. There are also too many charlatans and too many "men of faith" who are willing to take people for a ride as long as they can sell their religion. Given the trend in modern Indian education too, there are few of us who are willing to spend time digging into the texts of the past. Moreover, Indian texts were considered to be mostly spiritual-religious texts. The latest and most lucrative path is to "deconstruct" the texts through literary, political, philosophical, and psychological analyses. Thus it was that at the last South Asia Conference in Madison in October 1998, there were Sanskritists who "deconstructed" aspects of the Ramayana: one professor, wearing a ring in his left ear, speculated that when Hanuman "grew large" and lifted a mountain and transported it across the sea, it was merely a metaphor for Hanuman getting an erection after watching the many semi-clad and/or naked beautiful women in the gardens and palaces of Ravana. Professors from Berkeley, Columbia, Harvard and elsewhere cheered and commented on such "exegesis" (or you could say "excesses"), and there was only standing room in the conference hall to listen to such "deconstruction". I bring this up because we are more comfortable with such analyses, and believe they are "modern" and/or "scientific". In such a world it is rather difficult to make a new case for old texts. We believe linguists or literary critics, but we are skeptical of other kinds of "deconstruction," the ones that go against the grain.

The "traditional" take on the Rig Veda therefore would be that of scholars like Wendy Doniger O'Flaherty, who has selected, and translated 108 hymns out of the 1017 for a book (*The Rig* Veda) published by Penguins (1981). She basically claims that the Rig Veda contains details of daily life, the symbolism and mechanism of ritual, and that it provides insight into mythology, philosophy, and religion. Very few would argue about those aspects, and most are happy to accept the Rig Veda as such. Even the great commentators like Madhwacharya, or the great works like the Upanishads focus on the "spiritual-psychological-symbolic" aspects of the Vedas. We are happy when traditional texts or teachers tell us that the central teaching and the central aim of the Rig Veda is "the seeking after the attainment of Truth, immortality, and Light," and that the supreme goal of the Vedic sages was discovering the "One Reality". Thus the hymns on creation, especially the *Pirusha Sukta* ("the hymn of man" as it is ordinarily regarded), have been made famous.

According to the traditional reading of the *Pirusha Sukta* the gods created the universe by dismembering the cosmic giant, Pirusha, the primeval male who is the victim in a Vedic sacrifice (O'Flaherty, p. 29). She claims that the theme of cosmic sacrifice is a widespread mythological motif, and it is just a part of the Indo-European corpus of myths of dismemberment. So far, so good, you may say. But Roy argues that the Rig Veda is a book of ancient cosmology "where the authors have chosen fundamental particles and forces of nature to describe the cosmology in a dramatic way...." So, let us see how he interprets the particular verse in the *Pirusha Sukta* (10.90.15): "What does the sacrifice of Pirusa-animal mean" How can the God himself be sacrificed?

The sacrifice here means a change of form, a change from unmanifested form to a form of manifested universe.... As the Pirusa ceased to be what the Pirusa was before the creation, he was symbolically sacrificed. This had nothing to do with human sacrifice" (p. 37-38). Skeptical readers may say, "oh, it is just a little twist to the original formulation". But let us look at just one or two more verses, and see if we the "ordinary" or "literal" meaning makes sense. If it does not, then we need to try and figure out the symbolism. 10.90.01 is translated by O'Flaherty thus: "The Man has a thousand heads, a thousand eyes, a thousand feet. He pervaded the earth on all sides and extended beyond it as far as ten fingers". A thousand feet and a thousand eyes, we could say, is just a poetic metaphor for "God" who is "everywhere" and "sees everything". But what about the ten fingers? A thousand eyes and now "his" reach only as far as ten fingers? Roy says the ten fingers represent "ten dimensions".

In modern physics direction and dimension are synonymous. Thus, he claims, that in Vedic cosmology universe is seen as ten-dimensional. He quotes the Vayu Purana (4.74-75) in which it is said that the "whole universe including moon, sun, galaxies and planets was inside the egg and the egg was surrounded by ten qualities from outside". Roy provides a more careful context for the reader to speculate about the nature of the universe. There are numerous verses from the different hymns of the "ten books" of the Rig Veda that Roy translates, and provides a "context" which makes better sense than the merely poetic. A careful reader would therefore have the opportunity to compare both Roy's translation of the relevant verse and the analysis of the same.

The next important point that the author makes is that since the Rig Veda is a book of cosmology whatever "history" there is in it is not "real history". Similarly, he says that whatever else is there in it is merely tangential. For the establishment historians and other nay-sayers therefore this is a book that will befuddle and confuse. It is also a book that will undermine their claims about the Aryan invasion of India, for Roy musters some fascinating evidence (see p. 110 and p. 123) to support a fresh interpretation of the Harappan civilization.

Roy is aware of the argument by skeptics that the attempts at finding scientific meanings in scriptures is that they are made only after the discovery of those scientific facts. But the importance of his work is that he has tried to show how the scientific meaning contained in the Vedas is in many ways different from what modern scientists/physicists have put forward. Let us look at the difference. I will just summarize a few major points.

Roy summarizes for us the latest in modern cosmology, from the versions of Big Bang to versions of the Steady State models (Chapter 18). He summarizes their strengths and their weaknesses, and then he adumbrates what he believes (and provides evidence for) is the model that the Rig Veda constructs.

The sages considered the universe to be made of "fluid" (not as fluid as in water but "the flow of matter particles"), and that it was rotating. The rotation's effect on this spherical volume of fluid makes it take the shape of a spheroid (the shape of an egg). In the standard Big Bang model the universe is not rotating but its constituents are. The Big Bang theory has been challenged, for example, by those proposing a steady state model, and the book provides quick but precise summaries of those opposing theories. The Big Bang model also proposes that the mass-energy before the universe came into being was concentrated at a single point. The Vedas instead tell us that in the beginning there was no mass-energy. It was a complete void. Ed Tyron in 1973 put forward a theory that makes the same argument.

The Vedic sages considered the creation of mass-energy to be continuous and that it was being created on the surface of the universe. If you wonder how a void can have a surface Roy has some fascinating explanations. In the Vedic model the universe has a centre which is at absolute rest. There is an axis of the universe passing through this centre around which the universe is rotating. Space can be divided into two, manifested and unmanifested, and the creation of matter and antimatter will continue as long as the universe is expanding. While in the Big Bang model the universe can be open or closed, the Vedic model suggests differently.

And the cyclic model proposed by scientists, that is the universe will expand and contract continuously is also modified in the Vedic model. It suggests that each cycle is independent of the other and there is no limitation on how many cycles there can be. Roy supports all his claims by providing the specific location of the verse in the scriptures. The verses have been translated into English, and the scientific meaning of the verse is explained by dissecting the words and providing other supporting evidence from elsewhere in the Vedas.

The work of Roy is important in that he tries to figure out the hidden meanings in the Rig Veda by drawing careful analogies and comparisons, and telling us when he is not sure of a particular meaning of a particular word or hymn.

Thus the contracting universe is "Martanda", the living universe Vivasvana, the first pair of particle and anti-particle (matter and anti-matter) are "Yama" and "Manu", the early part of the universe when the surface tension was the most important force constraining the expansion of the universe the battle between these two forces is the immortalized epic battle of Indra and Vṛtra.

Radiation is Rudra, and the remnants of radiation from the early universe, the cosmic background radiation, is Visha. Brihaspati represents the expansion of the universe, gramya (the domesticated animal) is boson, aranya (wild animal) is fermion, and so on. All of Roy's claims are buttressed by relevant hymns, and he also provides interesting asides on how the myths and fables of other cultures and religions were borrowed from the latter Brahmanas and thus were misreadings and wrong or partial interpretations of Vedic knowledge.

At this point, skeptics may wonder how the Vedic sages knew what they knew. Roy claims that they arrived at their findings and conclusions based on sound reasoning. This may seem like the Vedic sages were the precursors of Descartes! I do wish that he had speculated more deeply on how these ancient people discovered these fascinating truths.

What was the Vedic methodology? Was the nature of the universe "revealed" or was it discovered? Readers may think this is a weakness of the book but he, however, makes it plain that modern scientific methods are not the only way one can investigate the "subtle nature of reality" (p. xiii). In his foreword to the book, Dr. Subhash Kak (author/co-author of books on astronomy, mathematics, and computer science, and a leading figure in the re-interpretation of Vedic knowledge) says: "Roy's basic premise is that the mind - by analysis, reflection on everyday phenomena, and grasping the nature of its own self - can discover a considerable amount of science, and this is what the Vedic rishis did.... Roy's method goes counter to the orthodoxy that outer knowledge cannot be discovered by an analysis of the inner.

But there is accumulating evidence from cognitive science and biology that the inner and the outer are connected. For example, biological systems are equipped with clocks tuned to the motions of the sun, the moon, and other astronomical phenomena. Indian thinkers have always insisted on the presence of such connections, claiming that this is how the mind is able to know the physical world. In Vedic thought this is expressed by the notion of 'bandhu' that connect the biological, the terrestrial, and the astronomical.... The Vedic focus on mind and consciousness is paralleled by the central place of the observer in modern physics. In quantum mechanics the state changes in an abrupt fashion when an observation is made and this has prompted some physicists to claim that consciousness should be the primary category of the universe, distinct from physical matter" (p. xiii, xiv).

CHRISTIAN CONTRIBUTION TO INDIAN NATION BUILDING

Introducing the Study

The arrival of St. Thomas to India around AD 50s marks the entry of Christianity nearly 1950 years back. He landed in the Malabar coast and went about doing his work till the Eastern coast and was buried in Chennai, the East coast. Francis Xavier who came to India in the 15th century, also started a new leaf in the historical contribution to Indian life. This paper tries to show some landmark contributions of the Catholic Church made to the mainstream life of India from a Socio-pastoral and sociological perspective. Today India is a nation with over one billion people with different colours, creeds, races ethnic groups, languages and cultures. This mosaic, called India, makes today important contributions in several fields though several see only the face of the advanced number of personnel working in information technology.

Situating India in the World scenario of religions we observe the following: India has given birth to four major religions of the World: Hinduism, Buddhism, Jainism and Sikhism. Hindus form the majority, (82%) in India. Buddhism, that originated in India and flourished till the 6th century A.D., was practically made to quit India and it spread to several countries in Asia, making itself a majority religion in Asian countries. Today Buddhists form only 0.5% in India. Besides Muslims form 12% in the Indian population. In spite of a long history of Christianity, Christians form today only 2.5% of the total population and the Catholics only 1.5% of the total population of India. In spite of this significantly tiny minority character, the Catholic Church in India made praiseworthy contributions in the life and development of Indians.

The aim of this paper is to explore a few areas wherein Catholic Church made significant contributions. Space and time does not allow one to bring out every detail. The main contours will be pointed out in a sociological and Socio-Pastoral perspective in the field of education, health care, Social development, Hindu religious revival movements, contribution to the secular polity of the country, offering of its personnel to the service of the people, and the field of the empowerment of women.

In the Field of Education

Though Christians and particularly Catholics are a tiny minority, the contribution in the field of education is not only impressive but shows the importance the Church has given to it in the Indian context. At the time of independence of India in 1947 only about 14% of the population were literate. If it has gone up to 55% of the population today, Christianity can be proud in playing its role in it. Some statistics will testify to it.

"The Catholic Church in India runs over 17,000 educational institutions, while over 11,000 are Nursery, Primary and Middle schools. There are also over 1500 professional and technical schools. In the year 2000, Catholic colleges numbered 175 including 2 Engineering and 2 Medical Colleges. What is impressive is that 70% of all these schools are in rural areas, serving the poor, especially the *dalits*, the *adivasis* and other disadvantaged groups. Only a meager 15% of the Church institutions are in the cities and large towns."

"At the close of the 19th century, India had only 26 Christian Colleges. At the time of independence in 1947, the number of Christian Colleges was 62 out of a total of 450. In 2000 Christian Colleges numbered about 250 out of the 11,089 Colleges. They catered to a total of 135,200 students of whom 28% were catholics. Nearly 50% of the Catholic Colleges are for women only. 17% are for men only and 33% are mixed". The Church gave a major importance to the education of women and we can proudly say that this led to the enlightenment of Indian women belonging to all religions, castes, tribes and different regions in the modern India. The Church had also given its due attention to technical education, and runs today 1514 technical and vocational training institutions in the country The historical contribution and breakthrough of the achievement of the Church in the field of education lies in the fact that it broke the monopoly of a single privileged caste and decentralized and democratized education. This made it possible for *dalits* and tribals not only to benefit by it but to have social mobility in life. Education of the masses in urban and particularly in rural areas has been the backbone of the development of India and for bringing about social changes.

Contribution in the Field of Social Development

The field of social development is another area that drew the attention of the Church. Church has considered social services as a way of demonstrating the compassion of Christ to the Indian Society. Hence specific attention to the development of the poor and downtrodden was given due importance right from the beginning. In certain areas like the tribal belt the liberation of the tribals from money-lenders and landlords served as the first contribution of the Church. E.g Fr.S.Lievens, Fr.J.B.Hoffmann, etc.

Today the Catholic Church allocates much of its finance in this field *e.g.* for tsunami relief and rehabilitation work it spent 150 million dollars through Caritas India. There are Diocesan Social Service Societies in all the 160 dioceses in India. There is the national organization of Caritas India and Catholic Relief Services and several Regional Societies like Don Bosco Reach Out in the North-East India. The Church changed and evolved in her services from relief and charitable works to Institutional model of educational and health Institutions and from there has adopted the empowerment approach of making the poor self-reliant, able to remake their future by a cooperative and collective action for social transformation.

The grassroots organizations of the poor and the downtrodden in villages are organized by the Church by giving them awareness education and motivation to act collectively. There are today thousands of such groups all over India which attempt to change their lives and build their future through savings, income-generation projects and collective actions to liberate themselves from oppressive forces.

Such actions have earned the anger of the rich and vested interested groups who today plan through fundamentalist groups to attack and eliminate the presence of Christians. You must have heard about the atrocities taking place in Orissa where no help is given to those victims of such attack.

Hindu Religious Revival Movements

In the pre-independence period some religious revival movements emerged (5). These religions movements were an outcome of the interplay of Socio-economic, political and cultural forces effecting a cultural transaction between Hinduism and Christian models of thought in a society in transition to answer to the existential needs of the people. Brahmo Samaj (1823) was founded by Raja Ram Mohan Roy. He assimilated several elements from the Western and Christian models and reformulated Hinduism by a new reinterpretation of the *Vedas*. He introduced a belief in monotheism and denied the caste-system and its ideology. He opposed vehemently child marriage and the practice of *Sati* (burning the widow in the funeral pyres of her husband). He encouraged the Western education system and himself ran several schools. His aim was to revitalize Hinduism without any feeling of antagonism towards other religions and cultures.

ARYA SAMAJ

It was founded by Dayananda Saraswathi in 1875. He tried to reinterpret the *Vedas* to say that the *Vedas* advocate monotheism and was against idolatry. He rejected the caste-system and child-marriage as having no basis in the *Vedas*. He took a different turn than Raja Ram Mohan Roy. "Back to *Vedas*" was his battle-cry to Hindus. He made it obligatory to read, teach, recite and listen to the recitation of *Vedas* which he interpreted in his way as said above. He gave an aggressive character to Hinduism as well as a militant spirit to attack anyone who would talk against Hinduism.

RAMAKRISHNA MISSION

It was inspired by Ramakrishna Paramahamsa and organized by Narendranath Datta, known as Swami Vivekananda. It had clear overtones of Hindu-Christian cultural transaction.

In Ramakrishna's attitude towards different religions he was both against the militant spirit of Arya Samaj and the reformatory character of Brahmo Samaj. He had a basis in Hinduism with an ecumenical spirit, showing the complementary character of all religions.

Thus he would first break the sectarian spirit within Hinduism by validating through his mystical experience the different sectarian Hindu gods and cults and, secondly, he would try to destroy the inter-religious rivalry by realizing a mystical experience of Mohammed and Jesus Christ.

Along with this mystical experience he would introduce the idea of social service to mankind by reinterpreting the *advaitic* principle of the basic unity of God and creatures to be the basis for all social service. Love of one's neighbour was the only form of adoration of God for Ramakrishna.

His disciple Swami Vivekananda founded Ramakrishna Mission on Christmas eve in 1897. Today it adopts several charitable and social works done by Hindus in several areas.

Contribution to the Secular Polity of the Country

"The Christian community has made a significant contribution when in the constituent Assembly, the Christian community through Fr. Jerome D'Souza renounced separate electorate and expressed trust in the majority community to respect and treat the minority community on a par with all as citizens of the country.

That was an important contribution of the Christian community to the secular nature of the Constitution of the Republic. For nation building the secular character and ethos of our polity is essential to shape and forge harmony and peace for all people of the country.

The Church remains committed to secularity of the Constitution of the Republic. Secular character of the Republic is a positive force for peace and communal harmony in a multicultural and multireligious society that India is."

The Religious Personnel

The Religious personnel working in different fields of Socio-Pastoral involvement is another contribution to the total services offered to build up India.

Diocesan priests	-nearly 9000
Religious priests	-nearly 15,000
Religious Brothers	-nearly 2,000
Religious Sisters	-nearly 77,000

Of these majority of Religious Sisters and Brothers serve in educational and healthcare institutions. A good number of priests also serve in such institutions and social service societies in the 160 dioceses in India. Practically all of them are professionally qualified and give a professional contribution in the building up of the nation.

Towards the Empowerment of Women

The development of women in different aspects is another specific contribution to the backbone of Indian development. It starts from working for the abolition of girl child feticide in the womb or outside by upholding the ethical values and supporting women to fight against such evil by giving protection to such women and the child they beget.

It continues by the education of the girl children through the schools and through the awareness given to women's grassroots groups to educate their girl children. Their higher education is also supported. One must recall the fact that out of the 220 Catholic Colleges in India 50% are meant only for women and 33% are mixed ones.

The awareness programmes and empowerment of women by thousands of grassroots groups where the Church is actively present, touch the majority of the illiterate adult women. Asserting equal participation in Church participative structures like Diocesan Pastoral Council, parish pastoral council and educating women to demand equal representation in decision-making in micro, semi-macro and macro political structures cannot be ignored by a honest observer as a sincere attempt of empowerment of women by both Catholics and others.

To Conclude

Besides what has been mentioned above, there have been several other fields like Indian Christian spirituality, Inter-faith dialogue, contribution to linguistic anthropology right from 16th century in several languages in India, contribution to ethnography and Tribal anthropology and Dalit Anthropology, contribution to the formation of the youth, etc. Catholic Church can be compared to leaven working in the mass of the Society. According to different periods this leaven has worked with various degrees of force. Hence it is very often not seen outside. The Church also does not seek publicity as it follows the principle of left hand not knowing what the right hand does.

3

Establishment of Brahmo Samaj

Brahmo Samaj is the societal component of Brahmoism. According to J.N Farquahar, "It is without doubt the most influential socio-religious movement in the evolution of Modern (Greater) India."

It was conceived as reformation of the prevailing Bengal of the time and began the Bengal Renaissance of the 19th century pioneering all religious, social and educational advance of the Hindu community in the 19th century.

From the Brahmo Samaj springs Brahmoism, the most recent of legally recognised religions in India and Bangladesh, reflecting its non-syncretic "foundation of Ram Mohan Roy's reformed spiritual Hinduism (contained in the 1830 Banian deed) and scientifically invigorated by inclusion of root Hebraic-Islamic creed and practice."

Meaning of Names

For Modern usage reflecting subsequent Legislation, Constitution and Legal rulings see Brahmo. The Brahmo Samaj is a community of people assembled for orderly public meeting, discussion or worship of the Eternal, Immutable Supreme Being, Author and Preserver of the Universe, "but not under or by any other name designation or title peculiarly used for and applied, to any particular being or beings by any man or set of men whatsoever". Brahmo literally means "one who worships Brahman", and Samaj mean "community of men".

History and Timeline

Brahmo Sabha: On 20 August 1828 the first assembly of the Brahmo Sabha (progenitor of the Brahmo Samaj) was held at the North Calcutta house of Feringhee Kamal Bose. This day is celebrated by Brahmos as Bhadrotsab. This Sabha was convened at Calcutta by religious reformer Raja Ram Mohan Roy for his family and friends settled there. The Sabha regularly gathered on Saturday between seven o'clock to nine o'clock. These were essentially informal meetings of Bengali Brahmins (the "twice born"), accompanied by Upanishadic recitations in Sanskrit followed by Bengali translations of the Sanskrit recitation and singing of Brahmo hymns composed by Ram Mohan. These meetings were open to all Brahmins and there was no formal organisation or theology as such.

On 8 January 1830 influential progressive members of the closely related Kulin Brahmin clan (scurrilously described as Pirali Brahmin *i.e.* ostracised for service in the Mughal Nizaamat of Bengal) of Tagore (Thakur) and Roy (Vandopadhyaya) zumeendar family mutually executed the Trust deed of Brahmo Sabha for the first Adi Brahmo Samaj (place of worship) on Chitpore Road (now Rabindra Sarani), Kolkata, India with Ram Chandra Vidyabagish as first resident superintendent. On 23 January 1830 or 11th Magh, the Adi Brahmo premises were publicly inaugurated (with about 500 Brahmins and 1 Englishman present). This day is celebrated by Brahmos as Maghotsab. In November 1830 Ram Mohan Roy left for England.

Decline of Brahmo Sabha

With Ram Mohan's departure for England in 1830, the affairs of Sabha were effectively managed by Trustees Dwarkanath Tagore and Pandit Ram Chandra Vidyabagish, with Dwarkanath instructing his diwan to manage affairs. Weekly service were held consonant with the Trust directive, consisting of three successive parts: recitation of the Vedas by Telegu Brahmins in the closed apartment exclusively before the Brahmin members of the congregation, reading and exposition of the Upanishads for the general audience, and singing of religious hymns. The reading of the Vedas was done exclusively before the Brahmin participants as the orthodox Telegu Brahmin community and its members could not be persuaded to recite the Vedas before Brahmins and non-Brahmins alike. By the time of Ram Mohan's death in 1833 near Bristol (UK), attendance at the Sabha dwindled and the Telugu Brahmins surreptitiously revived idolatry. The zumeendars, being preoccupied in business, had little time for affairs of Sabha, and flame of Sabha was almost extinguished.

Tattwabodhini Period

In 1839 Debendranath Tagore, son of (Prince) Dwarkanath Tagore, founded the Tattwabodhini (Truth-seekers) Sabha.

Foundation of Samaj

On 7th Pous 1765 Shaka (1843) Debendranath Tagore and twenty other Tattwabodhini stalwarts were formally invited by Pt. Vidyabagish into the Trust of Brahmo Sabha. The Pous Mela at Shantiniketan starts on this day which is considered as foundation of the 'Adi' (First) Brahmo Samaj which was named the Calcutta Brahmo Samaj.

First Schism

The admittance of Keshub Chandra Sen (a non-Brahmin) into the Calcutta Brahmo Samaj in 1857 while Debendranath was away in Simla caused considerable stress in the movement, with many old Tattvabodhini Brahmin members leaving the Samaj and institutions due to his high-handed ways. These events took place intermittently from 1859, coming to a head publicly between the period of 1 August 1865 till November 1866 with many tiny splinter groups styling themselves as Brahmo. The most notable of these groups styled itself "Brahmo Samaj of India". This period is referred to in the histories of these secessionists as the "First Schism".

Spread of Influence

Although the Brahmo Samaj movement was born in Kolkata, the idea soon spread to the rest of India. That happened to be the period when the railways were expanding and communication was becoming easier. Outside Bengal presidency some of the prominent centres of Brahmo activity were: Punjab, Sind, and Bombay and

Madras presidencies. Even to this day, there are several active branches outside West Bengal. Bangladesh Brahmo Samaj at Dhaka keeps the lamp burning.

Social & Religious Reform

In all fields of social reform, including abolition of the caste system and of the dowry system, emancipation of women, and improving the educational system, the Brahmo Samaj reflected the ideologies of the Bengal Renaissance. Brahmoism, as a means of discussing the dowry system, was a central theme of Sarat Chandra Chattopadhyay's noted 1914 Bengali language novella, Parineeta.

Focus of Modern Brahmo Reform:

• Denunciation of polytheism,
• Rejection of the caste system and its abolition,
• Rejection of the dowry system and its abolition,
• Emancipation of women,
• Widow remarriage,
• Reform of educational system,
• Opposition to sati (the practice of burning widows alive),
• Spread of knowledge by universal access to information,
• Legal reform especially in fields of personal and secular law,
• Simplicity and purity in public and private affairs
• Opposing corrupting influences like intoxicants, television, devadasi system, politicians etc.

After controversies, including the controversy over Keshub Chunder Sen's daughter's child marriage rituals wherein the validity of Brahmo marriages were questioned, the Brahmo Samaj Marriage Bill of 1871 was enacted as the Special Marriages Act of 1872 and set the age at which girls could be married at 14. All Brahmo marriages were thereafter solemnised under this law which required the affirmation "I am not Hindu, nor a Mussalman, nor a Christian". The Special Marriages Act 1872 was repealed by the new Special Marriages Act in 1954 which became the secular Marriage law for India. The old Special Marriages Act of 1872 was allowed to live on as the Hindu Marriage Act 1955 for Hindus-Brahmo Religionists are excluded from this Act; which is applicable, however, to Hindus who follow the Brahmo Samaj. On May 5, 2004 the Supreme Court of India, by order of the Chief Justice, dismissed the Government of West Bengal's 30 year litigation to get Brahmos classified as Hindus. The matter had previously been heard by an 11 Judge Constitution Bench of the Court (the second largest bench in the Court's history). As of 2007 the statutory minimum age for Brahmos to marry is 25(M)/21(F) versus 21(M)/18(or 15F) for Hindus.

It also supported social reform movements of people not directly attached to the Samaj, such as Pandit Iswar Chandra Vidyasagar's movement which promoted widow remarriage.

Doctrine

The following doctrines, as noted in Renaissance of Hinduism, are common to all varieties and offshoots of the Brahmo Samaj:

Brahmo Samajists have no faith in any scripture as an authority.

Brahmo Samajists have no faith in Avatars.

Brahmo Samajists denounce polytheism and idol-worship.

Brahmo Samajists are against caste restrictions.

Brahmo Samajists make faith in the doctrines of Karma and Rebirth optional.

RAM MOHAN ROY

The renaissance in modern Indian literature begins with Raja Ram Mohan Roy. Roy was born in Radhanagar village in west Bengal's Hooghly district on May 22, 1772, to conservative Bengali Brahmin parents. His father Ramakanta Roy's family belonged to the Vaisnava (who worship Lord Vishnu-the Preserver; followers of Sri Caitanya Maha Prabhu) a liberal sect that flourished in Bengal and South India. His mother Tarini Devi's orthodox priestly family (Bhattacharyas of Chatra) on the other hand belonged to the Shakta sect (worshippers of Goddess Kali-the Shakti-the Mother Energy of the universe). Roy did his elementary education in the village school in Bengali, his mother tongue. At the age of 12, Roy went to a seat of Muslim studies in Patna where he mastered Persian and Arabic. His knowledge of Arabic enabled him to read the Koran in the original, as well as the works of Sufi saints. He also devoured Arabic translations of the works of Aristotle and Plato.

When he was 16, Royclashed with his orthodox father on the issue of idol worship and left home. Toacquaint himself with the Buddhist religion, he travelled across northern India and Tibet for the next three years. Hisquestioning mind objected to the deification of the Buddha and this did not godown well with some of the lamas. He then visited Varanasi where he learnt Sanskrit and studied ancient Hindu scriptures.

In 1803, he secured a job with the East India Company and in 1809, he was posted to Rangpur. In Rangpur, he learnt about Jainism and studied the Jaintexts. Roy was drawn to certain aspects of Christianity that led some of the followers of the religion to suggest that he convert; but he politely declined.

Roy's understanding of the different religions of the world helped him to compare them with Vedantic philosophy and garner the best from each religion. Sufi mysticism had a great influence on Roy. He loved to repeat three of their maxims: "Man is the slave of benefits"; "The enjoyment of the worlds rests on these two points-kindness to friends and civility to enemies"; and "The way of serving God is to do good to man".

To pursue his interests, Roy resigned from the East India Company a few years later and came to Calcutta in 1814. Dissatisfied with the system of education and the rote method of teaching English, he formed an association of English and Hindu scholars. He also invested his own money in the starting of a school where he introduced subjects like science, mathematics, political science and English. Roy felt that an understanding of these" modern" subjects would give Indians a better standing in the world of the day. Though initially antagonistic towards British rule in India, Roy later began to feel that the country would benefit in terms of education and by exposure to the good points of Christianity. For this he was called a stooge of the British. Along with a group of like-minded people, Roy founded the Atmiya Sabha in 1814. The group held weekly meetings at his house; texts from the Vedas were recited and theistic hymns were sung. Roy was drawn to the Unitarian form of Christianity that resulted in him supporting a Unitarian Mission to be set up in Calcutta in 1824.

Historical Significance

In the early 1800s, the General Assembly of the Church of Scotland sent Reverend Alexander Duff, a young and dedicated missionary, to Kolkata to set up an English-medium institution. Though Bengalis had shown some interest in the spread of Western education from the beginning of the 19th century, both the local church and government officers were skeptical about the high-caste Bengali's response to the idea of an English-medium institution. Raja Ram Mohan Roy helped by organizing the venue and bringing in the first batch of students.

He also assured the guardians that reading the Bible did not necessarily imply religious conversion. Although his ultimate aim was the spread of English education, Duff was aware that without a good command on one's native language, it was impossible to master a foreign language. Hence in his General Assembly's Institution (as later in his Free Church Institution), the teaching and learning of the Bengali language and literature was given high priority. Duff was keen on sports and had accumulated different kinds of sports-related equipment for use in his institution. When he introduced political economy as a subject in the curricula, the Church strongly criticized him.

In 1840, Duff returned to India. At the Disruption of 1843, Duff sided with the Free Church. He gave up the college buildings, with all their effects and with unabated courage, set to establish a new institution, which came to be known as the Free Church Institution. He had the support of Sir James Outram and Sir Henry Lawrence, and the encouragement of seeing a new band of converts, including several young men born of high caste. In 1844, governor-general Viscount Hardinge opened government appointments to all who had studied in institutions similar to Duff's institution. In the same year, Duff co-founded the Calcutta Review, of which he served as editor from 1845 to 1849. These two institutions founded by Duff, *i.e.*, the General Assembly's Institution and the Free Church Institution would be merged later to form the Scottish Churches College. After the unification of the Church of Scotland in 1929, the institution would be known as Scottish Church College.

Along with Raja Ram Mohan Roy, the father of modern India, Dr. Duff played a significant role in supporting Lord Macaulay in drafting his famous Minute for the introduction of English education in India. Successive eminent missionary scholars from Scotland, *viz.* Dr. Ogilvie, Dr. Hastie, Dr. Macdonald, Dr. Stephen, Dr. Watt, Dr. Urquhart and others contributed to the spread of the liberal Western education.

Along with other educational institutions like Serampore College, Hindu College, the Scottish Churches College played a pivotal role in ushering the spirit of intellectual enquiry and a general acceptance of the ideals of the European Enlightenment, among Bengalis, in what came to be regarded as the Young Bengal Movement and later, the Bengal Renaissance.

Duff's contemporaries included such luminaries as Reverend Mackay, Reverend Ewart and Reverend Thomas Smith. Till the early 20th century the norm was to bring teachers from Scotland (like William Spence Urquhart, Leslie Stephen, H.M. Percival, Ian Fairweather etc.) but eminent Indian scholars were also engaged as teachers by the college authorities. Scholars like Surendranath Banerjea, Kalicharan Bandyopadhyay, Jnan Chandra Ghosh, Gouri Shankar Dey, Adhar Chandra Mukhopadhyay Sushil Chandra Dutta, Mohimohan Basu, Sudhir Kumar Dasgupta, Nirmal Chandra Bhattacharya, Bholanath Mukhopadhyay and Kalidas Nag had all contributed hugely to enhance the academic standards of the college.

Dr. Duff played a leading part in founding the University of Calcutta in 1857, he was associated with the Agro-horticultural Society and the establishment of a medical college, the first in India. He also aimed at breaking down caste-barriers by founding several girls schools. The Scottish Church College played a pioneering role in women's education as well as co-education in the country. Female students comprise half the present roll strength of the college. With the added interest of the missionaries in educational work and social welfare, the college stands as a monument to Indo-Scottish co-operation. The aims and principles of the College are essentially those of its founder namely, the formation of character through education based on Christian teaching.

Raja Ram Mohan Roy (1772-1833) was born into a Brahmin family in Bengal and experienced the orthodox practices of Hinduism in his youth. He studied the Quran, Buddhism and the New Testament. He disliked Idol worship and hated the practice of Sati, after seeing his brother's widow burnt alive on her husband's funeral fire. He fought to abolish polytheism, idol worship, the caste system, child marriage, animal sacrifice and Sati which is the practice of a widow being burnt alive on the funeral pyre.

In 1828, Raja Ram Mohan Roy founded the Brahmo Samaj (Society of Brahma) in an attempt to reform Hindu religious beliefs and practices. Brahmo Samaj's hall of worship has no images, statues or pictures. Only prayers and Hymns are sung, selecting one God for concentrating their prayers. Members offered prayers as a group. This community worship was a new aspect to Hinduism. The form of worship under Brahmo Samaj system was based on the Christian school of thought as the founder was inspired by the Western ideas. The Samaj inspired progressive development in Hindu Society, religion and politics. The indirect result of the reform movement of Ram Mohan Roy was the abolition of Sati, child marriage, untouchability, caste distinction, and established women's right to property and widow remarriage.

SCIENCE IN THE VEDAS

Vedic Physics by the 33-year old Dr. Raja Ram Mohan Roy is an ambitious work by a physical scientist who-thanks to his upbringing in a traditional household-also had the benefit of a Vedic schooling from childhood. His goal is to show that the Vedas, in keeping with their name meaning 'knowledge', contain a good deal of scientific knowledge that was lost over millennia, which he seeks to recover by suitably interpreting them. In particular, he regards the Rigveda as a book on particle physics and cosmology that has much in common with modern physics, but sometimes more subtle, especially when it comes to explaining the origin and evolution of the universe.

Such a claim is of course not new; there is no shortage of books claiming that the Vedic seers had seen everything and modern science is only a rediscovery. The author makes no such claim. His position is that by following a path of discovery quite different from that followed by modern science, the Vedic sages had arrived at a model of the universe, supported by a theory of atomic and subatomic particles that bears some similarity to modern physics; but Vedic cosmology is quite different from modern theories of the universe. What lends credence to the author's claim is his comprehensive grasp of modern physics. This allows him to construct-possibly reconstruct-a Vedic model of the universe that avoids some of the difficulties of modern theories like the Big Bang.

This may sound similar to some other books on the subject like Fritj of Capra's Tao of Physics, but there are important differences. For one, the author's grasp of the Vedic texts is surer, based on primary readings and often, original interpretations. Next, he offers some remarkable insights that go beyond contemporary knowledge of cosmology and even physics. Most significantly, he reconstructs a theory of the universe that may be a serious competitor to modern theories like the Big Bang. In other words, he is not satisfied with a comparison between Vedic knowledge and modern science; his goal is it to shed new light on important problems of nature. His approach is based on a careful reading of Vedic texts combined with a firm grasp of science. And therein lies the book's strength.

Before going into the details of Mr. Roy's book, it is useful to have an idea of different approaches to the study of the Rigveda. The most widely known is the nineteenth century reading favoured mostly-but not exclusively-by Western Indologists, which holds the Rigveda to be the record of 'Aryan invaders' from Eurasia and their conquest of India then populated by dark skinned natives. This has justly fallen into disrepute though some Western academics and their Indian followers continue to cling to some variant of it if only because they have nothing better. It is not hard to see that two dominant nineteenth century European ideas-colonial conquests and racism-went into this interpretation though political and Christian missionary interests also had major influence. The values underlying this version have fallen into disrepute, but their creation called 'Indology' continues to hold sway in academia, though it is rapidly crumbling.

When we turn to Indian interpretations, we run into problems of a different kind-break in tradition. Although we look at the four Vedas as from a single genre, there is considerable difference between the Rigveda and the other three. To take an example, the same verses from the Rigveda that appear in the Yajurveda are sometimes read and even interpreted differently.

Where the Yajurveda is generally treated as 'Karma-kanda'-or what may loosely (and incorrectly) be called 'ritualistic', the real meaning and purpose of the Rigveda remains something of a mystery. This is by no means a recent phenomenon. The ancient commentator Yaska (c. 3100 BC) tells us that even in his time scholars no longer had the intuitive grasp of the Vedic hymns that the ancients possessed. For whatever reason, even before the third millennium, the true meanings of the Rigveda had been greatly diluted if not lost, and various artificial interpretations like Karma-kanda came to be imposed on them.

Another point to be kept in mind is the extreme sophistication of structure and language of the Rigveda. Even superficially seen, its metrical forms and linguistic structures are the most sophisticated the world has even known. To go with this, its language, far from being elaborate, is concise yet flexible-at times bafflingly so. As Sri Aurobindo observed, the Vedic language is "just and precise and sins rather by economy of phrase than by excess, by over-pregnancy rather than by poverty of sense." From this it is possible to see that the Rigveda records not the beginning of a civilization but a culmination, containing knowledge-or 'Veda'-coded in the form of what we call Rigvedic hymns. In other words, the language of the Rigveda could well be technical in nature, like what we find in a modern book on physics or mathematics. A convincing key to unlocking this body of knowledge remains to be found. This is what the author in his book has set out to do. In his words: "Most of the verses in the Vedas are mysterious. This is so because we don't know the actual scientific meaning of these verses. My aim in furnishing complete hymns is to give my learned readers as much information as possible, so that they can help in finding the lost Vedic science." His book is an admirable step in that direction, and, as this review seeks to explain, a great deal more.

The message of the book under review may be summarized as follows: one of the keys to unlocking the secrets of the Rigveda consists in reading many of the words like 'gau' and 'ashva' as well as names of gods like 'Marut' and 'Indra' as technical terms used in the natural sciences, and the hymns themselves as descriptions of laws of nature. In other words, the Rigveda contains a description of the forces of nature and the laws that govern them, written in cryptic even coded language. The author's goal is to extract their meaning by making sense of important hymns that appear enigmatic or even incoherent when interpreted in a conventional way. Though his effort cannot be considered complete, it nonetheless sheds new light on important Vedic passages.

For example, in the Vedic literature we have frequent statements like 'agni was pashu' and 'pashus are agneya' that make no sense when read literally. The author, however, identifies 'pashu' with particle and 'agni' with energy. Then a whole series of Vedic passages including the ones just cited become comprehensible and even coherent. Similarly, he identifies Vayu with field-one of the most important concepts in physics. Surya of course stands for light, and the seven horses yoked to Surya's chariot are the seven colours of the light spectrum. The word 'gau' (cow), which Yaska tells us also means light, actually refers to the particle state of light or the photon. Based on his approach, the author suggests that the great

Rigvedic hymn 1. 123 by Dirghatamas, actually describes the creation and annihilation of particles, which some liken to Shiva's Dance of Creation. It should be emphasized that this brief description-necessarily simplified-does not do full justice to the author's interpretations.

This approach offers some interesting possibilities. The author observes: "Our universe is matter dominated. If matter and antimatter are created together in same amount, then we should find equal amount of antimatter. Whyis it we don't find much evidence of antimatter as far as we can observe? Are remote parts of the universe antimatter dominated? Did matter and antimatter somehow get segregated in different corners of the universe? Scientists don't think so. Scientists believe that when universe was very young, for some reason a small excess of matter over antimatter was generated. As matter and antimatter annihilated each other, this small excess remained, and this small excess is our universe. The Vedas take a different view. According to the Vedas, matter and energy are constantly being created at the surface of the universe, and there is an imbalance in their creation. Matter and antimatter continually annihilate each other and the small excess of matter has accumulated over the age of the universe."

This is a profoundly different cosmic view, which the author supports with the help of Rigvedic passages including 2.20.7 and 6.47.21. The latter may be read as: "Everyday Indra removes half of the people, similar to the other half but black in colour, born in his house." (The author uses the past tense, which I have rendered into the present following Panini's rule for the Vedic usage: chandasi lung lat litah.) The author goes on to observe: "Indra is considered responsible for killing the black people in the Rigveda. As matter and antimatter are attracted towards each other due to the opposite nature of electric charge resulting in annihilation, electric force is indeed responsible for this phenomenon."

So black refers to antimatter! In addition to the author's remarkably original reading of an obscure passage, it highlights the utter superficiality of European Indologists **and their** Indian followers in giving such passages a racial meaning. If the author's insights can be supported, this is the kind of knowledge that was lost over the millennia. There is evidence however, that some fragments of it survived as late as the time of Sayana (1315-87). In his Rigveda Bhashya he gives a value for the velocity of light that in modern units works out to 186,000 miles per second. So it is not easy to dismiss the author's interpretations as speculation, obtained by 'retrofitting' modern scientific findings on to the Vedas. In any event, the Vedic cosmology worked out by the author has important differences with modern theories of the universe.

After presenting his interpretation of Vedic passages in the light of modern physics, the author gives a lucid summary of modern theories (Big Bang and Steady State) followed by a discussion of the Vedic model. He points out some of the basic problems of the Big Bang theory, highlighting the following: singularity, horizon, flatness, age, monopole, entropy and antimatter. He discusses the same problems in the Vedic context and shows how they may be elegantly accounted for. This can be illustrated with the help of the singularity problem. In the author's words: "Universe started with an explosion according to the Big Bang model. At time equal to zero, all the mass-energy was concentrated in a point. This is certainly an unimaginable feat, as the universe is immense.

According to Pauli's exclusion principle, not even two electrons can occupy the same state, and here the whole universe is considered to be inside a point....

The situation is a direct result of the conservation of mass and energy [or mass-energy], the most sacred principle of physics. Considering that the universe is expanding, extrapolating backward in time, the universe was as small as a point. As mass-energy of the universe must be conserved, all the mass-energy must have been there at time zero as well. We should note that conservation of mass-energy is violated in this case as well. This is equivalent to saying that all the mass-energy was created at time zero. Mass-energy density of the universe was infinity at time equal to zero, which is called a point of singularity."

To get around this obvious difficulty, scientists have introduced an entity called 'inflation', which has mysteriously disappeared from the present universe. The singularity problem does not arise in the Vedic approach to creation. As the author observes: "Inflation has not solved the singularity problem, as inflation only produces part of the mass-energy of the universe, and as long as even a tiny amount of matter-energy was present at time zero, singularity problem will be there. The Vedas tell us that at time zero there was no mass-energy in the universe. It was a complete void. Space, mass and energy are continuously being created. As universe had zero mass-energy at time zero, the universe did not start with singularity."

This obviously violates the conservation principle. But Vedic cosmology has a conservation principle of its own that includes space along with mass and energy. It is a very subtle principle and yet stunning in its simplicity. The author describes it as follows: "... the Vedas have returned to tell an even greater truth [than mass-energy equivalence]: equivalence of space, mass and energy. Space is no different from matter and energy. In the beginning there was no mass-energy in the universe because there was no space. Mass-energy is created due to expansion of the universe. The universe cannot expand without creating mass-energy and universe cannot contract without annihilating mass-energy. Thus the universe started with zero mass energy and will end up with zero mass-energy as well. Thus there was no singularity in the beginning and there will be no singularity at the end."

The author recognizes that since the universe is now in an expanding mode, we must be witnessing the creation of mass-energy in the universe. As evidence he points to gamma-ray bursts that scientists have observed but have no clue as to its source. In 1973 it was discovered that about three times a day, the sky flashes with a powerful burst of gamma-rays. The author observes: "The gamma-ray bursts are intense, bulk of their radiation is in the range of 100,000 to 1,000,000 electron volts, implying a very hot source and its sources release more energy within minutes than sun will release in its entire lifetime."

Astronomers believe that these bursts are coming from distances that range from three to ten billion light years. Various explanations have been offered-from black holes to collapsing neutron stars-but none is satisfactory. It is possible to account for it using Vedic cosmology. According to Vedic science, mass-energy is continuously being created at the surface of the universe. This is related to the expansion of the universe. In the author's words: "As the universe is huge now, its expansion will create immense radiation." What is extraordinary is that these gamma-ray bursts-corresponding to the creation of mass-energy according to Vedic science-takes place three times a day. This is exactly the frequency given in the Rigveda in at least three passages. (3.56.6, 7.11.3, 9.86.18). The second of these tells us: "O Agni! We know you have wealth to give three times a day to mortals."

Another fundamental difference between the Big Bang model and the Vedic model is that the latter postulates rotation of the universe around an axis. This means it has a preferred direction, or, in the parlance of physics, the Vedic universe is non-isotropic. Here too the author invokes an unexplained scientific phenomenon in support-violation of parity observed in weak interactions. As the author observes: "It is obvious that model of the universe should not contradict the nature of these interactions. Weak interaction has complete disregard for many conservation laws including parity... What is so special about weak interaction? Why is it that it does not obey conservation laws like other interactions?... It has been more than forty years since the discovery of parity violation, but cosmologists have not taken into account what particle physicists have proved."

The author shows that this can be seen as an indirect proof of the rotating universe implied in the Vedic model. He then cites possible direct evidence also. He notes that observations by Borge Norland and John P. Ralston on the polarization of light from distant galaxies indicate that the universe is rotating. (This is on top of the well-known Faraday Effect. Since the rate of rotation is slow, one has to look very far to find physical evidence of it.) Their results are disputed by other scientists for the reason that it violates the idea of an isotropic universe, but that is only to be expected. As the author notes: "Rotation of universe and continuous creation of matter and energy are two salient features of the Vedic cosmology."

This brings us to the author's reconstruction of the Vedic universe, which he summarizes as follows: "Like the Big Bang model, the Vedic model assumes that the universe started from a point and is expanding. However, unlike the Big Bang model, universe starts cold with zero mass-energy, and is rotating as well as expanding. There is a similarity with the Steady State model that mass-energy is constantly being created. The difference is that [in the Vedic] the universe is not considered infinitely old, and the creation of mass-energy is only during the expansion phase of the universe. During the contraction phase, the mass-energy is annihilated, so that the universe ends without a singularity."

Clearly, the author's study of the Vedas combined with his knowledge of modern physics has allowed him to present an impressive synthesis of the two. There are some minor difficulties. His reading of the Vedas leads him to postulate the existence of particles not known to modern physics. His interpretations of the symbolism of the Harappan seals are speculative, and sometimes wrong. We are of course on much firmer ground today-thanks to Jha's decipherment of the Harappan script, and the subsequent work of Jha and this reviewer.

Also, it is a little puzzling that he should read the famous description of the Sarasvati River-giribhya a samudrat-to mean 'from the ocean', when the causative case (pancami vibhakti) suggests the opposite. The book also has passages on the Puranas and the development of Hinduism that add nothing to it but interrupts the flow of reasoning that is central to its theme. But these are minor quibbles that do not seriously detract from what is beyond doubt a significant achievement.

We are now in the midst of a Renaissance of sorts in the study of ancient India, including the Vedas. More are less coinciding with the collapse of the colonial-missionary creation known as the Aryan invasion model of India, a new school of research-inaccurately called the Indo-American school-has been pursuing a path of study that combines ancient learning and modern science. Freeing itself from the racial, political and religious biases that influenced Indology for more than a century, this new school has made significant contributions to the history of the ancient world. Among notable members of this school one may cite K.D. Sethna, David Frawley, Shrikanth Talageri, Natwar Jha and several others. Dr. Roy, the author of the book under discussion, is a major new entrant to the field. He has opened an important way of looking at ancient texts-and possibly also the universe.

All told Vedic Physics is an impressive tour de force by a young scholar, offering fresh insights into the Vedas without compromising on the science. At the very least, it has opened new avenues for research, which one hopes will be pursued by scientists working closely with traditionally schooled Vedic scholars. This alone holds promise of a sane approach to problems if we hope to avoid the inanities-and the insanities-that have plagued Indology for over a century.

Nineteenth century Bengal witnessed a few reform movements among Muslims as well as Hindus. The Islamic Reform movements, such as Faraizi, Tariqah-i-Muhammadiyah, Taaiyuni and AHL-I-HADITH, occupied a conspicuous position among them. These were revivalist in character and stirred deep religious sentiments among Muslims throughout east, west and north Bengal, and succeeded considerably in rousing the Muslim masses to action. The Tabligh Jamaat and Seerat Conference movements, which recently stirred similar mass enthusiasm in Bangladesh, are reminiscent, and to a great extent also the spiritual progeny, of these movements of the preceding century.

Universal Perspective Religious movements being social phenomena have to be studied in the wider context. Islamic revivalist movements had taken such hold of Bengal in the 19th century that historians rated them as the persistent sign of life in a subjugated and decadent Muslim community. Religious revivalism in itself was not, however, peculiar to the Muslims of Bengal, but had become widespread throughout the Muslim world, affecting the Muslim Ummah as a whole. There is a suggestion that it had cropped up in different parts of the world under the impact of imperialism.

Thus considered, the Wahhabism of Arabia appears to have arisen under the impact of Ottoman imperialism. Mughal and British imperialism produced the movement of Shah Waliullahi and the Teriqah-i-Muhammadiyah. The Fariazi, Taaiyuni and Ahl-i-Hadith movements arose under British imperialism. The Fulani and Sannusiyah of North Africa arose under French and British imperialism, and the Paduri and Muhammadiyah movements of Indonesia under the impact of Dutch imperialism.

In popular parlance these religious reform movements came to be associatively known as Wahhabism and Islamic revivalism, tajdeed al-Islam, as against a somewhat Western Renaissance-oriented Muslim modernism and Pan-Islamism, ittihad al-Islam. The movements, in general, were universal; both aimed at re-awakening Muslims all over the world; and both carried the slogan: 'Islam in danger'. Therefore, there existed considerable mutual sympathy and a good deal of unity of purpose and identity of sentiments between them. Yet, they pursued different goals and occasionally expressed disapproval of each other's programmes and scrupulously maintained exclusiveness and independence of each other's stance.

Local perspective Although Bengal was occupied by the Muslims in the beginning of the 13th century AD and ruled by them till 1757, it was not fully Islamised. It comprised a cosmopolitan society consisting of Muslims, Hindus and Buddhists, who lived side by side in adjacent but separate villages and hamlets under a tolerant regime that ensured universal justice and security. In this local cosmopolitan historical perspective, the social scene in Bengal in the 19th century, as far as reform was concerned, sharply contrasted with the slothful situation obtaining in the 18th century. Intellectual life in Bengal during the 19th century became especially quickened and enlivened by the impulse of socio-religious reform which took hold of both

Muslim and Hindu communities. In the second decade of the century, it made an intelligent section of both the communities question the compatibility of the current patterns of their life with their respective religious inspirational sources, and also with the immediate and future prospects of their communities. The immediate cause of such a reawakening was the impact of British rule on Bengal.

The rule of the EAST INDIA COMPANY in Bengal had completely shattered the social frame of the country, firstly, by sapping the authority and status of the Mughal Ruling class which comprised Muslims and Hindus in equal numbers; secondly, by destroying the traditional lifestyle of the rural well-to-do class; and thirdly, by setting up the Hindu Banyans of Calcutta, who were mainly marwari businessmen and moneylenders and worked as Gomastahs (commercial agents of the English in India), often styled as 'black Gomastahs of white men'. The zamindars, feudal lords newly created by the PERMANENT SETTLEMENT of 1793, perpetrated atrocities on the masses. The gomastas and the zamindars were joined by a third group of ambitious fortune hunters, Englishmen looking for opportunities for capital investment in rural Bengal. Many of them probably brought money and skills from the lost colonies of America, and as indigo planters gave a 'royal colour' to the scourging of the peasantry.

The combined impact of these developments upon the social structure of a subjugated people can be well imagined. Such a pattern of a 'protected scourging' thus formed a corresponding 'take-over process' of the East India Company's rule over Bengal (1757-1857) as against the systematic destruction of the Mughal administration, which has been designated by Lathrop Stoddard as the policy of 'pacific penetration' by Western imperialism. This policy had created many social and economic anomalies especially in the rural life of Bengal.

Little wonder, therefore, that it aroused a deep sense of pity in the minds of Christian missionaries, and a sense of remorse in some good souls from the ranks of English administrators, and also considerable sympathy amongst humanist groups in England. With their blessings, encouragement, help and participation, Raja Ram Mohan Roy laid the foundation of a 'Renaissance' type of modernist/ Western social reform movement in Calcutta around 1814, which spurred numerous other social reform movements in Bengal and India for remodelling the Hindu social system.

However, if the British challenge had produced a somewhat positive response among the Hindu elite of Bengal, during the corresponding period it produced a negative response among the Muslims and spurred a number of 'revivalist' religious reform movements, beginning with the Faraizi movement of HAJI SHARIATULLAH in Bengal and the Tariqah-i-Muhammadiyah movement of Sayyid Ahmad Shahid of Rai Bareilly in Delhi, both of which came into existence about the year 1818 AD.

In contrast to the Muslim revivalist movements, Raja Ram Mohan Roy's reform movement is generally regarded as a Renaissance movement. It should, nevertheless, be observed that it differed from the European 'Renaissance model', especially as it was deeply infused with a revivalist desire to restore a pristine Hindu or Aryan religious spirit. The European Renaissance aimed at integrating the classical, secular, Graeco-Roman spirit of the 'rationalism' of the 'past' with the merciful Christian 'morality' of the 'present', to create a 'humanism' that could be the foundation of a happy and civilized 'future' world. In comparison, however, Raja Ram Mohan Roy's Renaissance aimed at resuscitating a pristine Aryan 'Unitarianism of God' with the help of the modern Western rationalist spirit. In the heart of hearts, it was not secular but deeply religious. Consequently some other important Hindu reform movements, such as the Arya Samaj, were antagonistically spurred by Ram Mohan's reformist activities and inspiration.

Islamic revivalism and the Hindu Renaissance thrived within the same space and about the same time. They affected each other, unfortunately more by their mutually antagonistic revivalist impulse, than by the actual or imagined 'rational' impulse of the Renaissance. Thereby they tended to break asunder the time-honoured Islamic or Mughal peace of 'religious tolerance' and began fostering a new form of Hindu-Muslim communalism.

Local Islamic perspective Bengal, from the Muslim conquest (1205) till the Battle of Palashi (1757), continued to be a well-secured stronghold of the world Muslim community. Politically also, it remained a bastion of Muslim power in the Indian subcontinent. But the Battle of PALASHI brought in the English, and as a consequence, Muslim society decayed and shrank under constant stress. The period of subjugation under the British can be subdivided into two periods: first-pure slavery of 100 years under the East India Company's rule and second-protected subjecthood for 90 years under the British Crown, the Great Revolt of 1857 drawing the dividing line between the two.

In the first period, Muslim society moved from light to darkness, from hope to despair, from Darul Islam to Darul Harb, that is, from the abode of peace to the abode of war. Muslims waged a relentless and unlimited war against the enemies of Islam to defeat their conspiracy against Muslim society and the religion of Islam. It was a war unto death-Jihad or Hijrat, which eventually gave birth to the Faraizi movement of Haji Shariatullah and DUDU MIYAN, the Tariqah-i-Muhammadyah movement or so-called Indian Wahhabism of Sayyid Ahmad Shahid, TITU MIR, Maulana Wilayat Ali and Maulana Inayat Ali, the Ahl-i-Hadith movement of Shah Ismail Shahid, and Maulana Nazir Husain and also the Taaiyuni movement of Maulana KARAMAT ALI of Jaunpur.

In the second period, following the great shake-up of 1857, the Muslims-not as a community, but individually-endeavoured to adjust themselves to the alien political power, to tame their nature before adjusting to the modern civilization of the West, to compete along with other subject peoples of the British empire in order to grab the amenities of a happy and cultured life under Pax Britannica, to exchange jihad for the protection of the British law, Aman. In a word, they tried for a transition from the abode of war (Darul Harb) to an abode of protection (Darul Aman) by means of giving up political ambition and accepting wholeheartedly the administrative peace, the rule of law, as the be-all and end-all of a happy modern life. These ideals and the accompanying sentiments and emotions became crystallised in one word-loyalism.

The Islamic revivalist movements thrived in Bengal with high emotional fervour from about 1820 to 1870, most of the time at a frantic sentimental level until they were systematically destroyed or tamed as non-political, religious movements by the British government. Thus considered, they may be said to form a 'transitional bridge' from the state of slavery to the state of protectorate. Until the struggle fizzled out, the slogan of 'Darul Aman' and the idea of protectorate could not take hold of Muslim society. After the revivalist movements fizzled out the Renaissance type of Muslim modernism, overtly or covertly pronouncing the slogan of 'loyalism', took charge of leading the Muslim community nearer to the English rulers along the road of constitutional progress.

Functions Coming into being as a puritan reaction to the impact of imperialism, as an international jihad movement and as a move to re-organise and reintegrate local Muslim society in the local socio-political perspective discussed above, the first and foremost task before the Islamic revivalist movements of Bengal was to revive the original doctrines of religion. This was also the main task set before Hindu reform movements such as the Brahma Samaj and Arya Samaj. In their reformist endeavour, both the groups called for purging their respective societies, but offered grounds for the fresh community-wide contact between them and their like-minded co-religionists across provincial barriers.

One of the functions of Islamic revivalism was thus the 'breaking of isolation' of the Muslims of different parts of the Indian sub-continent which had been caused by the shrinking of the Mughal power during the preceding century.

Secondly, it may be noted that, in all, there were four Islamic revivalist movements that gained popularity in Bengal. Out of them, the Faraizi, Tariqah-i-Muhammadiyah and Ahl-i-Hadith aimed at reviving the pristine teachings of Islam and purging Muslim society of un-Islamic local accretions. The fourth, the Taaiyuni movement led by Maulana Karamat Ali Jaunpuri, had split off from the Tariqah-i-Muhammadiyah and wanted to retain some traditional institutions of Muslim society such as Fatiha, Milad and Urs, which were rejected by the other three. Moreover, following the revolt of 1857 the Ta'aiyuni movement joined hands with the Muslim modernists and declared India under the British Crown as an 'abode of protection' or protectorate (Darul Aman), which according to Maulana Karamat Ali absolved the Muslims from the religious obligation of jihad, that is, fighting unto death for the liberation of the Muslim community, and from Hijrat, that is, migration to an abode of Islam. Moreover, the reformist trend of Shah Waliullah of Delhi had influenced the Ahl-i-Hadith movement.

The Faraizi movement arose under the direct influence of the Wahhabism of Arabia and had no direct link with the movement of Shah Waliullah or the Tariqah-i-Muhammadiyah of Delhi. On the other hand, the movement of Titu Mir was a direct extension of the Tariqah-i-Muhammadiyah of Delhi.

Being manifestations of a universal type of Islamic revivalism, these reform movements emphasized the social egalitarianism of Islam, equality of mankind as the creation of one Allah, brotherhood of Muslims, the unity of the Muslim world and the need for waging jihad for the liberation of Muslim lands from the hands of the infidels. For this purpose, the upholders of these movements also sought to resuscitate the Islamic Ummah, which became in course of time a central part of their reform programme. For this reason, the Islamic revivalist movements everywhere in the world, overtly or covertly, aimed at establishing an Islamic social order and political State, and as a matter of policy, turned directly to the masses.

A second important function of Islamic revivalism was, thus, reinfusing a deep sense of organic unity of the Ummah and of the value of Islamic egalitarianism and brotherhood in the consciousness of the Muslims. Moreover, their strategy of mass contact and fiery speeches delivered with equal fervour from the pulpit and the political platform, for rousing religious sentiments against internal corruption of Muslim society as well as against the conspiracy of the foreign rulers, succeeded considerably in waking up mass consciousness to the deplorable political and economic situation of the Muslims all over the world.

A third important function of Islamic revivalism in Bengal was thus the widening of general awareness, psychological re-invigoration, and reform and re-organisation of society. In the early 1820s when Sayyid Ahmad Shahid visited the city of Calcutta, he apparently received no opposition from any quarters of the Muslims, Hindus or the government administration. But in the first flush of its mass popularity in rural Bengal, in parts of 24 Parganas and Nadia under Mir Nisar Ali alias Titu Mir from about 1827 to 1831, it came upon the quicksands of a conspiracy of the new class of Hindu zamindars and gomastahs with whom the European indigo planters also joined hands.

However, Haji Shariatullah had lived at Mecca from 1799 to 1818. While he was a student he had closely observed the conflict of the Wahhabis of Arabia with Ottoman imperial power and watched how they were destroyed by Khedive Mohammad Ali at the behest of the Ottoman sultan. The Haji took shelter in patience and sobriety, and saved his movement by retreating completely from politics into the arena of social and religious reform. [Muin-ud-Din Ahmad Khan]

PEACE ON EARTH

Peace on Earth: Time to Rekindle Passion for Unity

In India, many civilisations have come together over the years, creating new patterns of universal oneness. Raja Ram Mohan Roy ushered in the age of new thought in 1828. He wrote: "All mankind is one great family of which numerous nations and tribes existing are only various branches".

In Bengal, Rabindranath Tagore's father passed on these thoughts to the poet who wrote: "I love India not because I have had the chance to be born on her soil, but because she has saved through tumultuous ages the living words that were issued from the illuminated consciousness of her sons".

All religions tell us that the divine is within us. The Gospel according to St. Thomas says: "He who has heard and assimilated my word is as I". In Sanatana Dharma it is Tat Tvam Asi. To find divinity within oneself it is important to act with compassion towards all beings.

Mexican poet Octavia Paz wrote: "In India there is a passion for unity". Maulana Azad once asked: "If religion expresses the universal truth, why should conflicts arise amongst different beliefs, each claiming to be the sole repository of truth, and condemning others as false?"

One reaches the infinite through love, not through violence. "Ahimsa hi param dharma, Sarva dharma samabhava". The trishul of Shiva represents the three dimensions of space, earth and sky and the three gunas that each of us must strive to overcome in our own lives.

Guru Vyasa spoke of the folly of men who choose the way to destruction through discord when all legitimate material satisfaction could be had through the way of fellowship and harmony.

Ours is a multifarious heritage. On the Sindhu-Gangetic plains the tribes were known as Sindhus and Hindus. Hindu became Indus to the Greeks and the country on the bank of the Indus became India. There was no caste, no temple, only prayers in the oral tradition of the Rig Veda.

Caste became an ugly name much later. Yet, Rishi Parasar (the law giver) was the son of a Chandala, Rishi Vashishta's mother was a fisherwoman, Viswamitra was a Kshatriya, Valmiki a hunter. All became great gurus. In the oral verse of the Rig Veda, men and women were equal.

Sanatana Dharma was meant to be India's gift to the world, a way to realise peace and harmony. Increasingly, however, ancient customs are being taken out of context for political purposes. Cattle were extremely important for the Vedic people and so became symbols of spiritual experience. Go, the name for cow and bull, also connotes the earth and the speech of rishis. Gokula means temple; it also means Krishna's dwelling place.

Today, politicians fight over cow protection. Why protect only the cow? What about the beautiful birds of the sky? And the donkeys and the street dogs that are constantly being ill-treated? The environment, too, needs protection. Majestic trees are regularly being chopped down. This decreases forest cover and causes more pollution. So the list is long and painful. Ecological awareness is the intuitive awareness of the oneness of all life. Our ancient heritage advocates protection not only for human beings and animals but for the elements, too.

Listen to the words of the Atharva Veda, written 4,000 years ago: "We are birds of the same nest,/We may wear different skins,/ We may speak different languages,/We may believe in different religions,/We may belong to different cultures,/Yet we share the same home-Our Earth./For man can live individually,/But can survive only collectively/Born on the same planet/Covered by the same skies/Gazing at the same stars/Breathing the same air/We must learn to happily progress together/Or miserably perish together".

BRAHMO SAMAJ ("ASSEMBLY OF BRAHMAN")

Doctrines

Brahman is worshipped as the sole creator and supporter of the universe. This monotheism is based on the interpretation of the early Vedanta, the Upanishads, and the Brahma Sutra. Ram Mohan Roy, founder of Brahmo Samaj, identified the monotheism of Christianity and Islam as of universal validity. Codification of the doctrines came with the main principles of the Nava Samhita, New Dispensation, of Keshub Chandra Sen, the third leader of the movement, in 1881. These are: 1) Harmony of all scriptures, saints, and sects. 2) Harmony of reason and faith, of devotion and duty, of yoga and bhakti. 3) The church of the Samaj stands for One Supreme God, to be worshipped without form. No idolatry in any form may enter the precincts of the church. 4) The church stands for universal brotherhood without distinction of caste or creed or sect. One might add to this the principle of Roy that religious authority should be based on reason and ability, not on priestly caste. Texts from all world religions are used for prayer and worship.

History

Ram Mohan Roy was born in 1774 to a Brahmin family in the Bengal village of Radhanagar. He was influenced in his youth by studies in Advaita and the monotheism of Islam, and later by the Unitarian movement. The superior kulina castes stood aloof from the British. Roy however was the son of a non-kulina Brahmin and the non-kulina Hindus reaped the benefit of working with the British. By 1815 Roy was a financial success and went to live in Calcutta to devote himself to social, moral, and religious reform.

The non-kulina Hindus were being urged by Christian missionaries to convert. To keep their Hindu identity and to acquire Western culture as well as to improve their religious status-for their religious leadership came from the kulinas-a new form of Hinduism was needed. Ram Mohan Roy provided this by the creation of the Brahmo Samaj in 1828 and he became the religious leader. He was followed by other non-kulinas and this new type of religious leader also led other new religious movements in the nineteenth century.

Thus started the first modern Hindu reform movement. Roy sought to reform Hinduism from within, to restore Hinduism to its primitive purity. He started the restoration of the Vedas to public awareness for both study and religious inspiration, and he regenerated the Vedantic tradition, still of importance to educated Hindus today. Roy worked tirelessly to better social, moral, and religious conditions, one of his great successes being his contribution to the abolition of suttee in 1829.

Under the successors of Roy, Debendranath Tagore (1817-1905) and Keshub Chandra Sen (1838-1884), the work of Roy continued and the Samaj developed into a vital movement for social and religious reform. Swami Vivekananda as a young man was involved in the most westernising, reformist faction of the Brahmo Samaj. Gandhi too was a beneficiary of the vision of Roy. The Samaj contributed to the process of making the Vedas "the active basis of numerous ideologies for socio-religious change. In this way they played an important part in the creation of modern India..." (Lipner 1994, 66).

Symbols

Keshub gave concreteness to the otherwise abstract monotheism of the Samaj by introducing into the church the Pilgrimage to saints, the Homa ceremony, the Baptismal ceremony, the Lord's supper, the Flag ceremony, the Arati, the vow of Poverty, the Savitri Vrata, the Nightingale Vrata, and other innovations. He also introduced extempore prayers and speeches from the pulpit rather than fixed stereotyped liturgy. However, Keshub himself became a symbol as a master and avatar.

Adherents

The Brahmo Samaj survives as a relatively small but progressive sect mainly in West Bengal. The Tagore family supported the Samaj for three generations.

HINDUISM

The Religion of Divine Immanence and An Hereditary Graded Social Structure

Hinduism, dating from around 1500 B. C., is the oldest living religion having a membership (1982) of 477,991,300 confined largely to India. It is the most complex, diverse, and tolerant of the world's religions. One can find within Hinduism almost any form of religion--from simple animism to elaborate philosophical systems--which has ever been conceived or practiced by mankind. Hinduism has met the challenge of other religions, primarily, by absorbing them and their practices and beliefs into the mainstream of Hindu religious expression. The Aryans (noble ones) invaded the Indus valley from Persia in the second millennium B.C. They were basically wandering nomads who spoke an Indo-European language which became the basis for Sanskrit. This early Aryan society developed into three basic socio-economic classes. The priests or Brahmins became the ruling class. The tribal chieftains and their warriors or Kshatriyas were next in line, with the commoners and merchants or Vaishyas rounding out the Aryan society. A fourth group, the conquered pre-Aryan people or Shudras, were at the bottom of society. Eventually these divisions developed into a religiously supported caste system.

The Vedas are the sacred scriptures of Hinduism. The four basic Vedic books are the Rig-Veda, the Yajur-Veda, the Sama-Veda, and the Atharva-Veda. Each of the Vedic books is divided into four parts. Each contains a section of hymns to the gods (Mantras), a section of ritual materials (Brahmanas), a section of guidance for hermits (Aranyakas), and a fourth section of philosophical treatises (Upanishads). The Mantra and Brahmana sections are the oldest materials with the Aranyakas and Upanishads added later. This Vedic literature evolved during the classical period of Hinduism.

The fourteen principal Upanishads form the basis of Hindu philosophy. They assume there is one reality, the impersonal god-being called Brahman. All things and beings are an expression of Brahman. Everything in the world and experience which is not Brahman is illusion (maya). All phenomenal existence (pleasure, worldly success, wealth) is illusion arising from ignorance of the true nature of reality. Those who continue in this ignorance are bound to life by the law of karma which keeps them endlessly in the cycle of birth, life, death, and rebirth. When man discovers the Path of Desire is not fulfilling he is ready to start on the Path of Renunciation. Here he recognizes his duty to others, family and community, and dedicates himself to a life of service. This is rewarding but he still yearns for infinite being, infinite awareness, and infinite joy.

To achieve these ultimates of experience we must realize the basic purpose of life is to pass beyond imperfection. That which is beyond the limitations and imperfections of life can be found within. Underlying our physical existence and personality is an infinite reservoir of reality. This infinite centre of every life, this hidden authentic self or Atman is no less than Brahman, the Godhead. By detachment from the finite, illusory self and commitment to Atman-Brahman, we achieve infinite being, infinite awareness, and infinite joy.

This philosophy of the Upanishads is a reaction to the sacrificial, priestly form of worship in Hinduism. It emphasizes meditation as a means of worship and teaches that ignorance is man's basic plight. Historically, the priestly sections of the Vedas have directed the religion of the masses in India while the Upanishads have attracted a relatively small number of Indian intellectuals. Contemporary Western people who are attracted to Eastern thought tend to identify Hinduism with the philosophy of the Upanishads.

Classical Hinduism also produced the ethical Code of Manu which teaches that the caste system is divinely ordained. The first three castes (Brahmins, Kshatriyas, and Vaishyas) are "twice born" people while the Shudras are "once born" manual labourers. The only upward mobility through this caste system is by means of repeated incarnations. Although the caste system is outlawed in contemporary India, its social influence is still strong.

The Code of Manu also teaches the various stages through which a man is expected to pass in a successful life: student, householder, hermit, and wandering beggar. These stages are only for twice born men. Women should stay in the home under the protection and control of the chief male in the household. The code requires the cultivation of pleasantness, patience, control of mind, non-stealing, purity, control of senses., intelligence, knowledge, truthfulness, and non irritability. The killing of cows is listed among the greatest of sins.

The composition of the great epic poem, the Bhagavad-Gita, sometime between the second century B.C. and the third century A.D. marks the end of the period of classical Hinduism. The Bhagavad-Gita is found within the text of a much longer poem and is probably the most highly esteemed scripture of Hinduism. In the poem Arjuna, a Hindu knight, for the first time in the recorded history of Hinduism, raises the question of the propriety of killing people. He is answered by his charioteer, Krishna, who turns out to be an incarnation of the god Vishnu. Arjuna is told he must be loyal to his duty as a warrior and kill. The Gita also teaches a variety of means of personal salvation. One may achieve release from life (Nirvana) through asceticism, through meditation, through devotion to and worship of the gods, or through obedience to the rules of his caste,

After the close of the classical period subtle changes gradually appear in Hinduism. Out of the millions of major and minor gods, worship tended to centre around the Trimurti: Brahma, the creator; Shiva, the destroyer; and Vishnu, the preserver. Among this trinity, Brahma receives the least attention. Shiva is the most popular probably because he is the god of sex and reproduction and appeals to the deprivation experienced by the masses. His various goddess consorts such as Kali are equally revered. According to mythology, Vishnu has appeared on earth in nine forms and will come a tenth time to bring the world to an end. Among his appearances are Krishna; Gautama, the Buddha; Matsya, the fish who saved Manu from the great flood; and Christ.

The majority of the people of India seek salvation through devotion to the gods while many of the wealthy and educated seek salvation through the way of knowledge. This intellectual Hinduism centres around six systems of philosophy: Samkhya, Yoga, Mimamsa, Vedanta, Vaiseshika, and Nyana. All claim to be based on the Vedas and revolve about common themes. The only basic difference among them is their view of ultimate reality. The Vedanta system is monistic and asserts that the only essence in the universe is Brahman; all else is illusion. The Samkhya, Yoga, Vaiseshika, and Nyana systems are dualistic and assert that the universe is composed of two forces, matter and spirit. The Mimamsa system is basically atheistic and teaches that salvation comes through the correct observance of Vedic rituals. Jainism and Buddhism began as reform movements in Hinduism and it has absorbed much of their thinking. During the Middle Ages Hinduism and Islam competed for followers in

India. The two religions are in many ways opposites and there has been much bloodshed in their struggles. Sikhism arose in an attempt to bring reconciliation between the two. Tradition credits the disciple Thomas for bringing Christianity to India. During the three centuries of British rule Christianity had considerable influence on the growing edge of Hinduism.

The nineteenth and twentieth centuries brought three main reform movements in Hinduism. Ram Mohan Roy, called the Father of Modern India, was a monotheist who tended to agree with Christian missionaries in their attempt to suppress the suttee, child marriage, polytheism, and idolatry in Hinduism. The greatest reformer was Sri Ramakrishna, a follower of non dualistic Vedanta, who believed there was one single reality, God, behind all religions and that truth is essentially one. His disciple, Dutt, later known as Vivekananda, became the first Hindu missionary to the modern world. He described Vedanta Hinduism as the mother of all other religions. The best known Indian reformer is Mohandas K. Gandhi who was influenced by the teachings of Jesus and the Jain doctrine of non injury (ahimsa) espoused civil disobedience and nonviolence which were largely responsible for bringing India freedom from British rule. Gandhi, in turn, became a major influence in the political thinking of Martin Luther King, Jr. and many of the leaders of the "peace movement" in Western Civilization.

THE HINDU REFORMATION

"...Thus it may be said that as early as 1820 India had come into the direct current of European thought and had begun to participate in the fruits of Europe's intellectual quest. The Brahmo Samaj lived up to this ideal. Its social message was Westernization, to purge Hinduism of the customs and superstitions with which it was overlaid, to raise the status of women, to bridge the yawning gulf between popular and higher Hinduism, to fight relentlessly against caste, social taboo, polygamy and other well entrenched abuses. To the educated Hindu, who felt unsettled in mind by the attack of the missionaries, the Brahmo Samaj provided the way out.

The Brahmo tradition has become so much a part of the Indian way of life now, that one is inclined to overlook its distinctive contribution. It does not lie primarily in the fact that it enabled Hinduism to withstand the onslaught of the missionaries, but in that it introduced the modern approach to Indian problems..."

Introduction...

The Hindu Reformation of the nineteenth century is one of the great movements of the age which by its massiveness and far-reaching significance takes its place with the most vital developments of modern history.

As it was a slow process and took place under the cover of British authority and was not always obvious to the outsider, it has so far escaped attention. A further reason why, in spite of its tremendous import, it passed unnoticed is that, by its very nature, it was an internal movement which did not touch or influence outside events. But India's independence and emergence into the modern world would hardly have been possible without the slow but radical adjustments that had taken place within the fold of Hinduism for a period of over 100 years.

In order to appreciate this movement fully it is necessary to understand what the position of Hinduism was in the beginning of the nineteenth century. 700 years of Islamic authority over the Indo-Gangetic Plains from Delhi to Calcutta had left Hinduism in a state of depression. It was the religion of a subject race, looked down on with contempt by the Muslims as idolatry. It enjoyed no prestige and for many centuries its practice had been tolerated only under considerable disadvantage in various areas. It had no central direction, no organization and hardly any leadership. When the British took over the rulership of Northern India, Hinduism for the first time in 700 years stood on a plane of equality with Islam. But a new and even more dangerous portent appeared on the stage.

The missionaries, feeling that there was almost a virgin field here in a society which appeared to be on the point of dissolution, took up the work of conversion. Islam, though it proselytized by fits and starts, had no separate machinery for carrying its message to the people. The Christian missionaries were different. They used no physical force, which Islam did not hesitate to do at intervals and in limited areas. But they came armed with propaganda....

Brahmo Samaj...

The first result of the Christian attack on Hinduism was a movement among educated Hindus in favour of a social reform of religion. The leader of this was Ram Mohan Roy (1772-1833), who may be called the father of the Hindu Reformation.

Born in a Brahmin family, Ram Mohan was brought up as a strict Hindu, but educated, as all Hindus who hoped to enter public service had perforce to be at that time, in Islamic culture. He was a deep student of Arabic and Persian when he entered the East India Company's service, where also he rose to some distinction. During this period he took to the study of English, which opened to him the whole range of Western liberal thought.

It was the time when the mellowed glow of the Great European Enlightenment had cast on European intellectual life an amazing serenity and sense of certainty. The light of D'Holbach, Condorcet, Diderot and the great Encyclopaedists had not died down and the dawn of the great nineteenth century thinkers, especially Bentham and the Utilitarians in England, which was destined to have so powerful an influence in the development of ideas in India, had not begun.

What Ram Mohan witnessed around him in India was a scene of utter devastation and ruin. The old order of Muslim rule had disappeared overnight, leaving behind it utter chaos in every walk of life. Hinduism in Bengal, once the centre of a devotional Vaishnava religion of great vitality, had sunk to a very low level of superstition, extravagance and immorality. A seeker after truth, Ram Mohan turned to the new religion which the missionaries were preaching. He studied Hebrew and Greek to understand Christianity better. But his scholarship was taking him at the same time to the well of European liberalism. Ram Mohan Roy was in fact the last of the

Encyclopaedists. Thus he came to reject Christ, while accepting the
wide humanism of European thought, its ethics and its general
approach to the problems of life.

His book, The Precepts of Jesus, the Guide to Peace and
Happiness, is an interpretation of Christianity in this new light, a
reply to the missionaries rather than a call to Indians.

While Ram Mohan Roy thus rejected the Christian claims, he
realized that Hinduism had to be re-interpreted. That interpretation
he attempted in the Brahmo Samaj, a new reformed sect of Hinduism,
which he founded. The Samaj was not in its essence a Christian
dilution of Hinduism, as has often been said, but a synthesis of the
doctrines of the European Enlightenment, with the philosophical
views of the Upanishads. As a religion Brahmo Samaj was based
firmly on the Vedanta of genuine Hindu tradition, but its outlook
on life was neither Christian nor Hindu, but European, and derived
its inspiration from the intellectual movements of the eighteenth
century.

Thus it may be said that as early as 1820 India had come into
the direct current of European thought and had begun to participate
in the fruits of Europe's intellectual quest. The Brahmo Samaj lived
up to this ideal. Its social message was Westernization, to purge
Hinduism of the customs and superstitions with which it was overlaid,
to raise the status of women, to bridge the yawning gulf between
popular and higher Hinduism, to fight relentlessly against caste,
social taboo, polygamy and other well entrenched abuses. To the
educated Hindu, who felt unsettled in mind by the attack of the
missionaries, the Brahmo Samaj provided the way out.

The Brahmo tradition has become so much a part of the Indian
way of life now, that one is inclined to overlook its distinctive
contribution. It does not lie primarily in the fact that it enabled
Hinduism to withstand the onslaught of the missionaries, but in that
it introduced the modern approach to Indian problems. India started
on her long adventure in building up a new civilization as a synthesis
between the East and the West in the 1820's, and in that sense Ram

Mohan is the forerunner of new India. It has been well stated that 'he embodies the new spirit, its freedom of inquiry, its thirst for science, its large human sympathy, its pure and sifted ethics along with its reverent but not uncritical regard for the past and prudent disinclination towards revolt.'

Macaulay, English Education & Christian Missionaries...

The spirit of reform was entering Hinduism from other sources also. In 1835 the Government of India declared that 'the great object of the British Government ought to be the promotion of European literature and science among the natives of India', and embarked on a policy of Western education...

It was the devout hope of Macaulay, who was the champion of the scheme, and of many others, that the diffusion of the new learning among the higher classes would see the dissolution of Hinduism and the widespread acceptance of Christianity.

The missionaries were also of the same view, and; they entered the educational field with enthusiasm, providing schools and colleges in many parts of India, where education in the Christian Bible was compulsory for Hindu students.

The middle classes accepted Western education with avidity and willingly studied Christian scriptures, but neither the dissolution of Hindu society so hopefully predicted nor the conversion of the intellectuals so devoutly hoped for showed any signs of materialisation. On the other hand, Hinduism assimilated the new learning, and the effects were soon visible all over India in a revival of a universalized religion based on the Vedanta.

It is necessary to remember that, though the Hindu religion has innumerable cults and sects, the philosophic background of all of them-including Buddhism-is the Vedanta. The doctrine of the Vedanta is contained in three authoritative texts-which are not scriptures-the Brahma Sutras, the Upanishads and the Gita.

Every orthodox sect in India derives its authority directly from these and, as has been stated in the previous chapter, the protagonists of each new religious sect have had to demonstrate how their own teachings flowed directly from these three sources. Thus it was, that Sankara, the reformer of Hinduism in the eighth century, had to write his commentary on all the three. It is to the doctrines of the Vedanta, as embodied in the Upanishads, that Ram Mohan Roy turned when he also felt the need of a new religious interpretation.

Arya Samaj, Dayananda Saraswati...

The demand of new India was not for a new sect. It was for a universal religion acceptable to all Hindus. The first effort to provide such a basis was by Dayananda Saraswati who saw in the Vedas the revealed Word of God and felt that, as the Vedas were accepted by all who claimed to be Hindus, a religion based on the Vedas should have universal appeal in India.

The Muslims had a revealed book, the Holy Quran. The Christians had the Bible, and Swami Dayananda felt that the amorphous and indefinable nature of Hinduism, which exposed it to so much weakness, could be remedied by providing the Hindus also with a revealed book. This seemed all the more the right path since the Vedas gave no authority to the usages and superstitions that had come to be accepted by the masses as Hinduism.

There was no sanction in the Vedas for caste, for the prohibition of the marriage of widows, for untouchability, for the taboo on food and the other characteristics of popular Hinduism which had been seized upon by the missionaries in their campaign and were being widely rejected by Hindu intelligentsia.

Swami Dayananda in his Satyartha Praksah, or the Light of True Meaning, made a brave and ingenious attempt to see in the Vedas all that the Christians and the Muslims were claiming to be the basis of their religions, universal brotherhood and a direct and non-metaphysical approach to God.

His Arya Samaj, however successful as a militant organization for the protection of Hinduism from the onslaughts of Islam and Christianity, never appealed to the Hindus outside the Punjab. The reasons were simple.

The attempt to go back to the Vedas involved a denial of the Hindu culture of the last three thousand years, a refusal to see any good in the puranic religion, in the variegated traditions which had enriched Hindu thought in the Middle Ages, all of which the Arya Samajists rejected without hesitation and attacked without reservation.

Secondly, the Vedic religion had long ago ceased to be related to the religious experience of Hindus. The Gita had poured scorn on Vedic sacrifices and held up the Veda-vadaratas (those who delight to argue on the basis of the Vedas) to contempt. The exclusiveness of the Arya Samaj, amounting to the intolerance of other religious practices though but a reflection of its prolonged fight against the proselytizing faiths and therefore essentially defensive, was also against the tradition of Hinduism which held firmly to the doctrine that the Gita preached, 'men worship Me in different ways, I give them the fruits appropriate to their worship'.

The Hindu does not deny the truth of any religion, or reject the validity of another's religious experience.

But the Arya Samajists, at least in their polemical days, were rigidly exclusive. The movement, therefore, did not spread to other parts of India and its influence was limited mainly to the Delhi and Punjab areas.

Theosophical Society, Annie Besant...

The urge of educated Hindus to find a common denominator for their various sects, which neither of these movements provided, was for a time fulfilled by the activities of the Theosophical Society, of which Colonel Olcott, the American, and Madame Blavatsky, the Russian, were the founders. Educated Hindus all over the country turned to the Theosophical Society, which introduced into India the organization and propagandist methods of European religious activity. Its interpretation of Hinduism followed the more orthodox lines, and many of its Indian leaders, like Dr. Bhagwan Das, of Benares, and Sir S. Subramania Aiyar, of Madras, were also leaders of Hindu Orthodoxy. Its social doctrines, however, were progressive and more important, and it cut through the sectarian lines of Indian religious organization. Theosophic Hinduism was an All-India movement and it profoundly affected the outlook of the new generation. When Mrs. Annie Besant, an extremely gifted, persuasive and dynamic personality, became the President of the Society, its propaganda for a reformed universal Hinduism became more marked and was carried on incessantly through schools, colleges and an enormous output of popular literature. Mrs. Besant.had become steeped in Indian culture and her popular approach was Vedantic, as her translation of the Gita would testify.

Swami Vivekananda...

The Vedantic reformation which was thus in the air found its most widely accepted exponent in Swami Vivekananda. Vivekananda was a Western-educated Bengali who came under the influence of Ramakrishna, a mystic whose personality had made a deep impression on the Bengali society of his day. Vivekananda was fired by a desire to revive Hinduism and purify its religious and social teachings. Initiated a Sanyasi, he toured the length and breadth of India spreading the gospel of Vedanta. A prolonged visit to America and a tour in England inflamed his patriotism, his desire to rejuvenate Hindu society and to give Hinduism a social purpose. His fervent declaration that he did not 'believe in a religion that does not wipe out the widow's tears or bring a piece of bread to the orphan's mouth' expresses clearly the changed temper of Hinduism. His own mission he described as follows. Answering the question: 'What do you consider to be the function of your movement as regards India?' the Swami said: 'To find the common bases of Hinduism and to awaken the national consciousness to them.' That common basis he found in the Vedanta which he interpreted in popular phraseology and preached untiringly all over India.

'All the philosophers of India who are orthodox have to acknowledge the authority of the Vedanta and all our present-day religions, however crude some of them may appear to be, however inexplicable some of their purposes may seem, one who understands them and studies them can trace them back to the ideas of the

Upanishads. So deeply have these Upanishads sunk into our race that those of you who study the symbology of the crudest religion of the Hindus will be astonished to find sometimes figurative expressions of the Upanishads. Great spiritual and philosophical ideas in the Upanishads are today with us, converted into household worship in the form of symbols. Thus the various symbols now used by us, all come from the Vedanta, because in the Vedanta they are used as figures.'

Again: 'Thus the Vedanta, whether we know it or not, has, penetrated all the sects in India and what we call Hinduism, that mighty banyan tree, with its immense and almost infinite rami fications, has been throughout interpenetrated by the influence J the Vedanta. Whether we are conscious of it or not, we think that Vedanta, we live in the Vedanta, we breathe the Vedanta and we die in the Vedanta, and every Hindu does that.'

He not only preached this gospel, but trained up a body of missionaries, men of education, pure life and religious zeal to carry this message to the villages.

There were innumerable other Sanyasis and learned men who, though belonging to no particular sect, were preaching the same principles all over India. In fact, the revival of Vedanta in Hindu thought at the end of the nineteenth century constitutes a religious movement of national significance. It was at the end of this period that Aurobindo gave what may be called the classic exposition of the entire Vedanta doctrine in his Essays on the Gita and later his Life Divine. By this, Vedanta may be said to have been restored to its place as the common background of all Hindu religious thought.

Vedanta, Popular Hinduism and the Law...

The unifying doctrine was the Vedanta, but the abstract conceptions of this philosophical approach could only appeal to the elite. Popular Hinduism continued in the old way, sectarian, devotional and based on daily rituals. But it also underwent extraordinary changes. The gnarled branches of this ancient tree either fell away by themselves or were chopped off by legislative action promoted by the reformers. Child marriage, which many Hindu communities considered as an essential part of their religion, was abolished by law through the insistence of popular agitation. The remarriage of widows was permitted.

Social disabilities based on caste vanished by themselves, and the occupational basis of caste communities was weakened. Temples were thrown open to the untouchables, and in the most orthodox province of Madras, Hindu religious endowments were placed under the control of public bodies. The movement for the regeneration of the depressed classes assumed a national character, and their participation in social and political life became a major factor in the last days of British rule.

Popular Hinduism had a more vigorous life than it ever had in the immediately preceding times, but it had in the course of a hundred years changed its character and temper, though it had kept much of its form.

The major difficulty of Hinduism which had made it a wild jungle growth of widely varying customs, usages and superstitions was its lack of a machinery of reform and unification. The institutions of Hinduism, which in a large measure got identified with 'the religion itself, were the results of certain historical factors. They were upheld by law and not by religion. Vivekananda put the point well when he wrote:

> *'Beginning from Buddha down to Ram Mohan Roy, everyone made the mistake of holding caste to be a religious institution.... But in spite of all the ravings of the priests, caste is simply a crystallized social institution, which after doing its service is now filling the atmosphere of India with stench.'*

The caste organization, the joint family, the rights of inheritance and the relationships arising out of them, which in the main are the special features of Hindu society, are legal and not religious. They are man-made institutions which do not claim Divine origin or religious sanction, and are upheld by man-made laws and not by any church or priesthood. It is a truism to say that legislation of today meets the social needs of yesterday and, unavoidably, law, as a conservative force, lags one step behind social necessities.

When the great codes of Hindu Law were evolved, no doubt they represented the social forces of the time, but soon they had become antiquated. The succession of authoritative commentaries would show that the urge for modifications was widely felt and, in the absence of a legislative authority, the method of a progressive interpretation in each succeeding generation was the only one available to Hindu thinkers.

The immutability of Hindu law and customs was never a principle with the authors of the great codes or their commentators. In fact, the monumental volumes of Dr. Kane's History of Dharma Sastra would demonstrate clearly that in every age social thinkers tried to adjust Hindu institutions to the requirements of the time.

If the laws are changeable it follows that the institutions which were based on such laws are equally changeable. The great weakness of Hindu society was not that the laws had remained immutable but that the changes introduced had been spasmodic, local and dependent to a large extent on the ingenuity of individual commentators. They were not in any sense a continuous renovation of legal principles, nor a legislative approximation to changing conditions.

The reason for this lack of direction of social ideas and the failure to prevent the growth of anti-social customs was undoubtedly the loss of political power. Not only was India as a whole never under a single sovereign authority, but even the political unity of North India which existed with occasional breaks from the time of the Mauryas (320 B.C.) to that of Harsha (A.D, 637) was broken up by the political conditions of the eighth century and lost for a period of 700 years with the Muslim invasion of the twelfth century. As a result, the Hindu community continued to be governed by institutions moulded by laws which were codified over 2,000 years ago and which were out of date even when they were codified.

The Muslim State had no legislative machinery, and when for the first time India was united under the British and the entire Hindu community lived under a common administration, the authorities of the East India Company after a first effort at social reform withdrew, under the pretext of religious neutrality, from activities which they thought might cause popular upheaval. Perhaps it was a wise step, as the motive force of large-scale social reforms must come from the people themselves and legislation can only give statutory sanction to principles which have already gained wide acceptance. The reformation of the Hindu religion was therefore an essential prerequisite of social legislation.

It was only after the Great War that the legislating State came into existence in India. Under the scheme of partial self-government introduced in 1921, there was established a central legislative authority with a majority of non-official elected Indians, which; was both competent to change the laws of Hindu society and to enforce obedience to such laws through the length and breadth of India. In the provinces the direction of government passed in a large measure to elected legislatures.

The legislative achievements of the Central and Provincial Governments in the field of social reform have been fundamental, though they did not go anywhere as far as the public demanded. The Civil Marriage Act and the Age of Consent Act (raising the marriageable age of girls to 14) were among the more important pieces of legislation which the Central Indian Legislative Assembly enacted.

The Civil Marriage Act validates marriages between men and women of different castes of Hinduism. It strikes at the very root of the orthodox Brahminical conception of caste, and annuls the laws of Manu and the other orthodox codes of Hinduism.

'The immutable law', prohibiting Varna-Samkara or the mixture of castes, ceased by this single piece of legislation to operate through the length and breadth of India.

The Age of Consent Act was equally revolutionary. It was the custom for over two thousand years at least for large sections of people to have girls married before the age of puberty. There was not only long tradition behind the custom, but it was considered compulsory at least for Brahmins in the light of certain authoritative texts. The Indian legislature made this custom illegal, though it had so much religious authority behind it, and the performance of such marriages became a penal offence.

Thus by the end of the third decade, the Hindu reformation had made enough progress to enable the new society to direct its social forces towards general betterment.

The reformation of Hinduism has been treated in some detail, because without an appreciation of its consequences the effects of Western education on Indian society will not be fully clear.

BASED ON THE THOUGHT OF RAM MOHAN ROY
Hindu Sects

All religions, including Hinduism, have sects. A brief survey of Sects (past and present) in other religions produced the following results: (Religions listed in alphabetical order)

Some Buddhist sects: Mahayana, Hinayana, Vajrayana, or the Diamond Vehicle, the Theravada School. By the time of King Ashoka the Great, there were eighteen or twenty different cults of Buddhism.

Some Christian Sects: Christian Science, Jehovah's Witnesses, Mormonism, Rasfatarianism, Unification Church, Protestant Church, Roman Catholic Church, Seventh Day Adventists, Baptist, Lutheran, Methodist, Orthodox, Pentecostal, Presbyterian, Universal Church from Brazil, Awakening Churches, etc.

Islamic sects: Ahmadia, Ismail, Salafi, Shia, Sufi, Sunni, Nizari Isma'ilis, Wahhabism, The Submitters, Nation of Islam etc. Some sects in Judaism: Conservative, Hasidic, Humanistic, Karaite, Orthodox, Reconstructionist, Reform, Sephardic, Traditional, Essenes, Sadducees, Pharisees, Temple Israel, Zealots etc.

Some Shinto Sects: Tenrikyo, Konkokyo, Kurozumikyo, Shinto Taikyo, Fuso-kyo (which included Omoto-kyo), Izumo-oyashirokyo, Jikko-kyo, Misogi-kyo, Shinshu-kyo, Shinto-shuseiha, Shinri-kyo, Shinto Taisei-kyo, Ontake-kyo. etc

Some sects in Taoism: The Heavenly (or Celestial) Masters sect, The Supreme Peace sect, The Mao-shan (Mount Mao) sect, The Ling-pao (Marvellous Treasure) sect, The Ch'uan-chen (Completely Real) sect.

Hinduism is extremely catholic, liberal, tolerant, and elastic. This is the wonderful feature of Hinduism. A foreigner (visiting India) is struck with astonishment when he hears about the diverse sects and creeds of Hinduism. But these varieties are really an ornament to Hinduism. They are certainly not its defects.

There are various types of minds and temperaments. So there should be various faiths also. This is but natural. This is the cardinal tenet of Hinduism. There is room in Hinduism for all types of souls-from the highest to the lowest-for their growth and evolution. The term 'Hinduism' is most elastic. It includes a number of sects and cults, allied, but different in many important points. Hinduism has, within its fold, various schools of Vedanta; Vaishnavism, Shaivism, Shaktism, etc. It has various cults and creeds. Hinduism accommodates all types of men. It prescribes spiritual food for everybody, according to his qualification and growth. This is the beauty of this magnanimous religion.

This is the glory of Hinduism. Hence there is no conflict among the various cults and creeds. The Rig-Veda declares: "Truth is one; sages call it various names-Ekam Sat Vipra Bahudha Vadanti." The Upanishads declare that all the paths lead to the same goal, just as cows of variegated colours yield the same white milk. Lord Krishna says in the Gita: 'Howsoever men approach Me, even so do I welcome them, for the path men take from every side is Mine." All diversities are organized and united in the body of Hinduism.

Hinduism provides food for reflection for the different types of thinkers and philosophers all over the world. All sorts of philosophy are necessary. What appeals to one may not appeal to another, and what is easy for one may be difficult for another. Hence the need for different standpoints. All philosophies of Hinduism are points of view. They are true in their own way. They take the aspirant step by step, stage by stage, till he reaches the acme or the pinnacle of spiritual glory. Sanatana-Dharmists, Arya-Samajists, Deva-Samajists, Jainas, Buddhists, Sikhs and Brahmo-Samajists are all Hindus only, for they rose from Hinduism, and emphasized one or more of its aspects.

The Hindus are divided into three great classes, *viz.*,

1. Vaishnavas: Who worship the Lord as Vishnu;

2. Shaivas: Who worship the Lord as shiva; and

3. Saktas: Who adore Devi or the Mother aspect of the Lord.

In addition, there are the Sauras, who worship the Sun-God; Ganapatyas who worship Ganesh as supreme; and Kumaras who worship Skanda as the godhead.

THE VAISHNAVAS-SRI SAMPRADAYA

The Vadagalai School and The Tengalai School

The Vaishnavas are usually distinguished into four principal Sampradayas or sects. Of these, the most ancient is the Sri Sampradaya founded by Ramanuja Acharya about the middle of the twelfth century. The followers of Ramanuja adore Vishnu and Lakshmi, and their incarnations. They are called Ramanujas or Sri Sampradayins or Sri Vaishnavas. The teachers are Brahmins. The disciples may be of any caste. They all recite the Ashtakshara Mantra: "Om Namo Narayanaya." They put on (display) two white lines and a central red line on the forehead.

Vedantacharya, a follower of Ramanuja, made some reform in the Vaishnava faith. This gave rise to the formation of two antagonistic parties of Ramanujas, one called the Northern School (Vadagalai) and the other the Southern School (Tengalai). The Tengalais regard Prapatti or self-surrender as the only way to salvation. The Vadagalais think that it is only one of the ways. According to them, the Bhakta or the devotee is like the young one of a monkey which has to exert itself and cling to its mother (Markata-Nyaya or Monkey Theory);

whereas, according to the Southern School, the Bhakta or the devotee is like the kitten which is carried about by the cat without any effort on its own part (Marjala-Nyaya or Cathold Theory). The Northern School accept the Sanskrit texts, the Vedas. The Southerners have compiled a Veda of their own called 'Nalayira Prabandha' or 'Four Thousand Verses', in Tamil, and hold it to be older than the Sanskrit Vedas. Really, their four thousand verses are based on the Upanishad portion of the Vedas. In all their worship, they repeat sections from their Tamil verses.

The Vadagalais regard Lakshmi as the consort of Vishnu, Herself infinite, uncreated and equally to be adored as a means (Upaya) for release. The Tengalais regard Lakshmi as a created female being, though divine. According to them, she acts as a mediator or minister (Purushakara), and not as an equal channel of release.

The two sets have different marks on their foreheads. The Vadagalais make a simple white line curved like the letter U to represent the sole of the right foot of Lord Vishnu, the source of the River Ganga (Ganges). They add a central red mark as a symbol of Lakshmi. The Tengalais make a white mark like the letter Y that represents both the feet of Lord Vishnu. They draw a white line half way down the nose.

Both the sects brand the emblems of Vishnu-the discus and the conch-on their breasts, shoulders and arms.

The Tengalais prohibit their widows from shaving their heads. The usual surnames of the Ramanuja Brahmins are Aiyangar, Acharya, Charlu and Acharlu.

Ramanandis

The followers of Ramananda are the Ramanandis. They are well-known in upper Hindusthan (India). They are branch of the Ramanuja sect. They offer their worship to Lord Rama, Sita, Lakshmana and Hanuman. Ramananda was a disciple of Ramanuja. He flourished at Varanasi about the beginning of the fourteenth century. His followers are numerous in the Ganga (Ganges) valley of India. Their favourite work is the 'Bhakti-Mala.' Their sectarian marks are like those of the Ramanujas. The Vairagis are the ascetics among the Ramanandis.

Vallabhacharins or Rudra Sampradayins

The Vallbhacharins form a very important sect in Mumbai, Gujarat and the Central India. Their founder was born in the forest Camparanya in 1479. He is regarded as an incarnation of Krishna. The Vallabhacharins worship Krishna as Baba-Gopala. Their idol is one representing Krishna in his childhood till his twelfth year. The Gosains or teachers are family men. The eight daily ceremonials for God in the temples are Mangala, Sringara, Gvala, Raja Bhoga, Utthapana, Bhoga, Sandhya and Sayana. All these represent various forms of adoration of God.

The mark on the forehead consists of two red perpendicular lines meeting in a semicircle at the root of the nose and having a round dot of red between them. The necklace and rosary are made of the stalk of the Tulasi (holy Basil plant).

The great authority of the sect is the Srimad Bhagavata as explained in the Subodhini, the commentary thereon of Vallabhacharya. The members of the sect should visit Sri Nathdvara, a holy shrine, at least once in their lives.

The Chaitanyas (Hare Krishna Movement)

This sect is prominent in Bengal and Orissa. The founder Chaitanya Mahaprabhu or Lord Gouranga, was born in 1485. He was regarded as an incarnation of Lord Krishna. He took sannyasa (monkhood) at the age of twenty-four. He went to Jagannath where he taught Vaishnava doctrines. The Chaitanyas worship Lord Krishna as the Supreme Being. All castes are admissible into the sect. The devotees constantly repeat the Name of Lord Krishna.

Chaitanya's Charitamrita by Krishna Das is a voluminous work. It contains anecdotes of Chaitanya and his principal disciples and the expositions of the doctrines of this sect. It is written in Bengali.

The Vaishnavas of this sect wear two white perpendicular streaks of sandalwood paste or Gopichandan (a kind of sacred clay). Down the forehead uniting at the root of the nose and continuing to near the tip. They wear a close necklace of small Tulasi beads of three strings.

[Note: During the twentieth century, Swami Prabhupada, A.C. Bhaktivedanta became the founder Acharya of the International Society for Krishna Consciousness with branches all over the world. This movement urges devotees to recite with faith and devotion the following Hare-Krishna Mantra:

"Hare Krishna Hare Krishna Krishna Krishna Hare Hare,

Hare Rama Hare Rama Rama Rama Hare Hare"

'Rama' in the above mantra of the Hare-Krishna movement does not refer to Sri Rama from the Ramayana but to Balarama, the elder brother of Sri Krishna.]

You interestingly add in your text on Chaitanya philosophy that the Rama in the Maha-Mantra does not refer to the Sri Ramachandra from the Ramayana, but to Lord Balarama (Krishna's brother).

I'll just quote a little from Srila Prabhupada: "We may mention an incident that took place between two of our Sannyasis (monks).

While we were preaching the Hare Krsna Maha-Mantra in Hyderabad, one of them stated that "Hare Rama" refers to Sri Balarama, and the other protested that "Hare Rama" means Lord Rama. Ultimately the controversy came to me (Srila Prabhupada), and I gave the decision that if someone says that "Rama" in "Hare Rama" is Lord Ramacandra and someone else says that the "Rama" in "Hare Rama" is Sri Balarama, both are correct because there is no difference between Sri Balarama and Lord Rama.... Those who are aware of the Vishnu-tattva do not fight over all these details".

Sri Caitanya Caritamrita Adi Lila 5.132 purport

Hoping this is of some help.

Ys,

Yashoda Dulal Das

(TKG)]

The Nimbarkas

The founder of this sect was Nimbarka or Nimbaditya. He was originally named Bhaskara Acharya. He is regarded as an incarnation of the Sun-God (Surya). The followers worship Krishna and Radha (Krishna's consort) conjointly. Their chief scripture is the Srimad Bhagavata Purana.

The followers have two perpendicular yellowish lines made from Gopichandan clay and applied from the root of the hair to the commencement of each eye-brow and there meeting in a curve. This represents the footprint of Lord Vishnu.

The Nimbarkas or Nimavats are scattered throughout the whole of upper India. They are very numerous around Mathura. They are also the most numerous of the Vaishnava sects in Bengal.

The Madhavas

The Madhavas are Vaishnavas. They are known as Brahma Sampradayins. The founder of the sect was Madhavacharya, otherwise called Ananda Tirtha and also called Purna-Prajna. He was born in 1200 ad. He was a great opponent of Sankaracharya's Advaita system of philosophy. He is regarded as an incarnation of Vayu or the Wind-God. He erected and consecrated at Udipi the image of Lord Krishna.

The Gurus of the Madhava sect are Brahmins and Sannyasins. The followers bear the impress of the symbols of Vishnu upon their breasts and shoulders. They are stamped with a hot iron. Their marks on the foreheads consist of two perpendicular lines made with Gopichandana and joined at the root of the nose. They make a straight black line (using charcoal from incense offered to Krishna), which terminates in a round mark made with tumeric. The Madhavas are divided into two classes called the Vyasakutas and the Dasakutas. They are found in Karnataka. Truthfulness, study of scriptures, generosity, kindness, faith and freedom from envy form the moral code of Madhavas. They give the Lord's names to their children (Namakarana Sanskar), and mark the body with His symbols (Ankana). They practise virtue in thought, word and deed (Bhajana).

Radha Vallabhis

Radha Vallabhis worship Krishna as Radha-Vallabha, the Lord or the Lover of Radha.

Harivans was the founder of this sect. Seva Sakhi Vani gives a detailed description of the notion of this sect and more of their traditions and observances. Charana Dasis, Dadu Panthis, Hari Chandis, Kabir Panthis, Khakis, Maluk Dasis, Mira Bais, Madhavis, Rayı Dasis, Senais, Sakhi Bhavas, Sadma Panthis, are all Vaishnava sects.

THE SHAIVAS

Smarta Brahmins of the South

The Shaiva Brahmins of the Tamil India have their title Aiyer. They are called Smartas. They all wear three horizontal lines of Bhasma or Vibhuti (holy ash) on their forehead. They all worship Lord Shiva. The different sects are:

1. *Vadamas:* Vada Desa Vadamas, Chola Desa Vadamas and Inji Vadamas

2. *Brihatcharanam:* Mazhainattu Brihatcharanam, Pazhamaneri Brihatcharanam, Milaghu Brihatcharanam and Kandramanikka Brihatcharanam

3. Vathimars

4. Ashtasahasram

5. *Choliyas:* Otherwise called Pandimars and inhabitants of Tiruchendur, and

6. *Gurukkal:* A sub-sect of Vadamas not recognized as one amongst them and whose duties are to worship at temples. They are also known by the name of Oattar in southern districts of Madras. These are different from Archaks. Archaks belong to any of the above sub-sects and inter-marry with persons of other professions, but not Gurukkal or Pattar. While Gurukkal is used only for Saivites, Pattar and Archak are used for Vaishnavites also.

Shaiva Brahmins of Malabar

1.Nambuduri 2.Muse, and 3.Embrantiri

Shaiva Brahmins of Bengal

1.Chakravarti 2.Chunder 3.Roy 4.Ganguli 5.Choudhury 6. Biswas 7. Bagchi 8. Majumdar, and 9.Bhattacharji

Shaiva Brahmins of Karnataka

1.Smarta 2. Haviga 3.Kota 4.Shivalli 5.Tantri 6.Kardi 7.Padya

Telugu Smartas

1.Murukinadu, 2.Velanadu 3.Karanakammalu 4.Puduru Dravidis 5.Telahanyam 6.Konasima Dravidi and 7.Aruvela Niyogis

Lingayats

They are called Vira Shaivas. They are found in Mysore and Karnataka. They wear on their neck a Linga of Lord Shiva that is placed in a small silver box.

Other Shaiva sects

Akas Mukhis, Gudaras, Jangamas, Karalingis, Nakhis, Rukharas, Sukharas, Urdhabahus, Ukkaras are all Shaiva sects.

THE SAKTAS

The saktas are worshippers of Devi, the Universal Mother. Dakshinis, Vamis, Kancheliyas, Kararis are all Sakta sects.

Miscellaneous

The Sauras adore the Sun, the Ganapatyas adore Ganesh, and the Kaumaras adore Skanda.

The non-Brahmins of South India are Naidu, Kamma Naidu, Chetty, Mudaliar, Gounder, Pillai, Nair,Nayanar and Reddy.

Nanak Shahis of seven classes (*viz.*, Udasis, Ganj-bhakshis, Ramrayis, Sutra Shahis, Govinda Sinhis, Nirmalas, Nagas), Baba Lalis, Prana nathis, Sadhus, Satnamis, Shiva Narayanis are other miscellaneous sects.

The Arya Samaj

The founder of the Arya Samaj was Swami Dayananda Saraswati,· who was born in Kathiawar in 1824. This Samaj is more of a social institution, with a religious background. It has Gurukulas, schools, and Pathshalas. The Suddhi Sabha is a proselytizing branch of the Arya Samaj.

[Note: The followers of the Arya Samaj do not perform idol worship. Swami Dayanand Saraswati wrote "Satyarth Parkash" (Light of Truth). This volume serves as the principal guiding light of the Arya Samaj. Some of the principles of the Arya Samaj are: God is the primary source of true knowledge and of all that is known by its means.

The Vedas are the scriptures of all true knowledge. All acts ought to be performed in conformity with Dharma *i.e.* after due consideration of right and wrong. The primary object of the Arya Samaj is to do good to the world *i.e.* to ameliorate physical, spiritual and social standards of all men. All ought to be treated with love, justice, righteousness and due regard to their merits.]

The Brahmo Samaj

The Brahmo Samaj was founded originally by Raja Ram Mohan Roy, early in the nineteenth century. The Brahmo Samajists do not perform idol worship. Keshab Chandra Sen introduced some changes in the year 1860.

There are now two branches within the Samaj, *viz.*, Adi Brahmo Samaj which holds to the tenets laid down by Raja Ram Mohan Roy and the Sadharana Barahmo Samaj which is somewhat modern and which follows Keshab Chandra Sen more closely. This Samaj has followers in Bengal.

The Jains

The first founder of the sect was Parsvanatha. Its first active propagator was Mahavira. The Jains are found in great numbers especially in the western coast of India. They are divided into two principal sects-the Svetambaras (clothed in white garments) and the

Digambaras (sky-clad or naked). The Jains do not admit the divine origin of the Vedas. They do not believe in any Supreme Deity. They pay reverence to holy men or saints who are styled Tirthankaras, who dwell in the heavenly abode and who, by long discipline, have raised themselves to divine perfection. The images of one or more of these Tirthankaras are placed in every Jain temple.

The Jains are strict vegetarians. They attach great sanctity to life. They practise Ahimsa (non-killing, non-violence). Strict Jains strain water before drinking, sweep the ground with a brush before treading on it or before sitting, never eat or drink at night and sometimes cover their mouths with muslin to prevent the risk of swallowing minute organisms.

There are two classes of Jains, *viz.*, Sravakas who engage themselves in secular occupations and Yatis or monks who lead an ascetic life.

The Sikhs

"Sikhism, while some of its' founding Guru's were Hindu, was created as a response to Hinduism and the reign of the Muslim Mughal empires."-KS Gidda 'Obedience to the Guru brings release from future births' this is a firm conviction of the Sikhs. Sikhs adopt the five Kakas, *viz.*, 1. The Kes (uncut hair), 2. The Kachhca (short drawers), 3. The Kara (iron bangle), 4. The Kirpan (steel dagger), and 5. The Kangha (small-tooth comb worn in the hair).

The Udasis are an ascetic order of the Nanaksahi Sikhs. Srichand, son of Guru Nanak, embraced Sannyasa. Udasis are his followers. Lakshmichand, another son of Guru Nanak, led the life of a house-holder. Vedis are his followers. Nirmalas are ascetic followers of Guru Govind Singh.

The Akalis are brave warriors. The Akalis wear a distinctive dress of blue, and a black turban.

The teachings of Guru Nanak are contained in the first book of the Adi Granth.

No Sikh smokes tobacco.

Sadhus and Sannyasins

Salutations unto the ancient Rishis, seers, saints, paramhansa sannyasins and sadhus, who are the repositories of divine knowledge and wisdom and who guide the destiny of the world in the past, present and future.

Every religion has a band of anchorites who lead the life of seclusion and meditation. There are Bhikshus in Buddhism, Fakirs in Mohammedanism (Islam), Sufistic Fakirs In Sufism, and Fathers and Reverends in Christianity. The glory of a religion will be lost absolutely if you remove these hermits or Sannysins or those who lead a life of renunciation and divine contemplation. It is these people who maintain or preserve the religions of the world. It is these people who give solace to the householders when they are in trouble and distress. They are the messengers of the Atman-knowledge and heavenly peace. They are the harbingers of divine wisdom and peace. They are the disseminators of Adhyatmic science and Upanishadic revelations. They heal the sick, comfort the forlorn and nurse the bedridden. They bring hope to the hopeless, joy to the depressed, strength to the weak and courage to the timid, by imparting the knowledge of the Vedanta and the significance of the ""Tat Tvam Asi" Mahavakya (great saying).

Dasanama Sanyasins

Sanaka, Sanandana, Sanat-Kumara and Sanat-Sujata were the four mind-born sons of Lord Brahma. They refused to enter the Pravritti Marga or worldly life and entered the Nivritti Marga or the path of renunciation. The four Kumaras were the pioneers in the path of Sannyasa. Sri Dattatreya also is among the original Sannyasins. The Sannyasins of the present day are all descendants of the four Kumaras, Dattatreya and Sankaracharya.

Sri Sankaracharya, regarded as an Avatara of Lord Shiva and the eminent exponent of Kevala Advaita philosophy, established four Maths (monasteries) one at Sringeri, another at Dvaraka, a third at Puri and a fourth at Joshi Math in the Himalayas, on the way to Badrinarayana shrine.

Sri Sankara had four Sannyasin disciples, *viz.*, Suresvara, Padmapada, Hastamalaka and Totaka. Suresvara was in charge of Sringeri Math, Padmapada was in charge of Puri Math, Hastamalaka was in charge of Dvarka Math and Totaka was in charge of Joshi Math.

The Sannyasins of Sringeri Math, the spiritual descendants of Sri Sankara and Suresvacharya, have three names, *viz.*, Sarasvati, Puri and Bharati. The Sannyasins of the Dvaraka Math have two names, *viz.*, Tirtha and Asrama.

The Sannyasins of the Puri Math have two names, *viz.*, Vana and Aranya. The Sannyasins of the Joshi Math have three names, *viz.*, Giri, Parvata and Sagara.

The Dasanamis worship Lord Shiva or Lord Vishnu, and meditate on Nirguna Brahman. The Dandi Sannyasins, who hold staff in their hands, belong to the order of Sri Sankara. Paramhansa Sannyasins do not hold staff. They freely move about as itinerant monks. Avadhutas are naked Sannyasins. They do not keep any property with them.

The Sannyasins of the Ramakrishna Mission belong to the order of Sri Sankara. They have the name Puri.

Then, there are Akhada Sannyasins, *viz.*, Niranjana Akhada and Jhuni Akhda. They belong to the order of Sri Sankara. They are Dasanamis. They are found in the Uttar Pradesh State only.

Rishikesh and Haridwar are colonies for Sannyasins. Varanasi also is among the chief abodes of Sannyasins.

Shaivas

In South India, there are Tamil Sannyasins who belong to the Kovilur Math and Dharmaputram Adhinam. They do not belong to the Sri Sankara order. They are Shaivas.

Nagas

Nagas are Shaiva Sannyasins. They are in a naked state. They smear their bodies with ashes. They have beard and matted locks.

Udasis

Guru Nanak's order of ascetics is called Udasis. They correspond to Sannyasins and Vairagis. They are indifferent to the sensual pleasures of this world (Udasina). Hence they are called Udasis.

Vairagis

A Vairagi is one who is devoid of passion. Vairagis are Vaishnavas. They worship Lord Rama, Sita and Hanuman. They read the Ramayana of Tulasidas. The mendicant Vaishnavas of the Ramanandi classs are the Vairagis. Sri Ananda, the twelfth disciple of Ramananda, instituted this ascetic order.

Rama Sanehis

The founder of this order was Ramcharan who was born in the year 1718 in a village near Jaipur in Rajasthan. The Rama Sanehi mendicants are of two classes, *viz.*, the Videhis who are naked and the Mihinis who wear two pieces of cotton cloth dyed red in ochre. Their monastery is in Shahapur in Rajasthan. The Rama Sanehi sect has the largest following in Mewar and Alwar. They are found also in Mumbai and Poona (in Maharashtra State), Surat, Ahmedabad in Gujarat State), and Hyderabad and Varanasi.

Kabir Panthis (panthi = followers)

Kabir Panthis are the followers of saint Kabir. They are numerous in all the provinces of Upper and Central India. There are twelve branches. Kabir Chaura is at Varanasi. It is a big monastery of Kabir Panthis. Dharamdas was the chief disciple of Kabir. The followers are expected to have implicit devotion to the Gurus, in thought, word and deed. They should practise truthfulness, mercy, non-injury and seclusion. The followers of Kamal, son of Kabir, practise Yoga.

Dadu Panthis

The Dadu Panthis form one of the Vaishnava cults. Dadu, the founder of this sect, was a disciple of one of the Kabir Panthi teachers. The followers worship Lord Rama. Dadu was a cotton cleaner. He was born at Ahmedabad. He flourished about the year 1600. The Dadu Panthis are of three classes, *viz.*, the Viraktas who are bareheaded (clean shaven head) and have one cloth and one water-pot, the Nagas who carry arms and who are regarded as soldiers and the Vistar Dharis who do the avocations of ordinary life.

The Dadu Panthis are numerous in Marwar and Ajmer. Their chief place of worship is at Naraina, which is near Sambhur and Jaipur. Passages from the Kabor writings are inserted in their religious scriptures.

Gorakhnath Panthis

Gorakhnath was a contemporary of Kabir. He is regarded as the incarnation of Lord Shiva. He calls himself as the son of Matsyendranath and grandson of Adinath. There is a temple of Gorakhnath at Gorakhpur in Uttar Pradesh. Bhartrihari was a disciple of Gorakhnath. Gorakhnath wrote Goraksha-Sataka, Goraksha-Kalpa and Goraksha-Nama. They are in Sanskrit. The followers of Gorakhnath are usually called Kanphatas, because their ears are pierced and rings are inserted in them, at the time of their initiation. They worship Lord Shiva.

Nimbarka Sampradayis and Ramanuja Sampradayis

These are Sadhus of the Nimbarka Sampradaya. They are Vaishnavas. The Sannyasins of the Ramanuja Sampradaya wear orange coloured cloth, a holy thread and tuft and Tri-danda or three-staff. At present, they are very few in number.

Parinami Sect

Sri Pirannath was the founder of this sect. He was born in 1675 at Jamnagarh, district Rajkot, in Kathiawar. He was the Devan (chief minister) of Raja Jam Jasa. The followers are to practise Ahimsa, Satya and Daya-non-violence, truthfulness and compassion. They study the sacred book, Kul Jam Svarup or Atma-Bodha, in Hindi, which contains the teachings of Sri Pirannath. It contains 18000 Chaupais. They worship Bala-Krishna, *i.e.*, Krishna as a small child.

The followers are found mostly in the Punjab, Gujarat, Assam, Nepal and Mumbai. There are two Maths or monasteries-one at Jamnagarh and the other at Pamna.

Smarta Sect

What is the universalistic Smarta Sect?

Smartism is an ancient brahminical tradition reformed by Shankara in the ninth century. Worshiping six forms of God, this liberal Hindu path is monistic, nonsectarian, meditative and philosophical. Aum Namah Shivaya.

Smarta means a follower of classical smriti, particularly the Dharma Shastras, Puranas and Itihasas. Smartas revere the Vedas and honour the agamas. Today this faith is synonymous with the teachings of Adi Shankara, the monk-philosopher, known as shanmata sthapanacharya, "founder of the six-sect system." He campaigned India-wide to consolidate the Hindu faiths of his time under the banner of Advaita Vedanta. To unify the worship, he popularized the ancient Smarta five-Deity altar-Ganapati Surya, Vishnu, Shiva and Shakti-and added Kumara. From these, devotees may choose their "preferred Deity," or Ishta Devata. Each God is but a reflection of the one Saguna Brahman. Shankara organized hundreds of monasteries into a ten-order, dashanami system, which now has five pontifical centres. He wrote profuse commentaries on the Upanishads, Brahma Sutras and Bhagavad Gita. Shankara proclaimed, "It is the one Reality which appears to our ignorance as a manifold universe of names and forms and changes. Like the gold of which many ornaments are made, it remains in itself unchanged. Such is Brahman, and That art Thou." Aum Namah Shivaya.

MODERN HINDUISM

Following the decline of the Mughal Empire during the late 17th century, the British gradually succeeded in establishing themselves as the paramount power in India during the next century. The process began with a British victory in the Battle of Plassey in 1757, followed by the defeat of the Marathas in 1818. British victory over the Sikhs in 1846 completed the process. By this time the British had made two decisions of far-reaching importance for the future of Hinduism: to allow Christian missionaries to operate within the British dominions, in 1813; and to introduce English as the language of public instruction, in 1835. These decisions forced Hinduism to confront Christianity and Western modernity. At the same time, the Western world was exposed to Hindu scriptures translated into European languages.

Movements for Reform

One response to the encounter with Europe was reform. The Bengali scholar Ram Mohan Roy set the tone for reform in the early 19th century. Roy campaigned against medieval or regional Hindu practices that were objectionable in the modern world. He advocated allowing widows to remarry and abolition of the relatively rare practice of sati (self-immolation of a wife after her husband's death; see suttee). In 1828 Mohan Roy founded the Brahmo Samaj (Society of Brahma) to spread his ideas.

Another movement kept India from moving too far toward imitation of the modern Christian West. The movement was named after Ramakrishna, a Hindu spiritual leader who served as a priest at the Dakshineshwar Temple in the city of Kolkata (Calcutta). His reputation as a mystic drew many to him, including Swami Vivekananda, who founded the Ramakrishna movement after Ramakrishna's death in 1886. Vivekananda, a representative Hindu product of India's new English-language education system, became a devotee of Ramakrishna and renounced the world after the priest's death. His message was a return to the timeless wisdom of the Vedas. As an unknown swami, he turned up uninvited at the Parliament of World Religions in Chicago in 1893 to present Ramakrishna's teachings. He won instant celebrity and was hailed as a hero in India for his vigorous advocacy of Hinduism. In 1895 he founded the Vedanta Society in New York City to promote Hindu ideas.

Vivekananda primarily used English in his work of reforming Hinduism and stressing the inclusive aspects of Hindu spirituality over ritual and rules. Another reform-minded leader of the 19th century, Dayananda Sarasvati, used Hindi in responding to the challenges of Christianity and modernity. Sarasvati founded the Arya Samaj, a movement also dedicated to modernizing Hindu practices and asserting the universality of the Hindu tradition. These movements helped revitalize Hinduism.

Another issue that engaged Hindu reformers was the plight of the lowest social class, the panchama jatis who are also known as untouchables. Local movements, such as one led by Sri Narayana Guru in Kerala, were most successful at reform. Narayana, who was born in 1856, believed that education and greater self-esteem, rather than confrontation and blame, would elevate the untouchables. He established temples where all castes could pray together.

HINDU REFORMERS AND INDIAN NATIONALISM

Brahmo Samaj

In 1828, a man named Raja Ram Mohan Roy (1772-1833) founded an organization called 'Brahmo Samaj'. Indian historians consider this organization forerunner which paved the way for reformation in India and its establisher as the 'father of modern India'. Raja Ram was a Brahman from Bengal. He was a British civil servant in India. He saw in British rule of India the best things that were benefical to India. He adored the west European philosophy of democracy, liberalism and humanism. He had a great interest in non-Indian cultures and religions. He was especially impressed by Christianity and other religions which preached the existence of one Almighty God.

Raja Ram tried to create a new Hindu religion philosophy and enfolded in it the existence of one God and other beliefs, which were then not the predominant features in Hinduism. He attacked some Hindu traditions and features among them caste system, child marriages, Sati-burning of the live wife over her dead husband's pyre, idolatry and other beliefs. He tried to change the popular Hindu traditions and claimed that the popular Hindu traditions were different from the real Hindu beliefs. Raja Ram and his organization 'Brahmo Samaj' tried to change the social order of India. He established newspapers and schools all around India. He convinced the British in 1829 to outlaw Sati. But during that period there wasn't yet an Indian ethos among the Indians. Indians were never one nation but always a collection of different entities. They were used to different rulers including non-Indians. From their point of view the British were just another ruler over them (see India in the past). But the main contribution of the Brahmo Samaj to the society of India was that it evoked issues that were common to people all around the Indian sub-continent. The notions of this organization were the inspiration for other organizations and various secular political parties, like the Indian National Congress, which were later on created in India (see Creating the Indian identity).

Sati-The Burning of the Widow

Sati is described as a Hindu custom in India in which the widow was burnt to ashes on her dead husband's pyre. Basically the custom of Sati was believed to be a voluntary Hindu act in which the woman voluntary decides to end her life with her husband after his death. But there were many incidences in which the women were forced to commit Sati, sometimes even dragged against her wish to the lighted pyre. Though Sati is considered a Hindu custom, the women, known as Sati in Hindu religious literature, did not commit suicide on their dead husband's pyre. The first woman known as Sati was the consort of Lord Shiva. She burnt herself in fire as protest against her father who did not give her consort Shiva the respect she thought he deserved, while burning herself she prayed to reborn again as the new consort of Shiva, which she became and her name in the new incarnation was Parvati.

Other famous woman in Hindu literature titled Sati was Savitri. When Savitri's husband Satyavan died, the Lord of death, Yama arrived to take his soul. Savitri begged Yama to restore Satyavan and take her life instead, which he could not do. So Savitri followed Lord Yama a long way. After a long way in which Yama noticed that Savitri was losing strength but was still following him and her dead husband, Yama offered Savitri a boon, anything other than her husband's life. Savitri asked to have children from Satyavan. In order to give Savitri her boon, Lord Yama had no choice but to restore Satyavan to life and so Savitri gained her husband back.

These two women along with other women in Hindu mythology who were exceptionally devoted to their husbands symbolized the truthful Indian wife who would do everything for their husband and they were named Sati. The meaning of the word sati is righteous. But as written earlier the women named Sati, in Hindu religious literature, did not commit suicide on their dead husband's pyre. Therefore the custom of burning the widow on her dead husband's pyre probably did not evolve from religious background but from social background.

There are different theories about the origins of Sati. One theory says that Sati was introduced to prevent wives from poisoning their wealthy husbands and marry their real lovers. Other theory says that Sati began with a jealous queen who heard that dead kings were welcomed in heaven by hundreds of beautiful women, called Apsaras. And therefore when her husband died, she demanded to be burnt on her dead husband's pyre and so to arrive with him to heaven and this way to prevent the Apsaras from consorting with her husband. There are also other theories about the origins of Sati.

Even though Sati is considered an Indian custom or a Hindu custom it was not practiced all over India by all Hindus but only among certain communities of India. On the other hand, sacrificing the widow in her dead husband's funeral or pyre was not unique only to India. In many ancient communities it was an acceptable feature. This custom was prevalent among Egyptians, Greek, Goths, Scythians and others. Among these communities it was a custom to bury the dead king with his mistresses or wives, servants and other things so that they could continue to serve him in the next world.

Another theory claims that Sati was probably brought to India by the Scythians invaders of India. When these Scythians arrived in India, they adopted the Indian system of funeral, which was cremating the dead. And so instead of burying their kings and his servers they started cremating their dead with his surviving lovers. The Scythians were warrior tribes and they were given a status of warrior castes in Hindu religious hierarchy. Many of the Rajput clans are believed to originate from the Scythians. Later on other castes who claimed warrior status or higher also adopted this custom.

This custom was more dominant among the warrior communities in north India, especially in Rajasthan and also among the higher castes in Bengal in east India. Among the Rajputs of Rajasthan, who gave lot of importance to valor and self sacrifice, wives and concubines of the nobles even committed suicide, when they came to know that their beloved died in battlefield. In other parts of India it was comparatively low. And among the majority of Indian communities it did not exist at all.

A few rulers of India tried to ban this custom. The Mughals tried to ban it. The British, due to the efforts of Hindu reformers like Raja Ram Mohan Roy outlawed this custom in 1829.

There aren't exact figures about the number of Sati incidences. In general, before this custom was outlawed in 1829, there were a few hundred officially recorded incidences each year. Even after the custom was outlawed, this custom did not vanish completely. It took few decades before this custom almost vanished. But still there are rare incidences in which the widow demands to voluntary commit Sati. In 1987 an eighteen years old widow committed Sati in a village of Rajasthan with the blessing of her family members. In this incidence the villagers took part in the ceremony, praising and supporting the widow for her act. In October 1999 a woman hysterically jumped on her husband's pyre surprising everyone. But this incidence was declared suicide and not Sati, because this woman was not compelled, forced or praised to commit this act.

In different communities of India, Sati was performed for different reasons and different manners. In communities where the man was married to one wife, the wife put an end to her life on the pyre. But even in these communities not all widows committed Sati. Those women who committed Sati were highly honoured and their families were given lot of respect. It was believed that the woman who committed Sati blessed her family for seven generations after her. Temples or other religious shrines were built to honour the Sati.

In communities were the ruler was married to more than one wife; in some cases only one wife was allowed to commit Sati. This wife was normally the preferred wife of the husband. This was some kind of honour for the chosen wife and some kind of disgrace for the other wives. In other communities some or all of the wives and mistresses were immolated with the husband. And in some cases even male servants were immolated with the kings. This kind of Sati in which the wives and servants were treated as the ruler's property intensifies the theory that Sati was introduced to India by the Scythian invaders of India. In some very rare incidences mothers committed Sati on their son's pyre and in even more rare cases husbands committed Sati on their wives pyres.

RAJ RAM MOHAN ROY VS. DAYANANDA

Hindu Renaissance, which is referred to as a religious and political movement, is closely related to a burgeoning Indian Nationalism. Hindu revivalism is of vital importance in the development of Hinduism as a world religion. The Hindu Renaissance had a tendency to play down the difference between theological traditions and to regulate ritual level, below the ethical spirituality of the Upanishads and the Gita. Hindu reform movement developed to restore the perceived greatness of Hinduism's ancient past, to adopt rationalist elements form within Christianity, and to pay particular attention to social and ethical concerns. The leaders of Hindu renaissance like Raja Ram Mohan Roy and Dayananda Saraswati played an important role in the awakening of social and religious reforms.

Raja Ram Mohan Roy (1772-1833) was born of a distinguished Brahmin family in Bengal. He was educated at the Muslim University at Patna where he studied Arabic and Persian philosophical literature. He also studied Sanskrit in Varanasi, as well as English, Hebrew and Greek with a view to translating Bible into Bengali. Because of the Muslim influence, particularly Sufi, Roy was a St...

The main contribution of Brahmo Samaj to the society of India was that it evoked issues that were common to the people all around the Indian sub continent.

They make faith in the doctrines of Karma and Rebirth optional. He wanted to return to the "Sanatana Dharma", the eternal law, which Hindus have moved away from by worshipping icons and reading Epics and Purans. He also supported remarriage of widows, if their previous marriage had not consummated. marriage by choice? the most ancient form of marriage in India-is the best form of marriage. He lost his faith in the Shaiva religion of image worship, when he saw mice climbing over the temple icon, eating the food which had been offered to the deity.

Dayananda Saraswati (1824-1883) was born in Saurashtra in Gujarat to a Shaiva Brahman family. Raja Ram Mohan Roy, through his services, was considered the true leader of Renaissance and known as the "father of Renaissance". He believed that people should not be discriminating by their birth but by their Karma, actions. It was not a seperate religion but a reform movement within Hinduism.? Dayananda Saraswati opposed the Varna system. The four Vedas are; Rig Veda, Yajur Veda, Sama Veda, & Atharva Veda.? Roy founded the Atmiya Sabha in 1815.

BELIEFS OF THE BRAHMO SAMAJ

Fundamental Principles of the Brahmo Religion and Universalism

The fundamental principles of the Brahmo Samaj, founded by Raja Ram Mohan Roy in 1828 are:

1. There is only one God, who is the creator, and the saviour of this world. He is spirit, infinite in power, wisdom, love, justice and holiness, omnipresent, eternal and blissful.

2. The human soul is immortal and capable of infinite progress, and is responsible to God for its doings.

3. Man's happiness in this and the next world consists in worshipping God in spirit and in truth.

4. Loving God, holding communion with Him, and carrying out His will in all the concerns of life, constitute true worship.

5. No created object is to be worshipped as God, and God alone is to be considered as infallible.

To this, Raja Ram Mohan Roy added "The true way of serving God is to do good to man." Since no one person is considered to be infallible, the Brahmos hold all the great religious leaders of the world in respect, and believe that truth is to be gleaned from all the scriptures of the world. To that extent, the Brahmo religion is truly eclectic. Universalist in nature, it is "dogmatically undogmatic".

The Brahmo Samaj has a great deal in common with the other free churches of the world, and is one of the founding members of the "The International Association for Religious Freedom". Rationalist in everything, it does not deny the possibility of Divine Revelation, but reserves the right to test the validity of what is supposed to be revelation. The connection between the Brahmo Samaj and the other liberal churches of the world is best understood when we considered the basics of Universalism, which are dealt with in the following paragraphs:

Duncan Howlett has aptly described Universalism as a doctrine of "Testing, Questing and never Resting, with Open Mind and Open Heart."

Each of these items bears detailed examination. The root question is how can we be sure about the truth of our beliefs? After all, there is no doubt that we human beings are fallible. The only way we can surmount our human fallibility is by continually testing the validity of our assumptions. We have to accept that we are prone to making mistakes and deceiving one another all the time. Even in the age of computers, there is always the possibility of mistakes being made in programming or worse still, valuable data being lost on account of viruses deliberately planted by misguided souls. We must therefore check everything by all the means at our disposal. This is true even in the case of religion, where we can no longer be certain of the infallibility of scriptures or prophets.

If our human capacity for error is a severe limitation, then our imagination and probing curiosity are surely among our greatest assets. It is the human spirit of inquiry and questing, in other words, seeking for the truth, which is behind all advances in Philosophy or Religion. The enquiring mind pushes beyond ideas that we already have, in order to discover new perfections. In this process of Questing, we are never really satisfied until we feel that we have gone as far as is humanly possible. This is what is meant by "never Resting". On the path of discovery we are bound to meet like-minded souls also engaged in the same search for truth. We must be open to dialogue with them, and at least listen to them even if we do not agree. The spirit of the "open mind" is a safeguard against dogma, which has no place in Universalism.

While the open mind enlarges our own frontiers, it is not enough to merely be open to other ideas. Acceptance of the other person as a brother and a comrade makes religion truly universal. Merely accepting that "In the Father's house there are many mansions" does not better our human lot the way "Love thy neighbour as thyself" does. True Universalism is based on the "Fatherhood of God and the Brotherhood of Man" more than anything else.

Universalists believe that religion should be dynamic and not static. Everything in this world is evolving, and religion too, changes with time. Any religion that adheres to a set of unchanging beliefs is a dead religion. Of course, any change has to be tested for validity by applying our God given powers of logic and reasoning, and must be acceptable to our conscience. The Brahmos believe that God reveals Himself in His own creation, and speaks to man through his conscience. The relationship between God and man is one of loving and giving. Our life is a gift from God. What we do with our life is our gift to God.

HISTORY OF THE BRAHMO SAMAJ

As British rule consolidated in India during the 18th century, two factors contributed to the formation of the Brahmo Samaj in the following century. Firstly the Hindu social system had begun to stagnate and placed too much of an emphasis on traditional rituals. Secondly an English educated class of Indians began to emerge to fulfil the administrative and economic needs of British rule. Raja Ram Mohan Roy, a Bengali, was a product of the latter trend.

What made Raja Ram Mohan Roy stand out from his peers was his questioning mind.

Apart from knowing several languages he was a Sanskrit and an Arabic scholar, and studied several religions. He campaigned for social reform and women's education. He founded the Brahma Samaj at Calcutta in 1828, which was initially known as the "Brahmo Sabha." Later in 1868 it was changed to the "Adi" (Original) Brahmo Samaj. It rejected idol worship and the worship of multiple gods and goddesses of the traditional Hindu beliefs.

Raja Ram Mohan Roy was much influenced by western thought, especially Christianity. He was one of the first Hindus to visit Europe, where he was much admired by the intellectuals. He died in Bristol.

He was friendly with another famous Bengali, Dwarakanath Tagore. Prior to his departure to Europe, Raja Ram Mohan Roy had asked Dwarakanath Tagore's son, Debendranath Tagore, to continue his work in his absence. Debendranath Tagore took an active interest in the Brahmo Samaj, and began to transform the Brahmo Samaj into a spiritual fraternity. He formulated the "Brahmo-upadesa" which were a set of readings from the ancient Hindu book, the "Upanishads."

Debendranath Tagore's successor was Keshab Chandra Sen. He sought to incorporate Christian ideals into the Brahmo Samaj movement. He began the compilation of a scripture including passages from the Holy Books of many religions-Hindu, Buddhist, Christian and Muslim.

Gradually, due to differences in certain areas of religious beliefs, three institutions arose:

- The Adi (Original) Brahmo Samaj-founded by Debendranath Tagore
- The Naba-Bidhan (New Dispensation) Samaj-founded by Keshab Chandra Sen
- The Sadharan (Common) Brahmo Samaj-founded by Pandit Shivanath Shastri

The Sadharan Brahmo Samaj sought to provide a more rational and monotheistic interpretation of the Upanishads. A "mandir" (prayer house) was built in Cornwallis Street, (now re-named "Bidhan Sarani") Calcutta. Eventually these three Samajes united to form the "Brahmo Sammilan Samaj," and a "mandir" was built in Bhowanipur, Calcutta. This celebrated its centenary in 1997. The Brahmo Samajes grew in several Indian cities and abroad. There are records of one being present in Rangoon and in London as far back as 1911.

Social Welfare

Removing The Caste System: The caste system has been a part of Hindu society for hundreds of years. It's inherent divisive nature and social injustices were abhorrent to the early Brahmos. Therefore an important reform that the early Brahmos campaigned for was the removal of the caste system. Many of the early Brahmos came from the Brahmin caste, who wore a sacred thread around their body to signify their caste superiority. From the 1850's onwards the renunciation of the sacred thread came to symbolise this break with tradition. The equality of all men was fundamental to the Brahmo movement, and to them it did not matter what caste or indeed religion someone was born into. For example even in 1865 there was a case of a Muslim boy being attracted into the religion. Given the polarization of society between Hindus and Muslims at the time, this was revolutionary in those days.

Widow Remarriage: Despite Iswar Chandra Vidyasagar's campaign that led to the legalisation of widow remarriage (1856) in

India, Hindu society had many reservations on this issue. The Brahmos campaigned against such pre-judices. To reinforce their commitment to this many young men of the Brahmo movement made a positive point of marrying widows.

Saving of Upper Caste Unmarried Women: It wasn't just the lower castes who suffered in the caste system. Despite their caste status, the girls from the upper caste families suffered because of their position. If a suitable bridegroom could not be found for such a girl in their caste, their options were limited, as marriage to lower caste men was not permitted. These girls often found themselves being married off to very old men who were already married several times over. Or worse still, sometimes these girls would be poisoned to death. Again the Brahmos campaigned against such unjust practices and saved the lives of many such girls.

Women's Education and Status: Traditionally education had been primarily for the men. However during the 1860's and the 1870's the attitude of the Brahmos started to change. Education was encouraged among the Brahmo women. At the same time their equal status in society was emphasised by allowing women to pray with men at the prayer halls. In 1881 the Brahmo Samaj at Barishal (Bengal) appointed the first woman Brahmo preacher (Manorama Mazumdar). This article was written by Dr. Sumit Chanda, based on source material provided by the Brahmo Sammilan Samaj at Calcutta. The drawings originally formed part of the Poster Exhibition held in August-September, 1997, on the occasion of the Centenary celebration of the Brahmo Sammilan Samaj. These have been reproduced with the kind permission of Mr. P.R. Das Gupta, the Secretary of the Brahmo Sammilan Samaj.

Brahmo Wedding: In a Brahmo wedding, the bride and the groom, as adults, declare in an open house that each is willing to accept the other as a partner for life. Thus a Brahmo wedding has no tradition of "giving away" the daughter by her parents. The bride and the groom pray to God together and take their nuptial vows. The minister and the other fellow Brahmos pray for their welfare and future happiness. The bride and groom typically exchange garlands and rings, and the prayers are complemented by singing of hymns.

Millennium Sermon: On the first Maghotsav of this century and in the new millennium I would like to share with you some thoughts that have crossed my mind. The word January comes from the Roman God Janus, who had two heads-one pointing to the past, and one pointing to the future.

As we are celebrating Maghotsav in January at the beginning of the century, it is befitting that we first take a look at the past, and then into the future. A look at the past takes us to the Renaissance in India, and in Bengal in particular. In 1828 the Brahmo Samaj was established by Raja Ram Mohan Roy, who was followed by other leaders like Keshab Chandra Sen and Shivanath Shastri. It was a time of great spiritual social reforms against casteism and the emancipation of women. It was a period when superstitious and evil customs like the suttee were abolished. It an era when great educational institutions were established in Calcutta. That era has also seen the birth of men like Ramakrishna and Rabindranath and preachers of a non-violence like Mahatma Gandhi. We have seen the birth of the largest democratic nation when India achieved independence in 1947.

During the last century we have seen tremendous advances in the field of science and medicine. We have made great strides in developing transport-faster cars, trains and planes. Men have landed on the moon and we have watched it sitting in our own homes on TV. The past century has made enormous progress in the field of computers and satellite communication-the mobile phones and telecommunications by way of videoconferences in distant lands has brought the world closer. The world has become smaller and closer. Countries no longer think individually. They take a global view of trade and commerce.

However in spite of all the scientific achievements and material comforts have we made any real progress in moral and human values? Are human hearts and minds now closer to each other than 500 years ago? The 1900s have seen two World Wars-the people of the past century have experienced fighting and bloodshed and the horrific destruction of Nagasaki with the atom bomb. In spite of modern communications systems, communities seem to have grown apart and divided, as we have seen in Bosnia and very recently in the atrocities of Kosovo and now in Chechnya. At present and there are many wars going on in Africa and Asia with the devastating consequences of land mine injuries long afterwards.

Our social structure and family life has also changed. The extended family is on the brink of extinction. The advances in medicine have increased longevity, but are we able to provide a reasonable quality of care? Can we spare a little time for visiting elderly friends? Do we as human beings care for other humans and the plants and animals of this beautiful world?

Today at the beginning of the 21st century let us attempt to try to look at the future. We do not know what the future holds for us; but we can hope that the world will be a better place for all of us. The world, we can hope, will be a peaceful place-not only will there be peace among nations, but also in the hearts all men who will fulfil their duties towards the old, the sick and hungry. Societies and nations will not just think of their own survival but will work for the benefit of others, which is one of the ideals of the promise of the Brahmo Samaj, and that the other principles-"truth, justice and love" shall prevail in the hearts of men and women of the 21st century. We hope that the hearts and the minds of all the people in the world will be united and the century will be a happier place for all of us. It may seem like a dream but it is up to each one of us to make an effort, however small towards achieving this dream-and making this place a better place. May we find the world in the 21st century as Tagore has described in one of his poems:

THE NEW INDIA AND RAJA RAM MOHAN ROY

In spite of political convulsions and economic retrogression the first century of British rule in India (1757-1858) is in certain respects a memorable epoch in her history. The period witnessed a remarkable outburst of intellectual activity in India and a radical transformation in her social and religious ideas. The impetus to these changes came from the introduction of English education. Through this channel came the liberal ideas of the West which stirred the people and roused them from the slumber of ages. Reason and judgment took the place of faith and belief; superstition yielded to science. This great change affected at first only a small group of persons, but gradually the ideas spread among larger sections of the people, and ultimately their influence reached, in greater or les degree even the masses. The new spirit of this age is strikingly illustrated by the life and career of Raja Ram Mohan Roy, a remarkable personality, a great political and social reformer.

Raja bagan his reforming activity by preaching the unity of God, assailing the prevalent Hindu belief in many gods, and the worship of their images with elaborate rituals. He tried to demonstrate that the views were in accordance with the old and true scriptures of the Hindus, and that the modern deviations from them due to superstitions of a later age without any moral and religious sanction behind them. Ram Mohan's views stirred Hindu society to its depths, and bitter controversies followed. Ram Mohan published translations of ancient scriptures in order to defend his thesis, and carried on the contest, almost single-handedly, by the publication of a large number of Bengali tracts. Towards the close of his life he founded, in 1828, an organization for furthering his religious views. The organization ultimately developed into Brahma Samaj. It was meant to be an assembly of all who believed in the unity of God and discarded the worship of images. A house was built and handed over to a body of trustees. The Trust Deed which the Raja executed on 8th January 1830, directed that the building was to be used "as for a place of public meeting of all sorts of descriptions of people, without distinction ", for the worship of the one Great God, but that no image should be admitted or rituals permitted therein. The Raja however never regarded himself to be somebody else but a Hindu, and stoutly denied, up to the last day of his life that he was founding a different sect.

Ram Mohan was a great pioneer of English education. Not only did he himself found several institutions for that purpose, but he always lent a helping hand to others who endeavored to do so. He along with the active participation of the English man David Hare founded the Hindu College in Kolkata in the year 1817, which later on came to be called as the Presidency College. Ram Mohan's reforming activity was also directed against social abuses of Hindu society, notably the rigours of caste and the degradation of the position of women.

Those days a custom was prevailing in the society, known as the Sati daha prahta. According to this custom, a widow was forcibly immolated to death in the pyre of her husband. The word Sati means a chaste and virtuous woman but has by a curious process applied to the practice of burning chaste women along with the dead bodies of their husbands. This actually finds origin in the religious belief that there is a life after death and if the wife is burnt along with the husband, they will lead the life together after death. Such hopes and encouragements both to the victim and her natural protectors produced the inevitable consequences. In many cases the material interests of the male relations, added to religious faith induced them to persuade the unhappy victim to the tragic course. The British government tried to do away with this practice, but was bolted from the civil population. Thanks to the unwearied efforts of Raja Ram Mohan Roy. He stood firmly against the orthodox Hindus and supported the Government in its attempt. In a counter petition submitted by the Raja and his coadjutors against the petition of the orthodox Hindu section. After describing the horrors of the Sati in vivid terms, they declared that "all these instances are murders, according to every Shastra as well as to the common sense of all nations". To educate public opinion Raja Ram Mohan wrote a pamphlet on the subject and organized a vigilance committee in order to ensure that the Government regulations were followed in each instance. The Raja was bitterly opposed by the orthodox Hindus under the leader ship of Raja Radhakanta Deb. Feelings at last ran so high that even Raja Ram Mohan's life was threatened. Ultimately on 4th December 1829. The famous Regulation was passed, in which Sati was declared illegal and punishable by courts.

He also endeavoured to ameliorate the fate of helpless widows by many other ways, notably by changing the Hindu laws of inheritance about women giving them proper education. He was opposed to polygamy and various other abuses in the social system of Bengal. He also advocated remarriage of widows under specified circumstances. His ideals of womanhood and man's duty towards them, preached in forceful language in various tracts, were far ahead of his age and were inspired by the memories of the golden age of India.

In the field of Indian politics also Raja Ram Mohan was the prophet of the new age. He laid down the lines of political agitation in a constitutional manner which ultimately led to the birth of Indian National Congress half a century later. The Raja was a great champion of the liberty of the Press. Ever since 1799 there had been a strict censorship in the publication of journals. In 1817 Lord Hastings abolished the censorship, but laid down regulations, which among other things, prohibited the discussion of certain matters. Raja Ram Mohan presented petitions against the new Press Regulations both to the Supreme Court and to the King-in-Council. Though the petition was rejected but they form a noble landmark in the progress of Indian culture.

The Raja similarly drew up petitions against the Jury Act of 1827 The Raja had a clear grasp of the political machinery by which India was ruled and fully realized the importance of presenting India's case before the home authorities when the questions of the renewal of the Company's Charter in 1833 was being considered by Parliament. This was one of his main objects in under taking the voyage to England. These documents enable us to gather the view-point of Raja Ram Mohan and of the advanced Indian thinkers of his time, on the burning questions of the day. The Raja strongly championed the cause of the peasants. He pointed out that under the Permanent Settlement, the zaminders had increased their wealth, but the exorbitantly high rents exacted from their tenants had made the lots of the riots a miserable one. He advocated a reduction of the rent to be paid by the tenants by means of a reduction in the revenue payable by the zaminders. The consequent loss of revenue, he suggested, should be met by a tax upon luxuries or by employing low-salaried Indians as collectors instead of high-salaried Europeans. He favoured the Permanent Settlement but he rightly urged that the Government should fix the maximum rent to be paid by each cultivator.

Among the other measures advocated by the Raja may be mentioned the Indianisation of the British-Indian army, trial by jury, separation of the offices of judge and magistrate, codification of civil and criminal laws, consultation with the Indian leaders before enactment of new laws and the substitution of English for Persian as the official language of the courts of law.

Ram Mohan Roy and Social Reforms

Ram Mohan Roy was born into a Brahmin family near Calcutta on May 22, 1772. At Patna he learned Arabic and Persian, studying the Qur'an, Islamic law, and Persian poetry. By the age of ten he had two wives. Ram Mohan learned Sanskrit at Benares and studied Hindu philosophy for three years. He traveled, and some believe he studied Buddhism in Tibet. His father was a zamindar and collected taxes. Absorbed in Sufi and Vedanta philosophy, Ram Mohan criticized Hindu idolatry and soon became alienated from his traditional parents. Yet in 1796 his father gave him a house in Calcutta, and Ram Mohan began studying English. He loaned money to English employees of the East India Company. His father died in 1803, and years later his mother tried to disinherit Ram Mohan for heresy. His friend John Digby introduced him to western literature, and in 1805 he began working for Digby and the Company. Ram Mohan's first publication was in Persian and affirmed the unity of God; he warned against idolatry and religious doctrines that deceive. Ram Mohan may have witnessed a widow burned to death in sati at the funeral of his brother in 1812.

In 1814 Ram Mohan and a few friends began a friendship society called Atmiya Sabha. The next year he began translating some of the Upanishads and an abridgment of the Vedanta Sutra into Bengali and English. In 1817 he helped Edward Hyde East and David Hare found the Hindu College; but Ram Mohan's name was not associated with it because some Hindus considered him a heretic. In debate Ram Mohan defended Hindu theism and argued that people are harmed by myths about gods and goddesses that do not stand up to reason. In 1820 he began helping missionaries translate the Bible into Bengali to improve on Carey's version, and he published his book on the ethics of Jesus called The Precepts of Jesus, Guide to Peace and Happiness. In response to criticism, he wrote three appeals to Christians in which he argued that the humanistic ethics of Jesus is much more important than the miracles and theological doctrines on atonement and the trinity. Ram Mohan emphasized the oneness of God. Max Müller, the scholar who helped to found the modern study of comparative religion, said that Ram Mohan was the first person to synthesize eastern and western religion.

In 1818 Ram Mohan began an educational campaign to end the burning of Hindu widows (sati) by publishing and freely circulating a dialogue between an advocate and an opponent. He wrote,

In times of want the wife works like a slave.

In times of affluence the husband takes another wife and enjoys worldly pleasures.

Very often the wife is beaten up, discarded, accused of disloyalty, all because the husband feels that he has the right to do so.

Ram Mohan argued that nowhere in the Hindu scriptures is it demanded that a widow must commit suicide or be murdered. He charged that one of the main reasons for sati was the avarice of relatives who wanted to avoid the cost of supporting a bereaved widow. He advocated the custom should be abolished for humanitarian reasons. Most of the widows dying by sati were in Calcutta, and the number in Ram Mohan's own district of Burdwan was barely second to Hoogly. The number of such widow suicides in the six divisions of Bengal had gone from 378 in 1815 to 812 in 1818. These increases discouraged the efforts that were being made by the British government. Ram Mohan managed to prevent some burnings by personal persuasion. His writing must have had an effect because in 1819 the number of widow burnings in Bengal was 650. In a second tract that year he defended the rights of women by showing that they are not inferior to men but in some ways even superior. Orthodox Hindus organized groups to defend the atrocious tradition of sati against his campaign, and the number only gradually decreased in the next decade to 464 in 1828. However, the new Governor-General Bentinck made any support for sati a crime in 1829, and in gratitude Ram Mohan sent him an anti-sati address on behalf of more than three hundred supporters.

During its first year in 1821 Ram Mohan took over the editing of the Bengali weekly Sambad Kaumudi (Moon of Intelligence), the first newspaper published by Indians. Ram Mohan also founded and began editing a Persian weekly in 1822 called The Mirror of News (Mirat-ul-Akhbar).

He wrote a brochure demanding that Hindu women should have the same property rights as their fathers and husbands. In 1823 Chief Secretary John Adam got a regulation enacted that was called Adam's Gag because it required every periodical to obtain a license signed by the Council's Chief Secretary before it could publish each issue.

Ram Mohan closed down The Mirror in protest of this pre-censorship and sent a memorial to the Government. He explained why a powerful government should avoid censoring.

Another evil of equal importance in the eyes of a just Ruler, is, that it will also preclude the natives from making the Government readily acquainted with the errors and injustice that may be committed by its executive officers in the various part of this extensive country.

Every good ruler who is convinced of the imperfection of human nature, and reverences the Eternal Governor of the World, must be conscious of the great liability to error in managing the affairs of a vast empire and therefore he will be anxious to afford to every individual the readiest means of bringing to his notice whatever may require his interference. To secure this most important object, the unrestrained liberty of publication is the only effective means that can be employed.

When the British decided to spend its large grant for education on a Sanskrit College in 1823, Ram Mohan argued that Indians had a much greater need to learn science from Europeans. Just as the Baconian philosophy had replaced the medieval scholastics, India needed its own renaissance beyond its religious philosophy. Ram Mohan helped William Adam found the Unitarian Association, and with David Hare they started an Anglo-Hindu school with free tuition for Indians. The Vedanta College was founded to study Hindu scriptures. In 1825 the Parliament passed an East India Jury Bill that only allowed Christians to serve on grand juries. Ram Mohan criticized this discrimination by writing articles for Sambad Kaumudi, and the next year he demanded equal treatment in the Native Petition to Parliament. In 1827 he published the Sanskrit work Vajrasuchi that criticized the caste system. He believed that the most important moral principle is the golden rule: "Do to others as you would be done by."

Ram Mohan and his friends began the Brahmo Sabha on August 20, 1828 based on the idea of one God, one world, one humanity. Devotional songs, mostly by Ram Mohan, were interspersed between the invocation, prayer, meditation, and sermons. When they moved into their own building on January 23, 1830, their purpose was defined in the Trust Deed as to worship "the Eternal, Unsearchable, and Immutable Being who is the Author and Preserver of the Universe." All kinds of people were welcome as long as they behaved in an "orderly, sober, religious and devout manner." No objects were to be worshipped. No person was to be reviled. They aimed to promote "charity, morality, piety, benevolence, virtue, and strengthening the bonds of union between men of all religions, persuasions and creeds." The Brahmo Sabha did not recognize any priestly class as privileged mediators between God and humans. Their members worked on such reforms as abolishing child-marriage, polygamy, and caste persecution. They planned how to bring education to women and give them their proper status in society.

Conservative Hindus led by Radhakanto Dev, compiler of a comprehensive Sanskrit dictionary, tried to counter their progressive ideas by forming the Dharma Sabha. Young Bengalis responded to Ram Mohan's practical synthesis of eastern and western education, freedom of thought, freedom of the press, and intellectual idealism. Ram Mohan protested against the Government's salt monopoly, the high taxes on the cultivators, and worked for many progressive reforms. He criticized the East India Company for taking two million pounds out of India to London each year. He encouraged Dwarkanath Tagore to set up small industries in the Bengal countryside.

In 1831 Ram Mohan went against caste rules and became the first prominent Hindu to visit England. As the envoy of Mughal king Akbar II, he gained him an additional 300,000 rupees for his budget. His memorial to the House of Commons to counter the petition to repeal the abolition of sati was successful, and he presented in writing his reform ideas before the next renewal of the Company charter. He proposed reductions in the rents of the ryots (peasants), and he suggested that the decrease in revenue could be balanced by hiring native collectors at lower salaries. In his Questions and Answers on the Judicial System of India, Ram Mohan recommended replacing Persian with English as the official language in the law-courts, appointing native assessors, using trial by jury and the traditional panchayat system, separating the offices of revenue collectors from judges, codifying the criminal and civil law of India, and consulting with local leaders before enacting laws. His efforts helped persuade the House of Commons to repeal the clause disqualifying all but Christians from serving on grand juries, and the Indian Jury Act of 1832 allowed the governments of Bengal, Bombay, and Madras to appoint qualified Indians as judges. He urged the Tories to support the Reform Bill currently being debated. He did not think that a commercial organization should be ruling another country and suggested that a proper government would be easier for the natives, even though it would still be a foreign one.

Ram Mohan Roy also visited France before he died at Bristol on September 27, 1833. He lived according to the great humanistic saying of Sa'di that he wanted as his epitaph, that the best way of serving God is to do good to humans. He was one of the first pioneers for the ecumenical unity of all religions, and his outstanding efforts for modern education and social reform led some to call him the father of modern India.

The Young Bengal movement had been inspired by the poet Henry Derozio (1809-31), who had taught at the Hindu College and founded the Academic Association in 1828. After Ram Mohan Roy died in 1833, his disciple Vidyavagish led the Brahmo Sabha; but it languished until Dwarkanath Tagore's oldest son Devendranath Tagore joined in 1843 with twenty of his associates. Dwarakanath Tagore helped found the Landholders' Society in 1838, and the next year Ram Mohan's friend William Adam started the British India Society in England. They eventually merged into the British Indian Association, which paid agents to pressure in England and worked for reforms in local government. In 1846 Govinda-chandra Dutt denounced the unequal treatment of British and Indians before the law and urged the separation of the executive and judicial functions. Devendranath had founded the Tattvabodhini Sabha in 1839, and the monthly Tattvabodhini Patrika promoted Indian culture with western improvements. They changed the name of Brahmo Sabha to Brahmo Samaj (God Society) and in 1850 began agitating for social reforms such as widow remarriage, monogamy, and temperance. Vidyasagar discovered a verse in the Parashara Samhita that approved of widow remarriage, and his book Vidhava Vivaha led to the passage of the Widow Remarriage Bill in 1856. That year Devendranath withdrew for two years to travel and be more reclusive in the Simla hills.

DEROZIO AND THE HINDU COLLEGE

One of the main foundational principles of Hindu College was to "instruct sons of Hindus in the European and Asiatic languages and science" and it stayed the course till its transformation into Presidency College in 1854. The appointment of Henry Louis Vivian Derozio as a teacher of English Literature and History marked a new chapter in the rich cultural history of this institution.

Son of Francis Derozio, he was born at Entally-Padmapukur in Kolkata on 10th April 1809. While a student of David Drummond's school at Dhurmotalla (Dharmatala), he had his first lessons in superstition-free rational thinking, apart from the good grounding in history, philosophy and English literature. Drummond was a well known Scottish missionary famous for his free-thinking.

He quit education at the age of 14 and initially joined his father's concern at Kolkata and later shifted to Bhagalpur. Inspired by the scenic beauty of the banks of the River Ganges, he started writing poetry. Some of these were published in Dr. Grant's India Gazette. His critical review of a book by Emmanuel Kant attracted the attention of the intelligentsia. In 1828, he went to Kolkata with the objective of publishing a book of poems. On learning that a faculty position was vacant at the newly established Hindu College, he applied for it and was selected. Fakir of Jhungeera is one of his most famous poetic creations.

It may be recalled that Raja Ram Mohan Roy Bahadur established the Brahma Sabha in 1828. This event produced a massive commotion and backlash within the orthodox Hindu society. Efforts began to scotch this religious revolt. It is in the perspective of this backdrop that Derozio unleashed his ideas that culminated in what was to become a social revolt.

He introduced the first generation of English educated students in this country to the ideas then in vogue in the West. Although he was a teacher of Class Four (the highest class was Class One), he attracted students of other classes also. He helped them with their studies even beyond the officially allocated class hours. Many of them went to his home and he entertained them as friends He encouraged free thinking and a questioning of orthodox Hindu customs and conventions on the basis of Judaic-Christian rationalism. He infused in his students the spirit of freedom, the yearning for knowledge and the passion to serve their native country.

Through his efforts, he created a sensation as a lecturer in Hindu College. His students were known as Derozians a.k.a. The

"Young Bengal" group. He organized an Academic Association where topics such as free-will and fate, virtue and vice, patriotism, arguments in favour of or against the existence of deity, the shams of idolatry and priest craft, were discussed. A mere glance at the topics would show the direction the wind blew at that time. In 1830, they published a magazine called Parthenon. Apart from articles criticizing Hindu practices, the students wrote on women's emancipation and criticized many aspects of British rule. It was banned after publication of the first issue. The association survived till 1839.

A true poet at heart, he wrote about his students:

"Expanding like the petals of young flowers

I watch the gentle opening of your minds... "

Due to his unorthodox take on society, culture and religion, and for "corrupting the youths of the Hindus", he was expelled as a faculty member from the college by a majority 6:1 vote on 25th April, 1831. He faced penury and starvation. In the following days, while answering to the question of whether he had undermined his students' belief in the deity, he wrote: "If it be wrong to speak at all upon such a subject, I am guilty; for I am neither afraid nor ashamed to confess having stated the doubts of philosophers upon this head, because I have also stated the solution of those doubts. Is it forbidden anywhere to agree upon such a question? If so, it must be equally wrong to adduce an argument upon either side, or it consistent with and enlightened notion of truth to wed ourselves to only one view of so important a subject, resolving to close our eyes and ears against all impressions that oppose themselves to it?"

The removal of Derozio from the' staff of Hindu College could not, however, suppress the influence this free thinking scholar had on his pupils. He died shortly after he was expelled (23rd December, 1831). Even before his death Derozio founded a daily paper-The East Indian. He voiced the affliction of the Anglo-Indian community through this publication and went ahead and sent in a petition to the Parliament, with a request to ameliorate the anguish of the Anglo-Indians, conforming to his fighting zeal. Two other instances may be cited proving the liberalistic ideals of Derozio. In one of his poems he welcomed the independence of Greece at the battle of Navarino; again, he responded heartily to the legislation forbidding sati daha (widow burning) strengthening the hands of Ram Mohan Roy, the notable social reformer. Derozio was an atheist but his ideas were also partly responsible for the conversion of upper caste "twice born" Hindus like Krishna Mohan Banerjee and Lal Behari Dey to Christianity. Most of his other students joined the Brahmo Samaj in later life or even formally remained part of Hindu society but they certainly were path breakers.

WORLD RELIGIONS

Ancient impetus to religious innovation is kept alive. Social networks provided common link with religiously diverse ethnic groups. "Shiva" is same whether his idol in Nepal had Mongolian features Negroid or Dravidian features some Oliver places in India or outside India. Raama and Krishna were mostly depicted as having dark skin.. In the 17th Century Japan had closed its doors for merchant vessels from Europe because of Christian Missionary Activities which interfered with Japanese Faith. In the 19 century or little earlier Dutch merchant vessel showed their interest in trading with Japan on behalf of the Dutch government.

When the Vessel lay at anchorage the crew carried "cross" on the shore, laid it on the beach and went stamping over it to the king of Japan with a letter of intent for trade with Holland. They promised not to interfere with religion of the land and stopped the missionary activities of spreading Christianity in Japan. The trade was resumed, and Holland"s economy rose upward, In 1853 American warship forcibly entered Tokyo Bay, but Japan was receptive to the outside influences by them; and Japanese genius blended elements of many different spiritual and cultural traditions. In 1549, Francis Xavier, a Portuguese priest and a founder of the Jesuit order, arrived, in Japan at the head of a Christian Mission. Portuguese merchant vessels were going to Japan since 1545. The Christianity was supported by the warlord (daimyo in Japanese) Oda Nobunaga (1534-82), who made effective use of European weaponry. Psychological it gave the message that powerful weapons meant the powerful religion. As a general term it was effective all over the world.

Today Japanese Christians are in small number (about 600,000), but their devotion to Jesus and Mary has come to resemble the worship of Shinto "kami" or Buddhist "bosatsu". Japanese God must resemble and have Japanese features. Original Jesus could not have had features of a European man; though that is how he is shown on the "Cross". Buddhist temple, the Kiyomizu, at Kyoto attracts devotees even today. The city was Japan"s imperial capital from 794CE (A.D.); today it is called Tokyo. This is one of the most important centres of Japanese Buddhism. As Japan"s imperial capital in 794CE, it was known as Heian. This old name takes us to Sanskrit root: It suggests two words "Herambah" (Ganesha), and "Heli" meaning the Sun. Japanese always confuse "R" and "L"" in pronunciation-(" I play in temple and pray in bed" is the famous joke")-the word "Heian" is a suitable middle way of pronunciation. Japanese flag carries emblem of Sun in this centre; there are records Ga‚eaa idols were found in Japan. The indications are too obvious to be ignored.

Though the Japanese word "kami" (near to Sanskrit "karma") is often translated as deity, but in reality it designates an extremely wide range of spirit beings (as "Yakaa", "Gandharva", "Apsarᵢ", identified with Hindu concept) with a host of mysterious and supernatural forces and "essences" (something that exists). Where Hindus believe that there are 330 million (33 crores) gods; Japanese say, there are eight million "kami", tins is another way of saying that the number is infinite.

They include tutelary (having the guardianship) divinities of clans, villages, and town boundaries, mountains, rivers, caves, lakes are also included in these deities, "triptych" suggests a carving in three panels side by side. The central panel represents "Paraatatva", which is self expressive; when it becomes expressive it appears that sun emerges from the cave of darkness and the third dimension of space becomes active. The forth dimension of "Time" remains m comprehensible to the human intellect:

The oldest thoughts of ancient sages are found in "Rug Ved which took the form of various rituals and traditions. These ideas were made available for the future generations by way of stones or legends. Upanayan ritual had greater significance in Vedic rituals. It had two aspects as far as Guru is concerned. In a concept he is mother of a "Bata", at the same time he represents the god of death. When a child is prepared to start his education, it is tested to find if it deserved or worthy of education. "Kacha/Shukra" relationship is a good example of this concept.

The rationality of it suggests that true education is possible only when a disciple passed a test of death, the disciple literally enters the womb of his Guru and learns while there. There was yet another concept showing the relationship of the Sun and the planet "aukra" (Venus). This too has its roots in Rug Veda. Shukra was conceptualized as representing the Sun in "Yajnya" ritual. Hence, God is all pervading and his presence is eternal. His existence reflects in human mind but God is far from effects and causes of mental activities Himself.

The "code Book" is published in 2004; the book is written by Simon Singh, PhD, meteorologist. The study covers all the aspects of geology. The book "World Religions"" enclosed a section on Glossary; the Sanskrit word "Bodhisattva" is written incorrect and the meaning too is ambiguous. The meaning is indeterminate. The word should be written as "Bodhisattava" (n)-Buddhist ascetic; "Nirvana" is a state of mind, when such a mental status is reached a person is not affected by happiness or sadness. Sanskrit "Dhyaana"" is meditation.

Pundit Jawaharlal Nehru wrote in his "Discovery of India" a story of aankara. "He synthesized diverse currents troubling the mind of India and built a unity of outlook. In his life of only 32 years he did the work of many long lives and left such an impression of his powerful mind and rich personality of India that it is very evident right up to this day. He was curious mixture of philosopher and scholar, agnostic and mystic, poet and saint, practical reformer and able organizer".

There is a story of young "Nachiketa" who dares to go and meet the God of "Death". Emerson Ralph Waldo, American essayist and poet wrote: "Kathopanishad" helps to understand the Eternal Riddle of Death". Somerset Maugham borrowed the title itself from the Sanskrit words ". "kshurasya dhar nishita duratyaya"; the underlined words means "Razor"s Edge". The original Shloka goes like this: Oh! you, who are asleep, wake up, stand up, go to those learned Gurus and take lessons in "Atma Jnyjna"; it's difficult to walk on razor"s edge, and so is this subject of "Atma Jnyaana". All who are on this path of "Atma Jnyaana" are aware of the difficulties, but they don"t deviate from this path. Maugham seems to have caught the central idea of "Advaita" with great precision and indirectly supports the conviction of the universality of appeal of the "Advaita" doctrine.

General Editor Michael D. Coogan mentions the name of Raja Ram Mohan (miss-spilled as "Rohan"") Roy as Hind reformer in Chronology (Hinduism). He says he founded "society of Brahma" in 1828 meaning of "Brahma" again is miss-construed. Understanding "Brahma" is rare possibility. Out of a Billion one may approach near to what is understood by Veda Vyaasa as "Brahma". Others only keep walking on "Razor"s edge". The thought of Ram Mohan Roy who ushered in the modem epoch in India was firmly rooted in the "Vedanta"; and Vedanta is the manifestation of ""Advaita".

In 1981 the Encyclopedia of Indian Philosophies Vol.1 was published. It lists almost 700 titles a book on "Advaita Vedanta" and runs into about 30 pages. Vast and extensive literature was influenced by Advaita much before this volume was published. Fritz Copra"s "Tao of Physics, philosopher Hegel"s works, Philosopher.

HINDUISM-SOME PERCEPTION

The public debate regarding Hinduism and its various definitions has lately taken a curious turn, and has become a topic of animated political controversy. Hinduism is the world's most ancient living religion, going back to the very dawn of history, and is unique in that it is not tied to any one text, one individual or one point in time. This gives it a remarkable built-in pluralism which, down through the ages, has incorporated a wide spectrum of philosophical, theological and sociological concepts.

In fact the key to the continued dynamism of Hinduism over thousands of years, despite so many challenges and persecutions, lies in its remarkable capacity for creative re-articulation from age to age by a whole succession of seers and social reformers. The entire panorama of Hinduism from Vedic times down to the present day can indeed be looked upon as a series of challenges and creative responses. The latest of these was the 'Indian Renaissance' led by great social reformers such as Raja Ram Mohan Roy, Debendranath Tagore, Keshub Chunder Sen, Ishwar Chandra Vidyasagar in Bengal, R.K. Bhandarkar and M.G. Ranade in Maharashtra, Swami Dayanand Saraswati in the Punjab, and the great spiritual luminaries Sri Ramakrishna, Swami Vivekananda, Sri Aurobindo and Sri Ramana Maharshi. Gandhiji himself was essentially a profound social reformer and not only a political leader. Between them these thinkers were able to break through the accretion of superstition and dead habit that had gathered around this great inclusive faith over the centuries, and once again illuminate its essential core.

The ramifications of this would take us across vast oceans of thought, but the point to stress is that the master principles upon which Hinduism is based are to be found essentially in the Upanishads, which represent the high watermark not only of Indian but of world philosophy. It is in these luminous dialogues that the great issues confronting humanity have been addressed in a manner that seems to grow in relevance as we move into the global society. Out of the whole range of concepts found in the Upanishads, five deserve special mention..

The first and most basic concept is that of the all-pervasive Brahman-Isavasyam idam sarvam yat kincha jagatyam jagat--whatever exists and wherever it exists is permeated by the same divine power. This is an important realisation, because while many philosophies

have postulated unbridgeable dichotomies between God and the
world, matter and spirit, the Upanishadic view is that in the ultimate
analysis all that exists is a manifestation of the divine energy. Indeed,
there can be no manifestation without the light of consciousness
behind it, and this, in a way, is the realisation of the new science.
Previously, in the classical science of Newton and the Cartesian-
Marxist paradigm, there was an incurable dichotomy between matter
and energy; but in the post-Einsteinian situation there is a growing
realisation that whatever exists is really only a different manifestation
of the same energy. The unified-field theory which the scientists are
now seeking thus has its spiritual counterpart in the concept of the
all-pervasive Brahman of the Upanishads.

The second concept is that this Brahman resides within each
individual consciousness, in the Atman. The ktinan, as it were, is
the reflection of this all-pervasive Brahman in individual
consciousness; but it is not ultimately separate from the Brahman.
One of the examples given in the Upanishads is that as, when a great
fire is lighted, millions of sparks fly up out of the fire and then fall
back into it, so from the Brahman arise all these millions of galaxies
and into Brahman again they all ultimately fall back. The concept
of Isvarah sarvabhutanam hriddese tishthati the Lord resides within
the heart of each individual is the second great insight of the
Upanishads, and the relationship between the Atman and the Brahman
is the pivot upon which the whole Vedantic teaching revolves.

Yoga is aimed at bringing about the union between the Atman
and the Brahman. The word 'yoga' comes from the same root as
the English word 'yoke', to join. Yoga is that which joins the Atman
and the Brahman. There are in the Hindu tradition four major paths
of yoga-Jnana yoga, the way of wisdom; Bhakti yoga, the way of
emotional rapport; Karma Yoga, the way of dedicated action; and
Raja yoga, the way of psychic disciplines. All of them are directed
towards bringing about the union between the all-pervasive Brahman
without and the immortal atman within, call it God-realisation or
Self-realisation depending upon whether one is seeking a personal
or impersonal divinity.

Flowing from this we come to another important Vedantic concept, that all human beings, because of their shared spirituality, are members of a single family. The Upanishads have an extraordinary phrase for the human race-Amritasya putrah-children of immortality, because we carry within our consciousness the light and the power of the Brahman regardless of race or colour, creed or sex, cast or nationality, or any other differentiation. That is the basis of the concept of human beings as an extended family-Vasudhaiva kutumbakam-which is engraved on the first gate into our Parliament House. This great insight of the Upanishad is peculiarly relevant at this juncture in human history when science and technology have in fact annihilated distance and knitting the world into a global community.

A fourth major philosophical concept of the Upanishads revolves around the essential unity of all religions, of all spiritual paths ekam sad viprah bahudha vadanti-The truth is one, the wise call it by many names-as the Rg Veda has it. The Mundaka Upanishad has a beautiful verse which says that as streams and rivulets arise in different part of the world but ultimately flow into the same ocean, so do all these creeds and castes and religious formulations arise in different times and areas, but, if they have a true aspiration, ultimately reach the same goal. This is the philosophical basis of the Interfaith movement which aims at bringing together people of different religious persuasions in a friendly and harmonious dialogue.

Here is a philosophy which cuts across barriers of hatred and fanaticism that have been built in the name of religion. At its highest Hinduism is a universalist religion. It accepts the infinite possibilities of movements towards the divine, and does not seek to limit or confine us to any particular formulation. Each one of us has to seek our own path, and Hinduism welcomes and accepts the multiplicity of paths to the divine. It is like climbing a mountain. There are several different starting points, and if we keep arguing at those starting points we are miles apart. But when we start climbing and approach the summit our paths will begin to converge, and ultimately when we get to the peak we will all meet. Similarly, once we really start moving upwards in the field of spiritual endeavour, we will find denominational and theological differences gradually losing their importance, and as we rise to the summit we will realise the spiritual oneness of divinity. Thus the seers of the Upanishads, the great Christian mystics, the Muslim Sufis, the Sikh gurus all finally speak of a luminescent awareness of the divine presence.

A fifth Vedantic concept is that of the welfare of all beings Bahujana sukhaya bahujana hitaya cha. It is true, of course, that the lofty thought of the Upanishads coexisted with an iniquitous social order, much as the great Greek philosophy coexisted with the obnoxious practice of slavery. But at its highest, Hindu philosophy seeks the welfare of all creation, not only of human beings but of all life forms on this planet. In our arrogance we have destroyed the environment of this planet, we have polluted the oceans, we have made the air unbreathable, we have desecrated nature and decimated wildlife. But the Vedic seers knew that man was not something apart from nature, that human consciousness evolved out of the entirety of the manifested universe and therefore they had compassion for all living beings. That is why they constantly exhort us that while we are pursuing our own salvation, we must shun the path of violence and hatred. We need to develop both elements of inner aspiration and outer achievement-Atmano mokshartham jagath hitaya cha-we should work for our own salvation, but also for the welfare of the broader society in which we live.

These five concepts of Hinduism, if taken together, provide a comprehensive world-view which will be of real value to us in these troubled times. These principles are so universal that there is no scope here for a narrow interpretation. Indeed an exclusivist approach to Hinduism would constitute a grievous injustice to this great philosophy. It would be tragic if we do to Hinduism what the Jehadis have done to Islam. To seek to demonise an entire community comprising a significant section of our population is not only irrational and unjust, but could weaken the edifice of our national unity.

The confusion between Hindutva and Bharatiyata also needs to be clarified. It is certainly true that Hinduism has provided, down through the ages, the broad cultural and religious framework that has held India together despite its astonishing linguistic, ethnic and political diversity and divisions. Hinduism is as essential for an understanding of Indian culture and civilisation as Islam is for the Arab world and Roman Catholism for Latin America. But many other religions have also flourished in India for centuries, and there are today several States and Union Territories where Hindus are not in a majority. Three other world religions-Jainism, Buddhism and Sikhism-were born here, while four religions came to us from West Asia and also flourished here-Zoroastrianism, Judaism, Christianity and Islam. Along with the Baha'i faith as well as some new Buddhist sects, they represent a rich, pluralistic religious mosaic that needs to be carefully nurtured.

Also, India has by no means a monopoly over Hinduism. All Indians are not Hindus and all Hindus are not Indians. There are millions of Hindus living around the world who, while certainly having special regard for India as their spiritual motherland, are yet loyal and patriotic citizens of their respective countries. To equate Hindutva with Bharatiyata, therefore, is to create an avoidable semantic and conceptual confusion.

Certainly the great traditional centres of Hinduism lie in India, but there are also famous temples and pilgrimages in Nepal, Tibet and Sri Lanka, and new Hindu temples have now come up in almost every city in the West wherever there is a critical mass of Hindus. Hinduism is one of the great religions of the world, and to seek to confine it to India or to give it an exclusivist and majoritarian interpretation is to do it a disservice.

Anyone who lives by the great ideals of Hinduism should, by definition, adopt an attitude of amity towards other religious traditions. However, we have had in history figures like Hiranyakashyapa, Kansa and Ravana who were also Hindus but who took to the path of intolerance, cruelty and oppression. Incidentally, and this shows the essential liberalism of the Hindu tradition, Ravana, although bitterly opposed to and finally killed by Sri Rama, is nonetheless respected for his spiritual learning. His scintillating hymn to Lord Shiva-the

Shiva Tandava Stotra-is still recited with reverence by Shaivites around the world.

The real debate, therefore, is not between secularism and Hinduism. Secularism is built into the basic structure of our Constitution which also enshrines the freedom of religion, while Hinduism is the largest of the many religions that flourish in this country. The debate should be between differing versions of Hinduism. Let us never forget that one of the great glories of Hindu thought has been its capacity to embrace the entire human race with its concept of Brahman-Atman. While every nation and every community has the right, indeed the duty, to defend itself against attack and aggression, we must never take on the role of the aggressor. As the country with the largest Hindu population in the world, India should in fact be in the forefront of actualizing the highest universal principles upon which this great religion is based. Only then will we be doing justice both to Hinduism as well as to India itself.

THE HINDU ROOTS OF UNIVERSALISM, AND ITS RELEVANCE TO MODERN RELIGIOUS STUDIES

Universalism has been a very influential concept in Western thought, especially in the study of comparative religion. It is the belief in one universal religious truth, which can be reached or understood in many ways. This approach has promoted a sympathetic and tolerant attitude towards the world's cultures and religions, and emphasized the values common to different perspectives. While it is widely believed that universalism is a philosophy originating with Plato and Greek philosophy in the fourth century BCE, the concept is at least a thousand years older. We see universalism in the Rig Veda and the Upanishads, and it has continued to be an important concept in India to the present day.

Hindu interpretations of universalism have varied over time. This paper will examine the development of the idea of universalism in the Hindu context, discuss some relevant modern issues, and suggest some useful applications. The earliest statement of universalism comes from the Rig Veda, usually dated around 1500

BCE or earlier. The Rig Veda I.164.46 states "Ekam sat vipra bahauda vadanti" or "to what is one, the sages give many names (titles): they call it Agni, Yama, Matarisvan." This statement is echoed in Rig Veda 10.114.5: "Him with fair wings, though only one in nature, wise singers shape, with songs, in many figures."

These statements have been interpreted in two major ways. From the perspective of non-dual (and thus non-theistic) Vedanta, following Sankara and other writers, they mean that only the One or brahman is true. The world of names and forms is maya, it is false or illusory in relation to brahman. Thus, all form and human ways of understanding are false, including the gods, who participate in the realm of maya.

The schools of dualistic or theistic vedanta have interpreted "Ekam sat" differently. Brahman is true, and the names and forms used by the sages are also true (as sages are speakers of truth). Brahman is present in a particular god, and all of the gods, as well as such figures as Prajapati and Purusha. This interpretation came to include symbols, visible signs of the invisible truth, such as space, wind, fire, prana, and certain mantras like OM.

Thus, the "Ekam sat" line has been interpreted to mean that only brahman is universally true, and everything else (including all gods) is maya or illusion. It has also been interpreted to mean that all gods are true, as they participate in or share in the reality of brahman. Thus one interpretation says all gods are universally false, and the other says all gods are universally true.

We may also note that the range of the statement has grown over time. It has gone from a metaphysical statement (all is one), to a pan-Hindu statement (the various Hindu gods represent the same reality), to a pan-religious statement (all religions follow one truth, though their prophets use different names and forms to represent that truth). Some commentators have debated the legitimacy of this expanded interpretation.

Both non-dual and dualistic interpretations of universalism are also present in the Upanishads. The major texts of these Vedic commentaries range in dates from about the eighth century BCE to the fourth century BCE, though many were written later. We have the non-dual approach of "Neti, neti" or not this, not that" meaning that no physical object or mental concept fully embraces brahman. We still see this approach today in jnana yoga, in which illusion is peeled away by a process of denial and negation in order to reach ultimate truth.

We also have the theistic approach to Vedanta, in which brahman is the lord deep within the self, the inner controller within the heart, Isvara or Isa. This approach may be monotheistic, as we see in many Vaishnava interpretations of Vedanta, or it may be broader, including all gods. As the Mundaka Upanishad states, "This whole world is brahman, the hidden mover... within all that moves, breathes, and winks." (MU 2.2.1-3).

With Badarayana and other writers, this distinction developed into the doctrine of nirguna and saguna brahman, one term meaning absolute existence without form, the other with brahman taking on name and form, or nama-rupa. While non-theistic Vedanta emphasizes the nirguna aspect, most theistic Vedanta does not accept the lesser nature of the god with form, and understands both aspects to be of equal value.

In both the Upanishads and the brahmanas, we see a tendency to establish equivalences between beings and qualities apparently belonging to different levels and spheres. As Dandekar notes, one derivation of the word "Upanishad" is "placing side by side, equivalence, correlation." Such establishing of equivalents and correlations between different spheres acts as a precursor for the later universalist equating of different gods and symbols, all being part of the same underlying reality.

Another complex early text on universalism is the Bhagavad Gita, the conversation between the god Krishna and the prince Arjuna on the battlefield. The Gita is a text which integrates many different Hindu schools of thought: yoga, bhakti, samkhya, vedanta, and others. As Miller notes, the text is usually dated by scholars as being written between 400 BCE and 400 CE. On the topic of universalism, we have two opposing statements. When Krishna discusses other religions, he says to Arjuna,

When devoted men sacrifice

To other deities with faith

They sacrifice to me, Arjuna

However aberrant the rites. (BG 9.23)

Thus, whenever people worship other gods, they are really worshipping the one god, Krishna. Krishna's identity with all gods is also shown in his revelation to Arjuna of his universal form, in which he is the sun gods, the gods of light, the howling storm gods, and thousands of others. This is universalism-all deities are really the one Ultimate Truth. However, two lines later he states:

Votaries of the gods go to the gods

Ancestor worshippers go to the ancestors

Those who propitiate ghosts go to them

And my worshippers go to me. (BG 9.25)

Here, people who worship other gods do not go to Krishna, they go elsewhere.

But finite is the reward

That comes to men of little wit

Men who sacrifice to the gods reach the gods

Those devoted to me reach me. (BG 7.23)

Thus, the Gita has universalist ideas (Krishna is within himself all gods) and also non-universalist ones (that Krishna is different from other gods, who have different heavens).

With the rise of bhakti in the medieval period, universalist ideas tended to wane. The puranas emphasized the adventures of the gods, and often gave arguments for sectarian belief and practice. We do find, however, the concept of the istadevata, the personal god who is individually chosen, which means that people can choose any gods to worship. We also have the notion of avatar, in which deities can take on different forms. This implies that the deities of other religions can be true, because they could really be Hindu gods in disguise (thus, Buddha has been called one of Visnu's avatars). There have also been bhakti mystics like Kabir and Nammalvar, who have included universalist statements in their poetry.

Universalism returned as an important Hindu concept in the nineteenth century. Raja Ram Mohan Roy began the Brahmo Samaj, and sought to recapture the "purity" of older Hinduism, by following the non-dual interpretation of Vedanta. Thus, the Samaj forbade polytheism, worship of statues, caste restrictions, and belief in avatars. They were to follow the universal truth of Hinduism, not the mythic accretions that had been added over time, and they would not allow "graven images" (as they phrased it) within their buildings. Roy's successor Keshub Chandra Sen sought to incorporate Christian ideals in the Samaj, and began to compile a Samaj text with passages from many different religions: Hindu, Buddhist, Jewish, Christian and Muslim.

We also see universalism in the ideas of Ramakrishna and Vivekananda, though their approaches were different. Ramakrishna Paramahamsa of Dakshineswar was a Sakta devotee and temple priest. He danced and sang to the goddess Kali, and worshipped her all of his life. He followed Bengali Saktism as his primary practice, but he accepted the truth of other religions. He spent a week or so experimenting with Muslim and Christian worship, and he performed Vaisnava worship as well. He did meditation with a Vedanta guru, and with a tantric female teacher. He was a universalist and a passionate devotee of Kali.

His disciple Vivekananda had a more Brahmo approach to universalism. He felt that Hinduism should be rational, non-mythical, and activist, especially in the area of social service. He was not much interested in Ramakrishna's passion for Kali and worship of the goddess within statues-he took Ramakrishna's ideas of universalism and changed them, to bring them in line with his interpretation of

Vedanta philosophy. His ideas have come to dominate the Ramakrishna Mission, which he founded in Ramkrishna's honour. The last time I was in Calcutta, a swami of the Ramakrishna order told me that Ramakrishna was never a Sakta-he was only a Vedantin sage. I wondered if he had ever read Ramakrishna's biographies.

On occasion, Vivekananda also espoused what we might call evolutionary universalism-that all religions are true, but that they are evolving towards a superior form. We see this approach today in some forms of liberal Christianity, and also in Bahai religion. As Vivekananda stated. The idea of an objective God is not untrue-in fact, every idea of God, and hence every religion, is true, as each is but a different stage in the journey, the aim of which is the perfect conception of the Vedas. Hence, too, we not only tolerate, but we Hindus accept every religion... knowing that all the religions, from the lowest fetishism to the highest absolutism, mean so many attempts of the human soul to grasp and realize the infinite, each determined by the conditions of its birth and association, and each of them marking a stage of progress.

Some writers have called this "reverse colonialism"-for Vivekananda is saying that while all religions are true, they all evolve towards Hinduism, which is most advanced.

We also see universalism in the political sphere, mostly exemplified by Gandhi, who did not claim the superiority of a particular path. As he stated, After long study and experience, I have come to the conclusion that 1] all religions are true; 2] all religions have some error in them; 3] all religions are almost as dear to me as my own Hinduism, in as much as all human beings should be as dear to one as one's own close relatives. My own veneration for other faiths in the same as that for my own faith; therefore no thought of conversion is possible.

However, today there is conflict over the role of universalism in modern Hinduism. One one hand, it is the form of Hinduism followed by most Indians living and working in the West-especially scientists and engineers. It is "India for export"-the aspect of Hindu thought most widely known and respected around the world. As Carl Jackson notes in his book Vedanta for the West, universalism is Vedanta's greatest attraction to Americans-its all-embracingness, its tolerance, its ability to reconcile religious differences. For some, it is the basis for a claim of Hindu superiority-Hindus being more tolerant, loving and forgiving than Christians, who only claim to have these qualities.

On the other hand, some Hindu nationalists say that universalism condemns not only a Hindu state, but even Hindu devotional practice. This conflict comes out of different interpretations of the term. I shall give these names, in order to clarify them.

We might call one understanding intellectual or abstract universalism. It is a philosophical position, rather than a religious belief. It states that all religions are equal, as all go to the same goal, and therefore one should not follow a particular one. Here we have a universal truth at the expense of the particular, for the clarity and rationality of the philosophical position is preferred to the particularity of a specific belief and practice. When this is turned into a religious claim, it can become anti-religious, forbidding religious practice in the name of tolerant humanism. Here, humanism contradicts itself by negating the human right to religious freedom. From this perspective, practicing any religion constitutes religious prejudice or bias.

We might call the other understanding religious or sectarian universalism. In this approach, one religion is practiced, and others are accepted as valid and legitimate. It emphasizes the importance of particular or exclusive practice as a personal choice, but respect is given to other religions. In this approach, one can legitimately be both a Hindu or other religious practitioner and a universalist. One can support a religious nation, and still be a universalist.

This was also the real difference between Ramakrishna and Vivekananda-while Ramakrishna performed devotional bhakti practice and was a sectarian universalist, Vivekananda avoided devotion and ritual, and followed intellectual universalism.

I noted at the beginning of this paper that I would suggest some useful applications. In the field of Religious Studies in the USA, universalism has been under attack for over fifteen years. The universalism followed by Eliade and other scholars of comparative religion was based on the idea of the sacred as the common goal of religions. It is likely that Eliade was inspired in this idea by his study of Vedanta with Surendranath Dasgupta.

This idea has been attacked by a group calling itself Postmodernist, or sometimes Deconstructionist. They claim that all religious understandings are political, that belief in any common or universal religious truth is superstition and intellectual colonialism, the imposition of Western religious ideas (such as universalism) on non-Western victims. No legitimate comparisons can be made between world religions, as religions are only responses to social history and alien to each other.

Some suggestions:

- Indian scholars might note that India has its own tradition of universalism, and that it is not a Western Platonic or Eliadean idea forced upon India by colonialist thinkers. They can make clear that universalism is an indigenous category, thus giving permission to Western scholars to use the concept in the field of comparative religion without fear of practicing intellectual colonialism.

- Indian scholars with their long history of religious study and universalist philosophy are in a unique position to promote comparative religion and to argue against postmodernists who reduce religion to politics.

- India now has virtually no programmes in Comparative Religion, History of Religions, or Religious Studies in its universities. The tradition of universalism which respects all religions should lead to the formation of such programmes, so that scholars in India can understand the language of modern comparative religious discourse and effectively participate in global religious conversation and scholarship.

To speak metaphorically, both the idea of universalism and the study of religion itself have become recent victims of cultural theory and Postmodern reductionism in the USA. Nobody in the West has been able to liberate them. India has the most ancient ideas in this area-perhaps it can contribute some contemporary voices as well.

UPANISHADS AND MEDITATION

The subject is 'Upanishad and Meditation'. There is a reason why I have used this title because when we say 'Upanishad', normally people get worried and think that it must be something to do with sanyasins who have left the world and gone off into the forests. Also some people are actually quite worried about reading the Upanishads because they think that it is lot of theory and that it must be quite other-worldly. About meditation they feel that you must leave this world and go off to some forests and meditate.

'Meditation' is a word which has so many connotations because there are so many forms of meditation available today. Some meditate for physical health; some for mental health; some people meditate for what they call 'healing' and then there are people who just take up meditation as a hobby. So I want to show the connection between Upanishad and meditation. Therefore we will explain the terms one by one. We will start with the 'Upanishad' and then come to 'meditation' and see the link between the two.

There is also the basic question-why would one read the Upanishads in the first place? And why would one want to meditate? We have to find out the reason for that. There must be some deep lying reason-one does not do it because it is a fashion obviously. So I will begin with the basic question and then go into what the Upanishads say.

There is a very basic thing which we all seek-whether we have read the Upanishads or not; whether we are interested in religion or not; whether we are believers or atheists-and that is happiness. Happiness is one common factor, which is something that every sane human being looks for in this world. Happiness is the common factor which everybody seeks. Even when somebody commits suicide, it is usually because one wants to escape the unhappiness, the sorrow, the sadness, hoping that when one escapes from sorrow, there will be some kind of happiness.

This is the common search whether one is a believer or a non-believer, Hindu, Muslim, Christian or Sikh-everybody looks for happiness in this world. And all our attempts to grasp things and hold them to us, is a search for happiness. It so happens that we keep looking for this happiness. If drinking a cup of tea gives you a little happiness-then you make the tea and you drink it-and you are satisfied for a while. But tomorrow you have to drink the tea again to become happy!

The fact that from birth to death we keep seeking this happiness all the time, indicates that we have not got the happiness which we are looking for. We get it in small doses here and there sometimes; And it is such a rare thing that when we get it, we don't want to leave it. But it slips away from us. Usually happiness is a very rare thing because whenever I work for a certain object for the satisfaction of my desire and I find what I seek, then because it is such a rare commodity, I want to catch it and hold it to myself. What happens is that at that moment I get the feeling of insecurity that the object which has given me happiness or the state which has given me happiness, may slip away at anytime or somebody may take it from me; or it may happen that when I have found it, I may be gone! Nobody can stop death! So there is this constant search for complete happiness but it is always incomplete. It is unfulfilled totally.

I must tell you this-once in the United States, I went to Sunny Vale for a talk in the Hindu temple there. There was a gentleman sitting quietly in the last row who kept looking at me for a long time. After the talk was over, he took me to the garden. He said, "I want to speak to you" and just caught my hand. And instead of speaking he started crying. After he settled down, I asked him, "What is the matter? Please sit down. let's have a chat." He said that long ago, he had come away from India and settled down in the states. He worked very hard and had a big house, a swimming pool etc. but he had only one daughter. He said, "Everything I made was for my daughter because she was my only thing, my treasure! And then, just the day before, she was gone!" She was doing her medicine. She had come out of the airport and got into the car. She had a road accident and she died. Now his question was-'Why? Why did I work? For her? What is the meaning of all this? Because my whole life was centred on a particular thing, I had got everything for her. But then that person is no more here!'

Now this is one example. There are many such examples-but it need not necessarily mean that the person goes off! It is also true that what we acquire can go away. Therefore, any happiness which we acquire or we hold on to slips away for fear that it may slip away from us. So, from that insecurity, already the unhappiness has started. Although we thought that we are very happy, the unhappiness has already started with acquiring the object-because we don't want somebody else to take it away. In the New Testament there is a beautiful statement-the Sermon on the Mount-when Jesus says, 'Lay treasures in your heart where thieves do not break in and steal'-'steal' not 'steel'!

Therefore looking at this-that we keep working all our lives just trying to grasp this so called 'happiness' which always eludes us. Permanent happiness is only an idea with us because we know only this 'little happiness' that comes to us.

The great rishis-when I say 'rishis' it does not mean a set of people belonging to a certain culture only. What I mean by 'rishis' is all the wise men who looked into this system; who tried to find out what life is; who looked at human problems and researched and went deep into the subject-they are all rishis. They may be Buddhists, they may be Sufis, they may be Christians; they may be-anybody! Of course when you say, 'rishi'-it is a Sanskrit word which means 'A great Being' who has gone into and found out the spiritual truths by his own experience. Now the rishis, looking into these factors very carefully, seeing how people are constantly unhappy; seeking,

seeking and not getting the ultimate fulfillment which they seek-found out, discovered that there is a happiness, a complete fulfillment which is available to every human being-irrespective of caste, creed or community-within oneself, rather than without.

There is a beautiful verse of Kabir Das about the musk deer, the Kasturi Mriga, as it is called. It's a kind of deer which has just under its tail-a little bag, a sac, where it secretes musk and in a particular season, when the scent of the perfume of the musk begins to pervade the atmosphere, the deer, not knowing that this perfume is coming from right under its tail, begins looking for it all over the forest, wondering where this wonderful scent comes from. The rishis said that this happiness which you seek is not something outside-it is not something dependant on anything outside. Its is right inside-you just have to turn, reverse your search and look within. It does not mean that you should be un-operative in the outside world.

Great rishis have written hundreds of books, thousands of scriptures and commentaries on the shastras-that does not mean that they are lazy people who don't want to do anything outside. They are those who discover that real happiness and real fulfilment is to be found inside and not outside and it is independent of anything which you acquire or not acquire in the outside world.

Now to put it in another way. Say, when I am enjoying something, like a particular fruit, when I eat the fruit, what happens is that when the sense organ comes into contact with the fruit, I enjoy the taste of the fruit. But that enjoyment is not in the fruit-it is in me. I am the one who is enjoying it. The theory of Vedanta-it is also a practice if somebody can go into it practically-is that all bliss and happiness lies within every living being, every human being and when the senses come into contact with a particular object, a little bit of it is released.

The rishis said if you are satisfied with the little bit that is released, that's fine-stay with it. But if you want to go the reservoir from which the whole thing comes at once, then turn around and go within. That is why these two paths-one is called the Pravritti Marga or 'The path of action outside' and the other is the Nivritti Marga which is 'The path of action turned inward'-are all action, mind you, meditation is also an activity. And the most important scripture and perhaps the oldest written on the Nivritti Marga is the Upanishad, are the Upanishads, rather-it is not one book.

It is interesting to look into the word meaning of 'Upanishad'. It is formed of three words-'Upa' 'ni' and 'shad'. These are the three syllables which combine together to form the word 'Upanishad'. The word 'Upa' means 'closer'. It is 'to move closer', 'to go closer'. I'll explain; and the last word 'shad' means 'to sit down' or 'to settle down'. Adi Shankaracharya has also translated it as 'to shake up' or 'to loosen one's hold'; and the middle word 'ni' which connects the two.

Now first we will start with 'Upa' which means 'closer'. There are many meanings in this-one is 'to move closer to the Truth' or 'to move closer to the Absolute Reality' or 'to move closer to the complete happiness' which is the right of every human being. The other meaning is to go close and listen to what is being said-it is very important. Normally, when we say, 'we hear', we hear but we do not listen. So in the Upanishad listening is a very, very important factor because normally, when we say, 'we listen', we are not listening but generally comparing. If I say, 'Upanishad' then somebody will think, 'What did so and so say about the Upanishad?' So there is a comparison already started in the mind. Now if half the mind is comparing, then only half the mind is listening.

The subject matter of the Upanishad is 'Shruti' as it is called in the ancient scriptures. Vedas are Shruti; Upanishad is Shruti-Upanishad is part of the Vedas. The four Vedas are-Rig, Yajur, Sama and Atharva Vedas. They have four parts: Samhitas are the hymns; the Branhmanas are the ceremonial part of the Vedas; the Aranyakas are that part of the Vedas which were studied in the forests; and from them came the Upanishads which is the last part, which is known as the Gyana-Kanda-the wisdom section of the Vedas. So Vedas include the whole thing.

It is known as 'Shruti'. Shruti means Shrotrasya-'that which is heard'-not 'that which is read', but 'that which is heard'. So 'hearing' is a very important part of the Upanishad-hearing meaning 'listening'. And if the mind is open and clear and not comparing-and is listening carefully to what is being said, then as soon as you listen to Shruti, it immediately registers and you have understood what is being said-that is why it is called 'Shruti'.

It is not the same thing when you read and then think about it-that's a different matter. Shruti is immediate listening to what is being said. And therefore, Upa here means 'to go closer'. In the ancient hermitages, when the rishis taught the students, the condition was that there should be absolute listening. For that, one has to pay very close attention to what is being said. So that is why it is also known as 'rahasya'-'the secret'. Because if you find what is being said in the Upanishads, you have found the essence of the teaching of Vedanta.

The other reason is that one can only move as close as possible to the Truth-one cannot become the Truth. And if you have moved close enough, then you are no more and the Truth is...not that you are becoming anything.

You see, when the sculptor takes a piece of rock and tries to carve Krishna out of it-or Shiva or anybody-he does not put anything into it. He chips off what is unnecessary and then the image is left. What is not necessary or the Krishna which he has thought about, he chips off and the image is what is left...something like that.

When all the 'mala' or 'delusion' has been cleared; when all the agitations of the mind are cleared, then it is the true essence...what remains is complete happiness, the Truth, which is known as the Brahman. Now this is the teaching of the Upanishad. Therefore 'Upa' means 'to 'go closer'-as close as possible to the understanding of what is being said.

Then 'shad' means 'to sit down'. Why sit down? Because 'sitting down', even physically is an indication of 'settling down'. Now all of you are sitting down-if one person stands up, we know that person is distracted-he is going away somewhere. It not only means physically 'sitting down', 'shad' also means that the mind has 'settled down'-not just physical sitting down but when the mind has settled in complete calmness. The meaning that Adi Shankaracharya has given for 'shad' is 'to shake up'-you can never say its wrong because he was an expert in Sanskrit grammar. 'To shake up' means 'to shake the mind out of its delusion' that happiness is to be found outside and not inside. But in the ultimate sense, when happiness is found inside, one realizes that there is no difference between the inside and the outside! But first one has to start from the inside.

The word 'ni' in between 'upa' and 'shad'. The word 'ni' indicates the level of the receiver. The Hindi word 'neechay','down' comes from 'ni'. 'Down' does not mean that we should physically sit down and the teacher should sit on big platform high up above you. That is not the meaning. It means that if really one has to listen and move closer to what is being said, the level of sitting down must be low-in the sense that one should sit with the understanding that one does not know.

If I say 'I know', then there is no question of saying anything-it will never register. If I begin the enquiry by saying 'I know' then there is no enquiry. So one should sit with that humility that comes out of the understanding that learning has no end...one can learn any time.

The Avadhoot Gita-it's a beautiful book and very interesting. The Avadhoot Dattatreya had twenty four teachers in his life and one of them was the honey-bee. The Avadhoot says 'I learnt the lesson from the honey-bee-collecting and keeping something for a rainy day; and also how it goes from flower to flower, sucks the honey and gathers it all together'-which means there is nobody on this earth who knows everything. As long as you have a physical body, there is nobody who knows everything. So we need to learn. At any time, one should be prepared to learn. And for learning-especially deep things like the Upanishads-one needs to have the humility to think that, 'perhaps I am learning something new-let me listen and learn'. If I say 'I know' then I cannot learn; and in this field sometimes, all that we have studied also might act as an obstacle.

There is this beautiful story of the Zen master and the professor who came to him to study the teachings. So he went to the Zen master and said he was so and so, a professor and so on. And then he said 'Sir now please teach me the essence of Zen. Give me the experience of Satori.' Now 'Satori' is the Zen experience of samadhi-spiritual experience.

So the Master said 'Sit down-let's have a cup of tea.' The professor thought 'what's this? I've asked him a very serious question and he says-let's have a cup of tea! But then Zen masters are peculiar beings, so lets agree with him.' So he said, 'OK, we'll have tea.' So the master himself made tea, put it on the table and starting pouring the tea. So he poured and poured and he poured and after a while, the tea began to flow out of the cup!

The professor sat quietly for a sometime and then he said, 'Sir, the cup is overflowing!' And then the master to him and said, 'Your cup is overflowing. How can I give you Zen? It is already full-there is no space.' So therefore that space is required.

You would have also noticed, that in ordinary terms, if you have to pour a liquid from one vessel to another, you have to keep the other vessel down. You cannot pour it up. So that space is required. That is what is meant-not that the teacher should be elevated and put on a platform or a swing. It is just that one has to sit with humility to learn and understand. In fact, if one is really deep into the understanding of Vedanta, even the teacher has utter humility because he would like to know and also have a rapport with those who are listening and this is not possible if one feels that one knows everything.

Ultimately, what we are seeking from understanding the Upanishads is not something that can be known through the conceptual mind at all! When all the defenses have completely gone, then what remains is That! Now basically, these are the teachings of the Upanishads. They are usually in the form of a dialogue-

'samvad'. You need two people for a dialogue. It is not a monologue-
the teacher keeps on saying and one has to agree! It is not that. It
is a healthy way of looking at things. But it is not trying to prove
each others' point.

There is a beautiful shloka chanted before you start anything-
it is chanted even in some schools:

'Sahanav avatu sahanau bhunaktu saha veeryam karavavahe

Tejasvinava dhitamastu ma vidvishavahai'

It is a very important shloka if one looks into the meaning of
it. It means:-"May both of us be protected'-meaning the teacher and
the taught; 'May both of us be nourished'-the teacher and the taught;
'May the energies of both of us increase'-both, not one! So it is not
a competition between the listener and the person who is talking.
It is the sitting together and trying to understand something properly-
that's the meaning of samvad. And the last sentence 'ma
vidvashavahai'-'let us not fight with each other', 'let us not quarrel
with each other'. Because I am not trying to prove my point and
you are not trying to prove your point to me. Otherwise it is not
a samvad, it cannot be a dialogue. We are trying to look at one
problem-of trying to find our true self which is also our true
happiness-together! And since the teacher is supposed to have walked
the path, he is in a better position to explain-that's all. And if the
student is listening carefully with an open mind, he will also find
it and in turn, be the same as the Master! Now this is the Upanishadd.

When one studies the Upanishad it is preferable to do so with
a teacher because it is largely unexplored territory. To go on one's
own by reading the Upanishads which are available to us-even if we
do get a simple translation-the fact is that they have been interpreted
in different ways. Even then, it is better to listen to someone who
has gone into it rather than do it yourself. Reading it yourself is
better than not reading at all! That's fine!

But it is better to take guidance; otherwise one might take a
long time stumbling along the way because one does not know
where the pitfalls are. You must have heard the famous statement

which many people think is a modern English saying-'blind leading the blind'. Actually it is a very ancient statement. It comes from the Mundaka Upanishad-'andhenaiva niyamana yatha andhaa' It refers to those who have only learnt theoretically and think that they know-when such people lead others into spiritual matters, then it is like 'andhenaiva niyamana yatha andhaa'-like the blind leading the blind.

It is better to learn these things from someone who has gone into it. And one of the signs, perhaps, of a person who has deeply gone into it and has understood the Upanishads is that he will never try to exploit you in anyway. He needs nothing from you-he would like to give rather than receive. This is a very important factor for the study of Upanishad.

There are many Upanishads. In fact, there are one hundred and eight Upanishads. Out of that, there are ten main Upanishads on which Adi Shankaracharya has written commentaries. They are the major Upanishads and out of these ten, some of the most important ones are-the Kathopanishad, Ishavasya Upanishad, Mandukya Upanishad, Mundaka Upanishad, Shvetastavara Upanishad, Keno Upanishad and so on. Now I would like to pick up a few descriptions from a few of the major Upanishads...

There is one thing which I'm sure some of you know-that the first foreign language translation of this great, valuable-in fact, invaluable literature available in this ancient land, was made by Dara Shikoh. He translated the Upanishads for the first time. Dara Shikoh was the elder brother of Aurangzeb-he was killed by Aurangzeb. He translated the Upanishads for the first time into Persian and Arabic and then it went to Greece.

That was the first time the outside world was looking at the Upanishads in another language as it was always available in Sanskrit. And when the Greeks read it, they were astounded by the depth in so ancient a teaching. And then came the Greek translation which is known as the 'Upanikhat', where about sixteen Upanishads were translated. Although many people think that the first English translation was done by Max Mueller, it is not true. The first English translation was done by Raja Ram Mohan Roy. Then after that came Max Mueller and various others.

Now among these Upanaishads, one is very very interesting and I think everyone should read it and that is the Isha Vasya Upanishad. It has only 19-20 verses. It begins with the profound statement which illustrates so many things. The Upanishad begins with the sentence, 'Isha Vasya idam sarvam, yat kincha jagatyaam jagat, tena tyaktena bhunjitha, ma krudhah kasya svid dhanam'- which means-'Isha vasya idam sarvam', 'that Supreme Lord' or 'that Supreme Reality'-let us put it that way. 'Vasyam' means 'pervades'... 'present'... 'pervades everything here'. That means, there is no place or no locality or nothing, which is not pervaded by that Supreme Being, that Supreme Reality. 'yat kincha jagatyaam jagat'-'all that moves and all that does not move'...'jagat' actually means 'that which moves'-that's why the whole world is called 'jagat' because it is always, constantly moving.

And that constant motion also reflects on our mind which is also constantly moving. It is one big cycle of motion. Plato had put it in an excellent sentence. He said 'there are two eternal things in this universe-one 'Is' and is never becoming and the other 'is not' but is ever becoming'. That 'becoming' is what is known as 'jagat'. That movement-it comes physically as well as psychologically. For example 'I don't have something, I must get it'-psychological movement. Or 'my mind is in a bad shape today, tomorrow it must improve'-psychological. Physically-'I don't have this thing; I must get that thing' or 'I am in this location, I must move to that location'. The world is also revolving all the time and then revolving around the geocentric system. So that 'constant movement' is called 'jagat'.

'And that which does not move'-is that which is absolutely still like the eye of the cyclone... total motion but in the middle there is nothing-absolute calmness. And it is from that calmness that everything is sucked in because it's a vacuum. So vacuum-'nothingness' is very powerful. Therefore the Upanishad says, 'Isha vasya idam sarvam'-'That Supreme Being pervades everything here'. 'Idam' is very important-it does not say 'there' but 'here'-'idam'! 'Yat kincha jagatyaam jagat'-'that which moves and that which does not move'. That means, there is nowhere you can go where that Being is not present! It's wonderful!

And then it says 'tena tyaktena bhunjitha'-which some people have translated as 'give up and rejoice' but I like to translate it as 'let go and rejoice'. Now this is topsy turvy. Normally when we say 'enjoy', we like to acquire...gather. But here, the Upanishad says, 'let go and rejoice'. Why? Because that Supreme Being pervades everywhere. So why should you rejoice? Because you are a spark of that Supreme Being! That means, that all the happiness that is there-and all the sorrow and everything that happens is pervaded by that Supreme Being. Therefore, if you want to rejoice, 'let go'! 'Let go' does not mean you should throw everything away and go to the forest. It means-develop the quality of 'letting go'. Then there is absolute peace-and rejoice!

Now let us look at just one small aspect of 'letting go'-there are many aspects to it. The Upanishads are like the Sufi and the Zen teachings-these are loaded meanings in one thing-you have to look at it carefully. Suppose twenty years ago, one of you slapped me on my cheek. Just think about it seriously ...how many minutes does that slap last, really? Five minutes? Ten Minutes? If it is a very big slap then perhaps for the whole day. I might have a swelling on my cheek. But the next day it is gone! But do I let it go? No! I carry it for twenty years, till it becomes a festering wound in my whole psyche. Actually its not there-its gone; it is only in my tape here-its taped in my brain, that's all. But I stick to it-I make it so real-I don't let it go and I suffer. Actually the action is over but I don't allow it to go.

Now this is one of the aspects-'let go and rejoice'! All you have to do is to mentally let it go because the action is not present now-this logic; but the brain likes to think it is very logical but it is often very illogical. So 'let go and rejoice'!

Then the next sentence is:-'Ma grudhah kasya svid dhanam'-'after all whose wealth' or 'whose wonderful wealth is all this anyway?'

If it is pervaded by the Supreme Being everywhere and you are a spark of that Supreme Being yourself-then what is all this? Everything is after all yours-so what are you trying to grasp? Let go and rejoice!

It's a wonderful way of life-its not easy but it is possible. People have practiced it and it is possible. And actually, believe me, you don't lose anything by it!

In the New Testament also you will find a statement-'seek ye first the kingdom of God and the rest shall be added unto you.' Actually, the world is such a funny place-you try to go behind something and it always runs away from you...you leave it and it tries to follow you! It happens. Vishwamitra goes off to the forest for tapasya and Menaka follows him and dances before him! It is a very funny world. When you don't want it, it comes with you!

What I'm trying to say is that there is nothing to fear and to live with this understanding is what is called holistic living. Holistic living is to live with the understanding that the entire universe is pervaded by that blissful Supreme Being and we are a part of that! To live like that-this is not a fantasy which is to be worked out in your mind. It is a fact and the actual process by which this is made possible is what is known as sadhana-meditation. There are different forms of sadhana. What is suitable depends on the kind of person who is practicing it. We cant prescribe the same sadhana for everybody because all beings are made differently.

Now the same Upanishad-the Isha Vasya Upanishad-in the next shloka says, 'kurvan eveha karmani jijivishee chatam samaah, evam tvayi nanyathato sti, na karma lipyate nare' which means-'do all your works even for a hundred years, provided there is only one way for you that you understand what we said just now-that the entire universe is pervaded by that Supreme Being and you are a part of that'. If you live with the blissful awareness of that, then you can live for a hundred years and you also do all the work you want and the karma effect will not touch you. They don't say, 'Don't do any work-run away!' They say, 'Work...work for a hundred years, doesn't matter, the effects will not touch you. Nothing will happen to you if you keep this in mind-that the entire world is pervaded by that Supreme Being and you are a part of That.'

Then there is one part of this grand Upanishad where there is a complete analysis of what is knowledge and what is ignorance. It goes on to make a beautiful statement where the Upanishad declares...'He who worships ignorance enters into darkness'-this we can understand. But the next sentence is very shocking-'He who worships knowledge enters into greater darkness.' What's this? Is the rishi out of his mind? What is the rishi trying to say? There are so many different shades of meaning to it. We can look into it carefully. Meaning one is: when one is full of worldly knowledge, when one begins to feel that one knows everything, when one worships knowledge for the sake of knowledge and not for the sake of finding out Truth through knowledge-then one enters into greater darkness; because then the ego becomes quite swelled up and there is no possibility of a break through if I can put it that way. One is swelled up with the pride of knowledge. So, 'He who worships knowledge enters into greater darkness. The other chap does not enter into so much darkness because at least he knows that he is ignorant-that is one meaning.

The other is a much more subtle meaning. What is knowledge? Normally when we say 'knowledge'-what does it mean? First I don't know something and then I try to understand it and study it and when I feel that I have understood it, it means that I have stored it in my memory and I can recall it any time I want-that is what we mean by 'knowledge'. I have understood something, then I have stored it in my memory and anytime I can recall it.-this is what I call 'knowledge'. Therefore if you look carefully at it, all the knowledge that we have-all of this, including me-is stored in the brain in the form of memory.

The Upanishad says that Supreme Truth or Reality is not a thing which is in the past-it is right here now! So therefore because it is right here, now, all your knowledge has no meaning applied to that Supreme Being. It is not something which you can learn and store and then remember. It is an immediate Presence which is here, available all the time! So if somebody thinks he can know about the Supreme Being and store it and then open it when he wants and then look at it-that is not the knowledge of the Truth and therefore he is entering into 'greater darkness'.

There was a very simple fakir living in Shirdi, once upon a time, who was called Shirdi Sai Baba. Many people thought that he had no knowledge of the scriptures or anything of that kind. One day somebody was sitting in front of him and reading the Gita...about how Krishna teaches Arjuna about knowledge. Then suddenly Baba stopped him and said, 'See when you are walking in the garden and if a thorn pricks the sole of your foot-then what will you do? You will pick up another thorn, poke it and remove the other thorn and throw it off.' Then he asked, 'Will you stick the other thorn back here-the one which you picked up? No, you will throw both away.' He said that is the meaning! If you want to be free of ignorance, you need knowledge. But once you are free, you have to throw both away. Don't stick the knowledge thorn into your foot and think that 'I know everything'. It is a very simple rustic example coming from a person who was not a scholar. These are the matters discussed in the Upanishads. Then there is another beautiful Upanishad-Kena Upanishad. As this is a general talk we will not take up the Upanishad now because it will take time-one Upanishad takes many days to understand if you go sloka by sloka. So Kena Upanishad-the word 'Kena' means 'Who?' Here is a scripture that was written many thousands of years ago whose title is 'Who Upanishad?'. Or let us put it another way, 'What Upanishad?' 'What'-that is a question which occurs to everybody-'What?' 'Who?' 'Why?'...Kena Upanishad.

This Upanishad starts with a very beautiful question. It asks:

Keneshitam patati preshitam manah kena pranah prattamah praiti yuktah

Keneshitam vaachamimaam vadanti, chakshu shrotam ka u devo yunakti

Keneshitam patati preshitam manah

Which means, 'What is it' or 'Who is it that thinks? When the mind becomes active, who it is that feels and sees and is conscious?'

'Kena pranah prathamah praiti yuktah' When the breath begins to go in and out, who it is that controls it?

You would have noticed that we are not conscious of our breath normally-that is why many meditations are linked with the breath. We can live without food for quite some time; we can live without water also for quite sometime, but without breath we cannot live for more than a few minutes. It is a very important part of our nourishment-of the whole system. And yet we are not conscious of it normally.

There are many things which we are not conscious of-we are not conscious of our circulation; we are not conscious of our digestion-it just goes on happening. If we look into it carefully we think that we do many things to look after ourselves. But what is it that we do from the point of view of nourishment, lets say...? Maximum we can do is to put food in our mouth and chew it. Even the swallowing part is done by a motion called peristalsis, in the esophagus. If that particular brain center is not working, we cannot swallow it, however much we try. It is an automatic, autonomous process. Then, after going in, it has to be digested. It has to be split into various parts-glucose etc., the impurities have to be thrown out. We don't tell the intestines 'now start digesting, now take the glucose? We do nothing really. Some one is looking after everything...and from birth to death, mind you!

The other day, I was reading about how many liters of blood is pumped by the heart in one's life-from birth to death-it's unimaginable! It doesn't work under our command-it goes on.

But breath happens to be something which again works automatically and it is one vital process which also can be controlled by us. Normally we are not aware of our breath but we can also become aware of it and control it consciously. So therefore the yogis say that it is the link between the human and 'That' which controls the activities of the system.

Now the question in the Upanishad is a little more abstract.
It asks, 'When you breathe, what is it that makes you breathe?'

'Keneshitam vaachamimaan vadanti'

'When you speak who is the Being actually, who is understanding
the words you say?'

'Chakshu shrotam ka u devo yunakti?'

'When you see, who is seeing? When you hear, who is it that
hears?'

And then it says, 'That is the Being who is your real identity-
the one who is within, who listens, who hears, who breathes, who
sees, because of whom one can think-that is the true essence of
your being. Find it!'

We all know that to see an object, we need eyes. It is because
the eye exists that we are able to see. But we really cannot see our
own eye except in the mirror which is only a reflection of the eye.
And yet we cannot say that the eye does not exist-it is because the
very fact that eye exists that we can see everything.

Now our true self, our true identity-or what the Upanishads
call the 'Atman' is 'That Consciousness' because of which we are
conscious-and to reach that identity of ours by quietening the mind,
is the main function of meditation.

It is not an easy thing because the mind is always distracted.
It keeps wandering here and there. It is not possible to bring it under
control and make it quiet suddenly and go deep within. So therefore,
various paths have been given by the great teachers-worship of a
form, worship of the formless, chanting of a mantra, watching the
breath-these are all different techniques to be adopted.

The only thing is I do not believe that there is only one
technique which is suitable for all. That is not possible because all
human beings are different-their backgrounds are different; if I may
say so, their past births are different, whether you believe it or not.
Their genes are different. So therefore, the importance of satsang.
'Satsang' means to be together with the teacher for quite sometime

and to begin to understand each other properly so that the teacher knows whether this is the right path for the person and the person also understands if it is the right path for him. And if that particular teacher is not suitable for that student, if he is a real teacher, he will have no problem in saying, 'look you are not my cup of tea, you can go somewhere else'-no harm. So also, the student also learns to understand the teacher only by living with him. Unfortunately, today it has become a very difficult thing. You cannot live with the teacher and so we have many package deals-it's alright, it is better than nothing! But it is very important for true spiritual progress to live with the teacher and understand each other. Also, it is very easy for the teacher to sit here on the platform and say, 'I'm a very peaceful being, I have no jealousy and anger'-and all that. But if you see the teacher when he is getting into bus or driving down the road, then you will really discover his inner being…somebody crosses the road and he says, 'O stupid!' Then we know where we are! So therefore, it is very important to know the teacher at close quarters in all functions daily in life. So this is the importance of satsang.

There is one more point which I would like to touch upon-the spiritual understanding that this infinite Goodness or the infinite Bliss or the Supreme Reality also happens to be the reservoir of infinite power. But it is lucky that people do not believe it. It is so because unless one has become that selfless, it is dangerous to come across that kind of infinite power. It can work…it is very dangerous for the world. Therefore the safety switch is that nobody believes in it! Good! It is a wonderful safety device which nature has modelled out-nobody believes in it! It's fine! If you believe it can be dangerous, unless one is really selfless.

To give an example of this energy at work, imagine a very old man walking on the street-he cant even move. One step at a time he goes. Anytime you expect him to fall down and die. And then, visualize a situation where a car comes roaring near him and stops right in front of him-with the screeching of breaks and so on. Generally, nine times out of ten, this old man would have cleared all long jump records! You would not have thought he could do it because he was in a bad shape-you thought he might fall down in the next step and die-but he has managed to do it. Now the question is-where did this energy come from? I know there is a chemical explanation-somebody would say that the adrenalin was pumped into his system-but where is the switch?

Look at this very carefully-logic and thinking has two sides. It has a positive side and a negative side. If this man had logically and rationally thought, 'I'm sick, I've just come out of the hospital-therefore I cannot jump' which is quite true, then he wouldn't have jumped. For that split second when he jumped, he had forgotten all logic and everything. 'Save yourself'-came the command for survival-and he jumped.

The yogis say that the mind, which is always thinking negative or positive thoughts-if it can be quietened for a while and made to become still, you get access to the infinite reservoir of power, as long as you don't let your conditioned thinking interfere with it. That is the other side of thinking. Thought is very useful, but as you think, you discover that it can also be quite conditioning. To de-condition it is to be aware that beyond it, there is an infinite source of energy and goodness; therefore become still and quiet-that is one form of meditation. This is a very simple form of meditation which any one can do, even if one is following some other discipline. And it has no patent-so I don't have to charge you for it!

I will go into that a little bit. We were just discussing about the breath. It so happens that as you go along, if you watch yourself carefully in your daily activities, you will find that when you are very agitated, your breathing rhythm is also very agitated. And when you are very quiet, just listening to music or meditating, your breathing rhythm or pattern is also very quiet and calm. If you look at yourself normally, you will find this out for yourself. So there seems to be some kind of connection between your state of mind and your breathing pattern.

Therefore the yogis thought that since the state of mind is reflected in the pattern or the rhythm of breathing can we work on it the other way round, which is to quieten the breathing rhythm so that the mind can also become quiet? And from that came the science of Pranayama or harnessing the breath, not controlling the breath, really. One of the simplest ways of meditation which is practiced by the Buddhists, by the Sufis, by the Yogis-by everyone-is what is known as 'watching the breath.' It is also practiced in Vipassana in some form. Now 'watching the breath' simply means that you sit down quietly and watch the breath. You can practice it along with any other discipline. You can do it before mantra japa. You can do it after you do your puja, if you worship God with form. Or you can do it before you practice some other form of meditation where your attention is fixed on the chakrass.

This is a very useful exercise to calm the mind and free it from distraction. And it works, especially because the mind cannot think of two things at once; it can only think of one thing at a time and then from there, it will shift to another thing. And the mind cannot be kept in a vacuum. So if you don't want the mind to be occupied by the outside world which creates a lot of distraction and disturbance you have to engage it in something within. The easiest and the best thing to engage it in is the breath and the way tot engage it in the breath is to sit down quietly and watch your breath.-be aware of the breath. You can practice it-slowly breathe in and out-but put your mind entirely on this practice. That means-give your complete attention to your breathing. When you give complete attention to your breath, the mind is occupied within-therefore it is not occupied outside automatically. If some thought occurs bring the mind back to the breath again. As you continue watching your breath while you inhale and exhale for a few minutes continuously, after some time, you will yourself begin to notice that there is a quietness. Generally, quietness comes just after you feel like ... a deep sigh. When you are watching your breath, then slowly, after a while, you feel like giving a deep sigh-and that is the beginning of the relaxing of the mind. At that stage, take up the practice of what has been given to you-the chanting of a mantra or visualizing-or any of the different techniques which have been given to you; or you can just let the mind settle down. You will find that your mind has become very alert but quiet.

In the Buddhist Mahayana system also, there is a meditation where you watch your breath in and out. And when you exhale, you visualize that all your impurities are going out of your body and you are becoming clear and quiet and remain in your true, essential, original state, which means-free of all distractions. It can be done anytime because it is not a tough hatha-yogic exercise. So you can even do it after a meal-there is no harm. Or in the evening or morning or whenever you like-or combine it with your meditational practices. The other way of meditation is just to chant a mantra. One of the greatest, most important and effective mantras that one can chant is the Gayatri. Chant the Gayatri mantra repeatedly, if possible, combine or linked with your breathing. There is a simple mantra, an ancient mantra-'Om Namah Shivaya'. I'm not prescribing it because these are all personal matters which have to be done depending on various factors. Suppose somebody has prescribed it for you and while you are chanting it, you find that your mind is getting distracted. So, what you do is, take a deep breath-when you breathe in, chant the mantra once with the inhalation; when you breathe out, chant the mantra once with the exhalation. So, link your mantra with the breath-one 'Om Namah Shivaya' is one inhalation and one 'Om Namah Shivaya' is one exhalation.

Or there is another simple technique of chanting say 'So Hum' or 'Hum So'-or whatever you like. When you breathe in, chant 'Hum', when you breathe out chant 'So'. We don't want to get into a controversy-somebody might say it should be the other way round-it doesn't matter... 'So Hum' or 'Hum So'...let it go and come out. Keep your complete attention on what you are doing-that is the most important thing. Also one of the chief reasons why the mind is not able to quieten and settle down is because there are certain psychic centers in the human psyche-the human system, which are usually cluttered, covered and made impure. I don't want to go into the different centers and where they are and how they are. These are all personal matters again. But one of the effects of watching the breath-of following the inhalation and exhalation-is that these centres become cleared up. When the channel is cleared, then it is possible for the mind to relax and settle down and go to its very core.

So, since today's subject is 'Upanishads and Meditation' I have only explained it in a nutshell-you cannot explain the Upanishads in 45 minutes. And meditation, you cannot finish it in another 15 minutes. But I have tried to link the two-because many people think that the Upanishads and meditation are something different. It is the same. The Upanishad is the understanding of the Truth and meditation or sadhana is the practice by which you experience what you have understood. These are linked together.

Before we stop, it would be a good idea to do some meditation. Meditate in whatever way you have been taught by someone. Or just watch your breath, quietly chant OM mentally-whichever way you would like to do it. But first I will chant Om three times-those who like can join-others can just listen. Om ...Om...Om.

Hari Om Tat Sat. Thank you very much for listening patiently for so long!

PEACE ON EARTH

Time to Rekindle Passion for Unity: In India, many civilisations have come together over the years, creating new patterns of universal oneness. Raja Ram Mohan Roy ushered in the age of new thought in 1828. He wrote: "All mankind is one great family of which numerous nations and tribes existing are only various branches".

In Bengal, Rabindranath Tagore's father passed on these thoughts to the poet who wrote: "I love India not because I have had the chance to be born on her soil, but because she has saved through tumultuous ages the living words that were issued from the illuminated consciousness of her sons".

All religions tell us that the divine is within us. The Gospel according to St. Thomas says: "He who has heard and assimilated my word is as I". In Sanatana Dharma it is Tat Tvam Asi. To find divinity within oneself it is important to act with compassion towards all beings.

Mexican poet Octavia Páz wrote: "In India there is a passion for unity". Maulana Azad once asked: "If religion expresses the universal truth, why should conflicts arise amongst different beliefs, each claiming to be the sole repository of truth, and condemning others as false?"

One reaches the infinite through love, not through violence. "Ahimsa hi param dharma, Sarva dharma samabhava". The trishul of Shiva represents the three dimensions of space, earth and sky and the three gunas that each of us must strive to overcome in our own lives. Guru Vyasa spoke of the folly of men who choose the way to destruction through discord when all legitimate material satisfaction could be had through the way of fellowship and harmony.

Ours is a multifarious heritage. On the Sindhu-Gangetic plains the tribes were known as Sindhus and Hindus. Hindu became Indus to the Greeks and the country on the bank of the Indus became India. There was no caste, no temple, only prayers in the oral tradition of the Rig Veda.

Caste became an ugly name much later. Yet, Rishi Parasar (the law giver) was the son of a Chandala, Rishi Vashishta's mother was a fisherwoman, Viswamitra was a Kshatriya, Valmiki a hunter. All became great gurus. In the oral verse of the Rig Veda, men and women were equal.

Sanatana Dharma was meant to be India's gift to the world, a way to realise peace and harmony. Increasingly, however, ancient customs are being taken out of context for political purposes. Cattle were extremely important for the Vedic people and so became symbols of spiritual experience. Go, the name for cow and bull, also connotes the earth and the speech of rishis. Gokula means temple; it also means Krishna's dwelling place.

Today, politicians fight over cow protection. Why protect only the cow? What about the beautiful birds of the sky? And the donkeys and the street dogs that are constantly being ill-treated? The environment, too, needs protection. Majestic trees are regularly being chopped down. This decreases forest cover and causes more pollution. So the list is long and painful. Ecological awareness is the intuitive awareness of the oneness of all life. Our ancient heritage advocates protection not only for human beings and animals but for the elements, too.

Listen to the words of the Atharva Veda, written 4,000 years ago: "We are birds of the same nest,/We may wear different skins,/We may speak different languages,/We may believe in different religions,/We may belong to different cultures,/Yet we share the same home-Our Earth./For man can live individually,/But can survive only collectively/Born on the same planet/Covered by the same skies/Gazing at the same stars/Breathing the same air/We must learn to happily progress together/Or miserably perish together".

WOMEN EDUCATION

The status of women in the Indian society has been a complicated one. It passed through fluctuations over the ages. While it was high during the Vedic period, it slumped in the post-Vedic period. Again, in the modern period it rose. Education of women is directly dependent and closely related to the social status of them. Education of women is essential for happy and healthy homes, improvement of society, economic prosperity, and national solidarity. Education of women is more important that of men, if new generation is to be made cultured and educated, if social transformation is to be brought rapidly, and if moral character of the children is to be built during the most impressionable years of their lives.

Women Education During the Ancient Period

"The home has, verily, its foundation in the wife"-The Rig Veda.

In fact, the rights enjoyed by the present day modern women are sparse compared to that of their Vedic counterparts. There was no discrimination between sexes. Women enjoyed equal educational opportunities. They were allowed to participate in the educational discipline, to enter the order of brahmacharya and to pass through the upanayana ceremony.

In fact education was allowed for women not as an opportunity, but as a must. The women carried on not only learning but also teaching; that they professed teaching is understood from the word upadhayani by Patanjali. They also learnt the art of fighting.

When it comes to talking about significant female figures of Vedic period, Ghosa, Lopamudra, Sulabha, Maitreyi and Gargi-come to mind.

Women education during the Medieval Period:-In the post-Vedic period, that after 300B.C. a drastic deterioration took place in the women position. The degradation of women lasted till the beginning of the twentieth century. Reasons might be-the ruling Aryans were busy in war and for that a need for more men resulted and sons were valued. The other reason might be ancestor worship.

As the man gain paramountcy by virtue of the status, the women are made inferior class and degraded. A multitude of derogatory attributes were ascribed to them. They were denied access to educational opportunity. They were no more allowed to prosecute Vedic studies. Due to absence of education, the women were deceived to be fit for nothing. Since the girls were not educated, early marriages became common. The purdah also came into royal families. Sati-daho was also revived. Thus women were burdened with cumulative injustices and subjected t gross discrimination in all spheres.

Women Education During Modern Period (Pre-independence)

Towards the end of nineteenth century, the position of Indian women in the society improved a lot.

The social reform movements launched by Raja Ram Mohan Roy and his Brahmo Samaj, Iswarchandra Vidyasagar and Arya

Samaj among the Hindus and similar movements in other communities to improve the status of women led to the enactment of several laws: sati abolition in 1829, banning child marriage, permitting remarriage of widows. The recognition of equal right of women to education was recognized against all conservative opposition the pernicious practice of purdah began to diminish, particularly among Hindus. The East India Company attached no women education. There was not even a single government school for women. Only a few girls managed to find a place in boy's school with greatest difficulties. Missionaries and some institution were privately running a few schools for girls. The Roman Catholic Mission was also participating actively in this movement.

Glancing at the education of women from 1857 to 1902, the Indian Education Commission declared that women's education was in deplorably backward state, and that it should be improved scientifically as much as possible.

The Brahma Samaj, the Arya Samaj and the Parsi Community and Christians set up many colleges.

In 1902, women education assumed the form of a movement. Guardians, too, were becoming conscious about the need to educate their daughters. The education department began setting up schools for girls. In 1904, Mrs Annie Besant se up a Hindi Girl's College at Bananas. In 1916, the first medical college exclusively for girls was set up Delhi. The same year, the SNDT Women University was established at Bombay.

Between, 1917 and 1947, women education grew rapidly. In 1915 the National Council of Women was established. In 1927, the first All India Women Conference took place. Women took active part in the movement of independence. The change became evident when a number of women made their mark by becoming ministers, under-secreteries and deputy speakers of Provincial Legislation when Congress Government was formed in 1936.

Elite women (like Sorojini Naidu, Rajkumari Amrit Kaur, Durgabhai Deshmukh) who joined the freedom struggle were not imbued with the desire to emancipate but were committed to feminine roles.

Women Education in Post-independence Period

It is only after the constitution of independent India guaranteed equal rights for women not only in legal, social, political spheres but educationally also. Education panel of the Planning Commission at its meeting held in July 1957, reviewed that," suitable committee should be appointed to go into various aspects of the question relating to the nature of education for girls at the elementary, secondary and adult stages and to examine whether the present system was helping them to lead a happy and more useful life".

The Government of India in the Ministry of Education accordingly set up the National Committee of Women education. The resolution on the National Policy on Education stresses the importance of women education in these words," the education of girls should receive emphasis not only on grounds of social justice but also because it accelerates social transformation."

The United Nations declaration on the elimination of discrimination against women (1967) took note of the great contribution made by women to social, political, economic and cultural life and the part they play in the family and particularly in the rearing up of children and recommended the following Article 9 of the declaration: "All appropriate means shall be taken to ensure to girls and women, married or unmarried, equal rights with men in educating at all levels and in particular:

a) Equal conditions of access to and study in educational institutions of all types, including universities and vocational, technical and professional schools

b) The same choice of curriculum, the same examinations, teaching staffs with qualification of the same standards and school premises and equipments of the same quality, whether institutions are co-educational or not

c) Equal opportunities to benefit from scholarship and other study grants

d) Equal opportunities for access to programmes of continuing education, including adult literacy programme

e) Access to educational information to help in ensuing the health and well being of families

Causes of slow progress:

1. Economic backwardness of the rural community

2. lack of proper social attitude in the rural areas for the education of girls

3. lack of educational facilities

4. lack of women teacher

5. lack of proper supervision and guidance due to inadequate women personnel in the inspectorate

6. lack of proper incentives to parents and children

7. lack of suitable curriculum

8. co-educational aspects

The professional education of women has also attained a phenomenal growth in the post-independent era. Women have attained a good deal of progress in the sphere of employment. They are now entering into IAS, IFS and other prestigious services in increasing number. Whatever it may be, it is still evident that at each level of educational attainment, women lag behind man. The reasons might be:

a) Enrolment of women at all levels of education is far below than man

b) Greater rate of dropouts

c) Negative attitude of people towards higher education

As the National Committee on the status of women observed," the image of the Indian women created" by few women holding high positions or academic qualifications conceals rather than reflects the low status and educational level of the average women of India.(refer table 1,2,3)

Discussion: The result of discussion among the first semester M.Sc Nursing students, such as the effect of education over the social status of females is already incorporated in the topic wherever applicable. It was evident that wherever women are now today, is mostly the result of some eminent social reformers, though most of them are male. Throughout the history of evolution of women education it is clear that it was 'a woman' who opposed the most.

Conclusion: Researchers found that the sex differences have no scientific foundations. Intellectual differences are not there, the difference in academic and professional achievements are mainly due to lack of adequate opportunities or the influence of traditional cultural patterns. Psychological difference between sexes is purely because of social conditioning. So, through assessment of existing problems and immediate remedial measures to be taken up by Government of India. We can always hope for the best and actively put our efforts into action that will guide India to experience a bright sunrise with a educated family-cultured society-and prosperous nation.

CRITICISM OF HINDUISM

Hinduism is one of the most ancient world religions, tracing its origins back over 5,000 years. Today there are more than 900 million Hindu people worldwide, but mainly in Bharat (India), and the nations of the Indian subcontinent. As the Hindu religion was born in India, its criticism is irreversibly linked with the broader problems that India's people face today.

Social Oppression

Varna System: The division of society into four heirachial classes has resulted in much social oppression of the lowest caste, the Shudras. Critics also decry the socio-political fragmentation caused by the caste system. For example, there are over 80 subcastes of Brahmins, and the Jat Hindu communities of Punjab and Haryana are considered a separate caste by themselves.

The four varnas caste theory in theological Hinduism, while not initially rigid, came to be used with time as a device to maintain the domination of the upper castes, Brahmins and kshatriyas (the ruling order) over the rest of society, using divine doctrine and notions of racial purity. Many modern Hindus feel that the caste of the person should be not determined by birth, but by adult choice or individual tendencies.

India and all of modern Hindu society almost universally condemns untouchability, even if the caste system debate is open. Untouchability was outlawed after India gained independence in 1947, and people who were formerly identified as untouchables have made considerable economic, social and political progress in India. However, subtle discrimination and isolated acts of violence in the inner parts of India frequently cause political and sectarian tensions. It must be noted that untouchability was derived from the caste system, but is not supported by Hinduism in any of it's scriptures or texts. Hinduism, Hindu, Contemporary Hindu movements, Vedic religion, Jainism, Sikhism, Buddhism, Hindu Nationalism, Hindutva, Criticism of Religion.

Status of Women: The oppression of women through condemned practices like Sati (widow self-immolation), the restrictions against divorce, property rights, child marriage or widow re-marraige were practices that arose in India's Middle Ages.

Hindu Response and Reform: The Hindu scriptures have provisions for divorce, property rights for women and widow remarriage. Although, the practices restricting these rights developed within Hindu society in the middle ages, they are not supported by the religion. The diverse nature of hinduism and hindus doesn't provide the atmosphrere to have a common establishment encompassing all hindus together as one. Even though hindus are quite tolerant in general, when criticims or issues arise against hindus or hinduism, there is no invididual or organization present to address that. Though certain organizations play the role of self-appointed guardians of hinduism, the very nature of hinduism doesn't accord an official stature to such an organization.

Hindu Fundamentalism: Political ideologies subscribing to Hindu nationalism are termed as Hindutva. Many of these ideologies are alleged by some Indian and foreign critics to be close to fascism.

Hindutva is alleged by critics to be anti-Muslim, and symbolic of efforts of a small, radical group of Hindus to undertake ethnic and religious cleansing of millions of non-Hindus from India, and re-establishing a caste-based system of apartheid and untouchability, and brahmin domination.

Hindu Response: Contrary to allegations, most organizations (such as RSS) subscribing to Hindutva frequently campaign against untouchability and caste based discrimination. Some of Hindutva is considered by it's proponents as a means to reassert Hindu rights in a country where they are increasingly feeling marginalized despite being in majority. It is also considered to be a reaction to the forcible conversions of Hindus to Islam and Christianity, the Partition of India, increasing criticism of age-old Indian customs and an influx of Western cultural influences.

Ideology Clash with Abrahamic Religions: From the worldview of the three Abrahamic religions, Hinduism is criticized as being polytheistic, which they consider to be evil. It should be noted that many Hindus do not view themselves as polytheists, and some feel that monism or monistic theism would be more apt. Hinduism does, however, present an appearance of polytheism to external observers not familiar with its philisophy. More correctly, the Smarta view dominates the view of Hinduism in the West and has confused all Hindus to be seemingly polytheistic and is an inclusive monotheistic religion. In Hinduism, views are broad and range from monism, dualism, pantheism, panentheism, alternatively called monistic theism by some scholars, and strict monotheism, but are not polytheistic as outsiders perceive the religion to be.

Hinduism has often been confused to be polytheistic as many of Hinduism's adherents, *i.e.*, Smartas, who follow Advaita philosophy, are monists, and view multiple manifestations of the one God or source of being. Hindu monists see one unity, with the personal Gods, different aspects of only One Supreme Being, like a single beam of light separated into colours by a prism, and are valid to worship. Some of the Hindu aspects of God include Devi, Vishnu,

Ganesh, and Shiva. It is the Smarta view that dominates the view of Hinduism in the West. After all, Swami Vivekananda, a follower of Ramakrishna, along with many others, who brought Hindu beliefs to the West, were all Smarta in belief. Other denominations of Hinduism, as described later, don't hold this belief strictly and more closely adhere to a Western perception of what a monotheistic faith is. Additionally, like Judeo-Christian traditions which believe in angels, Hindus also believe in less powerful entities, such as devas.

Contemporary Hinduism is now divided into four major divisions, Vaishnavism, Shaivism, Shaktism, and Smartism. Just as Jews, Christians, and Muslims all believe in one God but differ in their conceptions of him, Hindus all believe in one God but differ in their conceptions. The two primary form of differences are between the two monotheistic religions of Vaishnavism which conceives God as Vishnu and Shaivism, which conceives God as Shiva. Other aspects of God are in fact aspects of Vishnu or Shiva; see Smartism for more information. Only a Smartist would have no problem worshipping Shiva or Vishnu together as he views the different aspects of God as leading to the same One God. It is the Smarta view that dominates the view of Hinduism in the West. By contrast, a Vaishnavite considers Vishnu as the one true God, worthy of worship and other forms as subordinate.

It is also charged with idolatry, which is defined as worship of God who does not conform to the Abrahamic YHVH. These accusations are natural because of the exclusive nature of Abrahamic religions. Hinduism on the otherhand, is more tolerant of God as defined by other religions and does not subscribe to similar ideas of false god or idolatry.

Hindu Renaissance

Hinduism has often proven to have one of the strongest currents of reform and adoption to change than any other world religion. Unlike other systems riveted to a particular set of books or doctrines, Hinduism is constantly evolving. The first reform and synthesis of modern currents of change came when the ancient

Vedic religion was synthesized with the religious practices and philosophies of the Dravidian peoples to form the basis of modern Hinduism.

India's independence movement, and the victory of freedom in 1947 helped the new democratic Government of India to end social, economic and political discrimination against women, children and members of different castes. It has been the result of a reformist effort by Hindu society, that the evils of customs like untouchability and caste discrimination, tracing back thousands of years, were significantly eliminated from most parts of India from 1947 till today, just around 60 years. Hindu women have today unprecedented access to higher education, and have rights to divorce, inherit property, run businesses and choose their own professions and are considered with respect and dignity in all Hindu religious activities.

Reform Leaders: Raja Ram Mohan Roy, Dayananda Saraswati, Adi Shankaracharya, Swami Vivekananda, Mahatma Gandhi, Sri Aurobindo

Rise of Organized Movements

The decades following the Sepoy Rebellion were a period of growing political awareness, manifestation of Indian public opinion, and emergence of Indian leadership at national and provincial levels.

The influences of socio-religious groups, especially in a nation where religion plays a vital role cannot be undermined. The Arya Samaj was an important Hindu organization which sought to reform Hindu society of social evils, counter-act Christian missionary propaganda. Swami Dayanand Saraswati's work was important in increasing an attitude of self-awareness, pride and community service in common Indian peoples. Raja Ram Mohan Roy's Brahmo Samaj was also a pioneer in the reform of Indian society, fighting evils like sati, dowry, ignorance and illiteracy.

The inculcation of religious reform and social pride was fundamental to the rise of a public movement for complete independence. The work of men like Swami Vivekananda,

Ramakrishna Paramhansa, Sri Aurobindo, Bankim Chandra Chatterjee, Sir Syed Ahmed Khan, Rabindranath Tagore and Dadabhai Naoroji spread the passion for rejuvenation and freedom. Lokmanya Tilak, though with non-moderate views, was very popular amongst the masses. He gave the concept of "Swaraj" to the Indian peoples while standing trial. His popular sentence "Swaraj is my Birthright, and I shall have it" became the source of inspiration for Indians. The flames of the spirit of freedom were ignited by learned men like them, who gave reason for common Indians to feel proud of themselves, demand political and social freedom and seek happiness. They were the teachers who sparked the passion of learning and achievement for thousands of Indians, and the poets expressing the inner fires of the freedom-fighter's soul.

Inspired by a suggestion made by A.O. Hume, a retired British civil servant, seventy-three Indian delegates met in Bombay in 1885 and founded the Indian National Congress. They were mostly members of the upwardly mobile and successful western-educated provincial elites, engaged in professions such as law, teaching, and journalism. They had acquired political experience from regional competition in the professions and by securing nomination to various positions in legislative councils, universities, and special commissions.

It should be noted that Dadabhai Naoroji had already formed the Indian National Association a few years before the Congress. The INA merged into the Congress Party to form a bigger national front.

At its inception, the Congress had no well-defined ideology and commanded few of the resources essential to a political organization. It functioned more as a debating society that met annually to express its loyalty to the British Raj and passed numerous resolutions on less controversial issues such as civil rights or opportunities in government, especially the civil service. These resolutions were submitted to the Viceroy's government and occasionally to the British Parliament, but the Congress's early gains were meager. Despite its claim to represent all India, the Congress voiced the interests of urban elites; the number of participants from other economic backgrounds remained negligible.

By 1900, although the Congress had emerged as an all-India political organization, its achievement was undermined by its singular failure to attract Muslims, who felt that their representation in government service was inadequate. Attacks by Hindu reformers against religious conversion, cow slaughter, and the preservation of Urdu in Arabic script deepened their concerns of minority status and denial of rights if the Congress alone were to represent the people of India. Sir Syed Ahmed Khan launched a movement for Muslim regeneration that culminated in the founding in 1875 of the Muhammadan Anglo-Oriental College at Aligarh, Uttar Pradesh (renamed Aligarh Muslim University in 1921). Its objective was to educate wealthy students by emphasizing the compatibility of Islam with modern western knowledge. The diversity among India's Muslims, however, made it impossible to bring about uniform cultural and intellectual regeneration.

Partition of Bengal

In 1905, Lord Curzon, the Viceroy and Governor-General (1899-1905), ordered the partition of the province of Bengal for improvements in administrative efficiency in that huge and populous region, where the Bengali Hindu intelligentsia exerted considerable influence on local and national politics. The partition created two provinces: Eastern Bengal & Assam, with its capital at Dhaka, and West Bengal, with its capital at Calcutta (which also served as the capital of British India). An ill-conceived and hastily implemented action, the partition outraged Bengalis. Not only had the government failed to consult Indian public opinion, but the action appeared to reflect the British resolve to divide and rule. Widespread agitation ensued in the streets and in the press, and the Congress advocated boycotting British products under the banner of swadeshi. During this period nationalist poet Rabindranath Tagore penned and composed a song (roughly translated into English as "The soil of Bengal, the water of Bengal be hallowed... ") and himself led people to the streets singing the song and tying Rakhi on each other's wrists. The people did not cook any food (Arandhan) on that particular day.

The Congress-led boycott of British goods was so successful that it unleashed anti-British forces to an extent unknown since the Sepoy Rebellion. A cycle of violence and repression ensued in some parts of the country. The British tried to mitigate the situation by announcing a series of constitutional reforms in 1909 and by appointing a few moderates to the imperial and provincial councils. A Muslim deputation met with the Viceroy, Lord Minto (1905-10), seeking concessions from the impending constitutional reforms, including special considerations in government service and electorates. The All-India Muslim League was founded the same year to promote loyalty to the British and to advance Muslim political rights, which the British recognized by increasing the number of elective offices reserved for Muslims in the India Councils Act of 1909. The Muslim League insisted on its separateness from the Hindu-dominated Congress, as the voice of a "nation within a nation."

In what the British saw as an additional goodwill gesture, in 1911 King-Emperor George V visited India for a durbar (a traditional court held for subjects to express fealty to their ruler), during which he announced the reversal of the partition of Bengal and the transfer of the capital from Calcutta to a newly planned city to be

Occupation: Philosopher

Raja Ram Mohan Roy was born of a distinguished Brahmin family in Bengal. After liberal education he entered the service of the East India Company and rose to high office. (Image courtesy of the Bristol Central Reference Library, Braikenridge Collection).

Essentially a humanist and religious reformer, he left the Company to devote his time to the service of his people. Profoundly influenced by European liberalism, Ram Mohan came to the conclusion that radical reform was necessary in the religion of Hinduism and in the social practices of the Hindus. He founded the Brahmo Samaj at Calcutta in 1828, which was initially known as the "Brahmo Sabha." Ram Mohan's is remembered in Indian history is as the originator of all the more important secular movements in that country. His services to the cause of the abolition of suttee are well-known. He was the first feminist in India and his book, Brief remarks regarding modern encroachments on the ancient rights of females (1822), is a reasoned argument in favour of the equality of women. He argued for the reform of Hindu law, led the protest against restrictions on the press, mobilised the Government against the oppressive land laws, argued the case for the association of Indians in Government and argued in favour of an English system of education in India.

Ram Mohan Roy arrived in England in 1831 as the ambassador of the Mughal Emperor Akbar Shah II. He came to stay at Beech House, Stapleton Grove, Bristol in 1833.

However, ten days after arriving in Bristol he fell ill with meningitis, and died on 27 September 1833. He was initially buried in the grounds of Beech House, but ten years later his friend Dwarakanath Tagore had him reinterred at Arno's Vale. A chattri (funerary monument or mandir (shrine) was designed by William Prinsep and built with sponsorship from Dwarakanath Tagore. In 1997 a statue of Raja Ram Mohan Roy was placed on College Green.

SOME OPINIONS

Rabindranath Tagore: When Ram Mohan Roy was born in India, the darkness of a moonless night was reigning. Death was roaming in the skies...When Ram Mohan Roy awoke and spread his sight on Bengali society it was an abode of the spirits...At that time, only the ghost of the living ancient Hindu religion held its sway in the funeral grounds. It had no life, it had no vitality, it only had its strictures and threats...In the days of Ram Mohan, the tattered foundations of Hindu society, with thousands of holes filled with creatures, progressively growing from generation to generation, was bulging with the impact of age and immobility.

Ram Mohan proceeded fearlessly to free society from the serpent-like bondage... Today even our youngsters will kick such dead serpents with a smile on the face, we will laugh them off as common field snakes without any poison-we have forgotten their enormous power, the magnetic attraction of their eyes and the dangerous embrace of their long tails.'...When the Bengali students came out of Hindu College, imbibed with the new English education, a certain type of intoxication grew in them... They took the blood that oozed from the deeply injured heart of the ancient Hindu society and used it as a plaything... To them nothing was good or sacred in Hindu society, they did not even have that respect for ancient Hindu society that they should pick up its skeletons, scattered hither and thither, cremate them properly and return home with a heavy heart after sprinkling the ashes in the waters of the Ganges... Considering the conditions of the period, they cannot be blamed that much...But the man who scotched the first flames of revolutionary fire in the present Bengali society, that Ram Mohan Roy was not intoxicated in that manner. He observed everything, good and bad, patiently. He enlightened the dark Hindu society of those days, but did not light the all-consuming fires of cremation. That was the greatness of Ram Mohan Roy.

5

Mohan Roy's Contribution to English Literature in India

Though foreign in its origin, English has been adopted in India as a language of education and literary expression besides being an important medium of communication amongst the people of various regions. The beginning of Indian literature in English is traced to the end of the 18th century and the beginning of the 19th, by which time English education was more or less firmly established in the three major centres of British power in India-Calcutta, Madras and Bombay. Ram Mohan Roy (1774-1833), a social reformist from Bengal who fought for widow remarriage and voting rights for women, was the pioneer of Indian writing in English. Roy insisted that for India to be included among the world's nations, education in English was essential. He, therefore, campaigned for introduction of scientific education in India through the English medium.

Raja Ram Mohan Roy was followed in the early 19th century in Bengal by the poets Henry Derozio and Michael Madhusudan Dutt. Dutt started out writing epic verse in English, but returned to his native Bengali later in life. The poems of Toru Dutt (1855-1876), who died at a tender age of 21, and the novel Rajamohan's Wife by Bankimchandra Chatterjee have received academic acceptance as the earliest examples of Indian literature written in English. Toru Dutt not composed poetry in English, but more interestingly, translated French poetry as well. Her best works include Ancient

Ballads and Legends of Hindustan. However, the most famous literary figure of this era was Rabindranath Tagore (1861-1941), who won the Nobel Prize for literature in 1913 for his book Gitanjali, which is a free rendering of his poems in Bengali.

Sarojini Naidu (1879-1949) was a great poetess whose romanticism charmed readers in India and Europe. Her Golden Threshold (1905) and The Broken Wing (1917) are works of great literary merit. Aurobindo Gosh (1872-1950) was a poet philosopher and sage, for whom poetry was akin to a form of mediation. His epic, Savitri and Life Divine (2 vols.) are outstanding works in English literature. It may be mentioned that most Indian writers in English from the early period hailed from Calcutta, the first stronghold of the British, than other places in the country.

The freedom struggle resulted in a revolutionary brand of writing that voiced sentiments against the British Empire. Several political leaders from different parts of the country emerged as literary figures such as Bal Gangadhar Tilak, Lala Lajpath Rai, Kasturi Ranga Iyengar and T. Prakasham. The English language became a sharp and strong instrument in the hands of Gandhiji, who edited and wrote for papers like 'Young India' and 'Harijan'. He also wrote his autobiography, 'My Experiments With Truth', which is known for its literary flair. Jawaharlal Nehru (1889-1964) stands out as another prominent leader who excelled in writing prose. He is particularly remembered for his Glimpses of World History, Discovery of India and An Autobiography (1936).

Mulk Raj Anand, R K Narayan and Raja Rao were among the earliest Indian novelist writing in English, who began to write in the early thirties. Mulk Raj Anand (b.1905), best known for his short story 'The Lost Child', has written numerous works of prose, poetry and drama. His novels Coolie (1933), Untouchable (1935) and The Woman and the Cow (1960) reveal his concern for the downtrodden and underprivileged in India. R.K. Narayan is another prolific figure in Indian English writing. Most of his work, starting from his first novel Swami and Friends (1935) is set in the fictional town of

Malgudi, which captures the Indian ethos in its entirety while having a unique identity of its own. Malgudi is perhaps the single most endearing "character" R.K.Narayan has ever created. Bachelor of Arts (1937), The Financial Expert (1952) The Guide (1959) and Waiting for the Mahatma (1955) are his other popular novels. The last of the harbingers of Indian English literature is Raja Rao (b.1909), whose novel Kanthapura (1938), set in rural India, established him as a major figure on the Indian literary scene. Raja Rao's other three novels are The Serpent and the Rope (1960) and The Cat and Shakespeare (1965). Nirad Choudhuri (1897-1999) was another internationally renowned Indian writer whose autobiography An Unknown Indian (1951) catapulted him into a celebrated international author.

Later novelists like Kamala Markandaya (Nectar in a Sieve, Some Inner Fury, A Silence of Desire, Two Virgins), Manohar Malgaonkar (Distant Drum, Combat of Shadows, The Princes, A Bend in the Ganges and The Devil's Wind), Anita Desai (Clear Light of Day, The Accompanist, Fire on the Mountain, Games at Twilight), and Nayantara Sehgal captured the spirit of an independent India, struggling to break away from the British and traditional Indian cultures and establish a distinct identity.

In the 1980's and 90's, India emerged as a major literary nation. Salman Rushdie's Midnight's Children became a rage around the world, even winning the Booker Prize. The worldwide success of Vikram Seth's The Golden Gate made him the first writer of the Indian Diaspora to enter the sphere of international writers and leave an indelible mark on the global literary scene. Other novelists of repute of the contemporary times include Shobha De (Selective Memory), G.V. Desani, M Ananthanarayanan, Bhadani Bhattacharya, Arun Joshi, Khushwant Singh, O.V. Vijayan, Allan Sealy (The Trotternama), Sashi Tharoor (Show Business, The Great Indian Novel), Amitav Ghosh (Circle of Reason, Shadow Lines), Upamanyu Chatterjee (English August, The Mammaries of the Welfare State), Raj Kamal Jha (The Blue Bedspread), Amit Chaudhuri (A New World), Pankaj Mishra (Butter Chicken in Ludhiana, The Romantics) and Vikram Chandra (Red Earth and Pouring Rain, Love and Longing in Bombay). The latest Indian writer who took the world with a storm was Arundhati Roy, whose The God of Small Things won the 1997 Booker Prize and became an international best-seller. Rohinton Mistry, Firdaus Kanga, Kiran Desai (Strange Happenings in the Guava Orchard), Sudhir Kakar (The Ascetic of Desire), Ardeshir Vakil (Beach Boy) and Jhumpa Lahiri (Interpreter of Maladies) are some other renowned writers of Indian origin.

Former Prime Minister P.V.Narasimha Rao's The Insider; Satish Gujral's A Brush with Life; R.K.Laxman's The Tunnel of Time, Prof. Bipin Chandra's India After Independence, Sunil Khilnani's The Idea of India, J.N.Dixit's Fifty Years of India's Foreign Policy, Yogesh Chadha's Rediscovering Gandhi and Pavan K.Varma's The Great Indian Middle Class are notable works of the recent times.

The mid-20th century saw the emergence of poets such as Nissim Ezekiel (The Unfurnished Man), P Lal, A K Ramanujan (The Striders, Relations, Second Sight, Selected Poems), Dom Moraes (A Beginning), Keki Daruwalla, Geive Patel, Eunice de Souza, Adil Jussawala, Kamala Das, Arun Kolatkar and R. Parthasarathy, who were heavily influenced by literary movements taking place in the West such as Symbolism, Surrealism, Existentialism, Absurdism and Confessional Poetry. These authors used Indian phrases alongside English words and tried to reflect a blend of the Indian and the Western cultures.

Ram Mohan Roy, Translation of an abridgment of the Vedant, or Resolution of all the Veds; the most celebrated and revered work of Brahminical theology; establishing the unity of the Supreme Being; and that He alone is the object of propitiation and worship.

Calcutta, No printer, 1816. Contemporary blindstamped red goatskin (spine darkened and minor chipping). BOUND WITH RAM MOHAN ROY. Translation of the Cena Upanishad; one of the chapters of the Sama Veda: according to the gloss of the celebrated Shancaracharya: establishing the unity and the sole omnipotence of the Supreme Being and that he alone is the object

of worship. Calcutta: Printed by Philip Pereira, at the Hindoostanee
Press. 8vo. vii, 11 pp. BOUND WITH RAM MOHAN ROY.
Translation of the eshopanishad, one of the chapters of the Yajur
Veda: according to the commentary of the celebrated Shankar çcharya;
establishing the unity and incomprehensibility of the Supreme Being;
and that His worship alone can lead to eternal beatitude. Calcutta:
Printed by Philip Pereira, at the Hindoostanee Press. 8vo., xxiii, v,
8 pp. 4to and 8vo. FIRST EDITIONS of these very rare Calcutta
publications of the first appearance in English of excepts from the
sacred Sanskrit Upanishads, translated and published by Ram Mohan
Roy (or Ram Mohan Roy) who is considered by many "the father
of modern India."

Of the first work on the resolution of the Veds (Upanishads;
Kenopanisad) the OCLC locates only one incomplete copy (Boston
Athenaeum); of the second work from the Cena Upanishads OCLC
locates only one copy (University of Wisconsin); the last work is
from the Sankara Acharya which OCLC finds four copies (Columbia,
Harvard, NYPL and Mass Hist. Society). Ram Mohan Roy (1774-
1832), a highly educated Bengali brahman from a well-to-do landed
family: "also spelled Ram Mohan, Ram Mohan, or Ram Mohan;
Indian religious, social, and educational reformer who challenged
traditional Hindu culture and indicated the lines of progress for
Indian society under British rule. He is sometimes called the father
of modern India. "Little is known of his early life and education,
but he seems to have developed unorthodox religious ideas at an
early age.

As a youth he traveled widely outside Bengal and mastered
several languages-Sanskrit, Persian, Arabic, and later Hebrew, Greek,
and English, in addition to his native Bengali and Hindi. "In 1803
he composed a tract denouncing India's religious divisions and
superstition. As a remedy for these ills, he advocated a monotheistic
Hinduism in which reason guides the adherent to '. the Absolute
Originator who is the first principle of all religions.' He sought a
philosophical basis for his religious beliefs in the Upanishads and
Vedas, translating these ancient Sanskrit treatises into Bengali, Hindi,

and English and writing summaries and treatises on them. The central theme of these texts, for Roy, was the worship of the Supreme God, beyond human knowledge, who supports the universe. By translating the sacred Sanskrit Upanishads into modern Bengali, Roy violated a long-standing tradition, but, in appreciation of his translations, the French Societe Asiatique in 1824 elected him to an honorary membership. "In 1815 Roy founded the short-lived Atmiya-Sabha (Friendly Society) to propagate his doctrines of monotheistic Hinduism. He became interested in Christianity and learned Hebrew and Greek in order to read the Old and New Testaments. In 1820 he published the ethical teachings of Christ, excerpted from the four Gospels, under the title Precepts of Jesus, the Guide to Peace and Happiness.

"In his newspapers, treatises, and books, Roy tirelessly criticized what he saw as the idolatry and superstition of traditional Hinduism. He denounced the caste system and attacked the custom of suttee (ritual burning of widows upon the funeral pyres of their deceased husbands). Roy's actual influence on the British East India Governing Council's prohibition of suttee in 1829 is not clear, but it has been widely accepted that he had the effect of emboldening the government to act decisively on the matter. "Roy's importance in modern Indian history rests partly upon the broad scope of his social vision and the striking modernity of his thought. He was a tireless social reformer, yet he also revived interest in the ethical principles of the Vedanta school as a counterpoise to the Western assault on Indian culture. In his textbooks and treatises he contributed to the popularization of the Bengali language, while at the same time he was the first Indian to apply to the Indian environment the fundamental social and political ideas of the French and American revolutions."

WILLIAM ADAM

William Adam (November 1, 1796-February 19, 1881), born in Dunfermline, Fife, Scotland, began his ministry as a Baptist missionary in India. His labours in India made him into a linguist, a biblical scholar, and a Unitarian. Thereafter for years, Adam tried to elicit support for his work as a Unitarian missionary, first in India and later in the United States and Canada.

His career illustrates the meager support for and the difficulties of Unitarian missionary endeavours of the 19th century. As a young man Adam was deeply influenced by the famous Scottish churchman Thomas Chalmers. Chalmers interested Adam in India and got him to join the Baptist Missionary Society. The Society sent him for his education to the Baptist College in Bristol and to the University of Glasgow. Adam set out in September, 1817, for William Carey's Baptist mission station in Serampore, India, north of Calcutta. He reached his destination in six months, in March, 1818.

After mastering the classical Sanskrit and Bengali languages, Adam joined a group of men who were revising the Bengali translation of the New Testament. The group included the cordial and scholarly Hindu, Ram Mohan Roy. Roy convinced Adam that the meaning of the Greek preposition dia required that Jn 1:3, a verse of the prologue to John's Gospel, be translated as the Bengali equivalent of the English words, 'All things were made through the Word...' not 'by the Word'. Translators of New Testament Greek in later generations would come to agree, but in 1821 the view of nature of Christ, supported by this translation and espoused by Adam and Ram Mohan, was rejected by orthodox Christians as the Arian heresy (named for the 4th century CE dissident, Arius). For this reason colleagues nicknamed him 'the second fallen Adam'.

Adam soon resigned his position as a Baptist missionary and, along with Ram Mohan and a few other Indian and European friends, formed the Calcutta Unitarian Society. Adam sent ardent appeals to British and American Unitarians for financial support. Support was both slow in coming and quite inadequate when it came. Nevertheless, the Calcutta Unitarian Society remained fitfully active and viable for seven years. But in 1828 its Hindu supporters finally chose to create a new Unitarian form of Hinduism, Brahmo Somaj, leaving behind Unitarian Christianity.

In need of income, Adam turned to clerking and journalism. Working for the British governor of Bengal, he did a three volume census and analysis of native education in Bengal.

With help from the Dixwell family, New England merchants in the India trade, Adam's wife and family left India to go to the United States. Adam followed four years later, in 1838. Travelling from Boston, he attended in London the first meeting of the British India Society, an anti-slavery organization. Members of the Society introduced Adam to leading Garrisonian abolitionists from the United States. When he returned to Boston he took up the position of professor of Oriental Literature at Harvard, which he had been offered before his trip. Adam found Harvard's academic atmosphere did not suit him, however, and he resigned after just one year.

Finding himself consumed by the anti-slavery cause, he returned to London for the World Anti-Slavery Convention in June, 1840. He vigorously protested the exclusion of women from the meetings. Afterward, remaining in London, he began working as editor of the British Indian Advocate, the journal of the British India Society, then called for his family to join him. Eighteen months later the Adam family once again journeyed to America to join a new utopian community in Massachusetts, the Northampton Association of Education and Industry. Adam became the Association's secretary and director of education. He also invested money in the project, but after control of the capital was taken away from investors, he resigned. For a while the Adam family lived in the town of Northampton. William sought work as a lecturer and conducted classes for Boston women during the winter of 1844-5.

He met Charles Briggs, Secretary of the American Unitarian Association, who told him Unitarian ministers were desperately needed in the "west," which at that time meant west of the Appalachian Mountains. On his way to Illinois, Adam stopped in Syracuse, New York where the Rev. Samuel J. May, also an active Garrisonian, was minister of the Unitarian Church. May told Adam of a new opening for a Unitarian minister in Toronto on the British side of Lake Ontario. After hearing Adam preach, on two Sundays and one mid-week evening in early July, 1845, Toronto Unitarians called him as their first minister.

But the match between minister and congregation was not a good one. After some early success-the securing of a church building and a strengthening of the congregation-financial problems soured relations. Adam, with a family to support, was feeling constraint. He also felt let down by Charles Briggs, the AUA and Toronto Unitarians. Only the Toronto physician, Joseph Workman, tried hard to raise fit support for him. He resigned and resumed his journey to Illinois. There, within weeks, in late July, 1846, the First Unitarian Church of Chicago, without a minister for two years, called him as minister.

Manuscripts of some of Adam's Toronto and Chicago sermons and lectures survive in Dr. Williams's Library in London. Their titles show the range of issues addressed by this scholarly, socially active world traveler. They include 'Truth and falsehood in man', 'Labour', 'The River and Harbour Convention', and 'Temperance'.

After yet another negative experience in Chicago, Adam withdrew from the Unitarian parish ministry. He is known to have traveled to New Orleans, Louisiana shortly afterward. There is no record of Adam's activities over the next five years. Sometime before 1855, he returned to Britain, perhaps without his family. He is known to have preached in December, 1855, at a small Unitarian church in High Garret, Essex, England. Charles Dall, the missionary to India of the American Unitarian Association, 1855-86, visited Adam in London in 1861 on his way to India. Adam made it clear to Dall that he had altogether renounced Unitarianism and its ministry. He was writing a book critical of Comte's philosophy of history, which was published anonymously that year.

Adam lived obscurely another twenty years. He died at Beaconsfield in Hampshire in 1881, aged 84, and was buried, on his instructions, without ceremony in Woking Cemetery. He left his money to Dumfermline Grammar School for University scholarships, stipulating that the funds should be distributed "irrespective of sex or creed or no creed, parentage, colour or caste, nationality or political allegiance".

Adam was the first international Unitarian of modern times. His convert's enthusiasm was much damped by the lukewarm response of both British and American Unitarians to his requests for their support of his work as a Unitarian missionary in India. Ultimately, he was disappointed in the Unitarian movement as a whole. At the time Adam regretted that Ram Mohan Roy and his Hindu friends chose a Unitarian Hindu faith in preference to Unitarian Christianity. Yet without Adam's dedicated initiative and drive, the reformed Unitarian Hindu movement, the Brahmo Somaj, might never have come into being. The distinguished leaders of the Brahmo Somaj nurtured and propagated what became, in effect, a 'school of thought', which flowered into the famous Bengal Renaissance, a great burst of modern, yet distinctively Indian political theory, idealism and poetry. The Brahmo Somaj, first established in part by an ill-supported and mostly forgotten Unitarian missionary, influenced immensely the intellectual and political culture of all India.

There are letters from and referring to Adam in the Baptist Missionary Society Library at Didcot, Oxfordshire; in the Houghton Library at Harvard, Cambridge, Massachusetts, and in the anti-slavery collections in the Boston Public Library. The minute book of the Calcutta Unitarian Committee is at Unitarian Headquarters, Essex Hall, London. There are 50 manuscript sermons from the Toronto and Chicago period at Dr. Williams's Library, London. Correspondence regarding Adam's appointment at Harvard is in the Harvard University Archives. The minutes of The Society for the Promotion of Christianity in India and the record of the 1860 conversation between Charles Dall and William Adam are in the Andover Harvard Theological Library. The Dixwell family papers, with their many references to Adam and his family, and the archives of the Northampton Association are at The Massachusetts Historical Society in Boston.

The recent discovery of the Calcutta Unitarian Society minute book gives primary documentary support for the reports published in the Unitarian periodical press in both Britain and America. Letters from, to, and referring to Adam and members of his family appear in Clare Taylor, British and American Abolitionists: an episode in transatlantic understanding (1974); Walter M. Merrill, Collected letters of William Lloyd Garrison (1971); Sophia Dobson Collet, The life and letters of Raja Rammoun Roy, 3rd ed. (1962); and Dilip Kumar Biswas, The Correspondence of Raja Ram Mohan Roy (1997). There are several biographical articles on Adam: S. C. Sanial "the Rev. William Adam", Bengal Past and Present (1914); Andrew Hill, "William Adam: Unitarian Missionary", Transactions of the Unitarian Historical Society (1995); and Andrew Hill, "William Adam: a noble specimen", Canadian Unitarian and Universalist Historical Society (1995). For general information on Unitarianism in India, see Spencer Lavan Unitarians and India (1977). For more on the Northampton Association, see Christopher Clark, The Communitarian movement: the radical challenge of the Northampton Association (1995).

New Life for Raja's Tomb

Bristol, June 13: That there's some corner of a foreign cemetery that is forever Bengal is thanks to the generosity of Aditya Poddar, a Calcutta-born and bred businessman who handed over a $100,000 cheque in Arnos Vale cemetery in Bristol yesterday to prevent Raja Ram Mohan Roy's dilapidated tomb from collapsing. "It is a very proud heritage that we have-I want to contribute to that," said Poddar, 39, who studied at St. Xavier's College, Calcutta, after having a broad and secular vision of India ingrained in him at the Scindia School in Gwalior.

Now chairman of a timber company, Wellside International, based in Singapore and with concessions in many Latin American countries, including Panama, Costa Rica and El Salvador, Poddar explained his philosophy-and his sentiments which he said had been echoed in Mira Nair's film, The Namesake.

"Our roots are very important to us," he said. "We relate to where we come from. Heritage is very, very important. As a businessman, you don't want only to make money, you want to contribute back to society because that is where you are making your money."

He readily agreed to donate the entire sum required for renovation work after being approached last year by the mayor of Calcutta, Bikash Ranjan Bhattacharyya, and the municipal commissioner, Alapan Bandyopadhyay, who had visited Arnos Vale cemetery in the company of Rajat Bagchi, minister (coordination) at the Indian high commission in London. "It is an Indian looking monument," observed Poddar.

Although Ram Mohan Roy was one of the foremost social reformers of India, his story-why he set up the Brahmo Samaj, how he fought against the practice of sati and undertook a trip to England in 1831 to ensure that Lord Bentick's law abolishing the burning of widows was not reversed by the Hindu men who had hired an English lawyer for that purpose-is almost completely unknown to most Indians in Britain and perhaps a significant section of the diaspora.

The man considered to be "the Father of the Bengal Renaissance" was born, not in 1774, as the inscription on his tomb says, but on May 22, 1772, in Radhanagore, Bengal, the author Krishna Dutta, who was present yesterday, pointed out.

"He was also not a Bahadur (as the inscription also claims)," she said: In 1833, during his visit to England, Ram Mohan Roy accepted an invitation from Lant Carpenter, a sympathetic minister in the Unitarian Church, to stay at his home, Beech House, Stapleton Grove, in Bristol. But the Raja contracted meningitis and died 10 days after arriving on September 27, 1833.

He was initially buried in the grounds of Beech House in accordance with his own wishes but his remains were reinterred a decade later in Arnos Vale cemetery where the tomb was funded by his friend and a co-founder of the Brahmo Samaj, Dwarkanath Tagore.

Yesterday, Poddar handed over his cheque to a local amateur historian, Carla Contractor-she is married to a Parsi, Phiroze

Contractor-who has long campaigned for the restoration of some of the tombs in Arnos Vale, including notably that of Ram Mohan Roy. "I had been trying in vain for a long time but out of the blue, the mayor of Calcutta arrived and offered to find the money to restore the tomb because the Raja is such an important hero in West Bengal," commented Carla, who is a member of the Raja Ram Mohan Roy Trust given responsibility for the restoration work by the Indian high commission in London.

Carla also accepted a £500 cheque from the Brahmo Sammilan Samaj in Calcutta handed over by Rita Bhimani, who had come accompanied by her cricket writer husband, Kishore Bhimani.

The tomb, began Carla, "needs a lot of restoration. The foundations are sinking, the pillars have got cracks down them because they are in sandstone, the canopy is leaking. Basically, the whole thing needs to be taken down, cleaned, solidified and reassembled. It is a major job but it will be done".

She Promised: "When this is done, it will look as it did in 1842. It was William Princep from Calcutta who designed this tomb and I am in touch with the Princep family." She described the tomb as "a site of pilgrimage. Whenever I come here (I find) somebody has left flowers, a little memento, something touching. It is a source of pride for the Indian community-and my husband is Indian".

Prayers remembering Ram Mohan Roy as well as Lant's daughter, Mary Carpenter, who nursed the Raja and later visited India four times to do social work, were led by Bernard Omar, president of the Unitarian Church in Bristol. "Across our different faiths we unite in gratitude to the lives of two great people, one of whom came from India to this country and one, Mary Carpenter, who travelled to India," he said. "Both are buried in this cemetery. We pray in our different ways that they may continue to be remembered and honoured-that the essence of their work may continue. Amen."

Richard Smith, chairman of the Arnos Vale Cemetery Trust, told his Indian guests: "There are somewhere in the region of 50,000 graves and round about 170,000 people buried here. There used to be a crematorium here and over 120,000 people were cremated here as well. This cemetery was set up in 1837 and the first burial was actually in 1839. The crematorium, the first one in the west country, did not start until 1928."

The repair and renovation work will be undertaken to the highest standards under the guidance and watchful eyes of both English Heritage and Bristol City Council. Philip Davies, planning development director for the south of England at English Heritage, declared: "The monument is of very considerable interest and importance in England. It is one of the highest grades of listed buildings for a historical monument in England-Grade Two Star. It is something we are very keen to celebrate and the role of English Heritage here is provide advice and guidance and to make sure that the restoration and repair work is carried out to the best possible standards and does justice to the monument of such an important man."

He, too, Confirmed: "It is vulnerable, in need of repair and restoration. It is partly the age and vulnerability of the materials that were used originally. This is a very, very important step in conserving a very important monument in England."

He also Said: "It is particularly appropriate to do this in the 60th year of Indian independence. Britain and India have enjoyed a special relationship for 300 years and it is very important that we continue to celebrate this and develop that relationship with tangible projects like the restoration of this monument." Yesterday, the sun glittered on the gold chains of office worn by The Rt Hon. The Lord Mayor of the City and the County of Bristol, Royston Alan Griffey. He disclosed that the previous private owner had wanted to sell the cemetery to private developers who had intended either to bulldoze or relocate the memorials and use the land to build residential property.

Griffey Said: "This cemetery was in private ownership and the last 20 years or so it was in terrible condition. The previous private owner was not looking after it so the city (council) had to start compulsory purchase proceedings. That took quite a long time to do)."

He Went On: "That was successful and the compulsory purchase order has fairly recently been confirmed. The ownership was transferred (for a nominal £1) from a private company to Bristol City Council who then, in turn, transferred it to some trustees to look after the restoration of this beautiful cemetery, including the Raja's tomb."

He Insisted: "Without the city taking back the cemetery I am afraid it would have been in a very, very badly neglected state and it would have eventually deteriorated and a lot of the monuments, including this tomb, would have collapsed." He also believed the Raja's message had contemporary relevance. "I certainly do-the Raja has the benefit of not one but two statues in Bristol. There is one outside the Bristol Council offices, a full-length statue, very imposing in robes, but inside the Council House is also a smaller statue, a bust of the Raja. And Bristol is interested in India because there is a large Indian population in the city."

He Commented: "Of course, he was a great man, benefactor, linguist, ahead of his time with human rights. I am a lawyer so I know how difficult battles can be to achieve civil liberties and human rights."

He was frank about Bristol's dark past, in every way as shameful as sati. "This is the 200th anniversary of the abolition of the slave trade act passed in 1807 and we have been having commemorations in Bristol and other places-Liverpool, London, Hull-who were also ports involved with the slave trade. Bristol was one of the major trading posts in the triangular trade-ships from Bristol went to west Africa and then over to the Caribbean and North America and then back to Bristol with tobacco and other products."

Alapan Bandyopadhyay, the Calcutta's municipal commissioner, paid tribute to the dedication shown by Carla. "Carla had taught at Sophiya College in Bombay-and she rediscovered Raja Ram Mohan Roy. She rightly thinks mere restoration is not enough unless the memory is kept alive. The trust could repair other conservation projects. The cause could be made wider."

INDIAN PHILOSOPHIC PROSE IN ENGLISH

The use of English for the exposition of Indian philosophy has opened up new avenues of interpretation involving pluralistic responses and redefinitions growing out of already existing tenets. Beginning as it does with the predominantly zealous missionary approach, which was an attempt by thinkers such as Carey, Marshman, Ward, Monier-Williams and others to find footholds for Christianity, through the memorable episode of European philosophical responses to India represented by Hegel, Schelling and Schopenhauer, followed by the Orientalists of the stature of Muller and Farquhar responding to the neo-Hindu inclusivism of Ramakrishna, Keshab Chandra Sen, Vivekananda and such others, to the later engagement and preoccupation with ideas of Indian philosophy by eminent Indians for social reform and national and cultural revival-the dimensions of Indian philosophic prose in English spread over areas as diverse and extensive as politics, religion, sociology, economics, ethics, culture, spirituality and so on, thus putting an end to narrow, authoritarian, critical tenets prescribed for the study of philosophy. Also, here the foregrounding of English as a language of discourse where the original Sanskrit is no longer privileged offers an important shift in the politics of Indian thought.

The continuing tension between Western responses and indigenous interpretations, the conceptual frames formulated to accommodate Western assumptions in order to invest Indian thought with a sense of universal acceptability, the impact of Indian philosophic and religious texts on the Western consciousness, and their global dissemination due to the use of English have considerably altered the philosophic and religious maps of the world.

Considering this, it is interesting to approach the issue in question from the perspective of New Historicism. In his seminal work The New Historicism Reader (published in 1994 by Routledge) Aram Veeser gives the five fundamental assumptions of New

Historicism thus: 1) every expressive act is embedded in a network of material practices; 2) every act of unmasking, critique and opposition uses the tools it condemns and risks falling prey to the practice it exposes; 3) literary and non-literary 'texts' circulate inseparably; 4) no discourse, imaginative or archival, gives access to unchanging truths or express unalterable human nature; and 5) a critical method and a language adequate to describe culture under capitalism together participate in the economy they describe. The present paper attempts a survey of the New Historicist perspective of Indian philosophic prose in English based on these assumptions.

Embedded Texts: Written and Non-Written

The expressive acts of Indian philosophy from its earliest oral tradition-the Vedas, Vedanta, Puranas, Itihasas, Yoga, Mimamsa, bhakti poetry and music-have been influenced by and in their turn have also influenced the dominant material practices of their respective ages. Coming to the origin and development of Indian philosophic prose in English over the last two centuries, the discussions generally begin with Raja Ram Mohan Roy, whose contribution most often acclaimed is largely restricted to the field of political and social activism. This marginalizes the fact that these had their foundation in his vast acquaintance with Hindu philosophic texts which he commented upon in English. Till recently his writings have failed to receive due recognition. The quality of embeddedness indicated by Roy's Vedanta Chandrika and such other works is as obvious as it is in Vivekananda's thoughts on the Upanishads and the Bhagavadgita. Gandhi's use of ahimsa, the dominant ideal of Jainism, to give direction to the nationalist movement, Tilak's reinterpretation of the Bhagavadgita in justification of the lesson of violence for justice taught to Arjuna, Dayananda Saraswati's 'purification' of Vedic knowledge for inculcating a temper of self-confidence and his insistence on the universal global significance of the Vedic teachings are all illustrations of one crucial idea: in all of these philosophy was a response to the external challenges of life. Philosophy as an academic discipline was more or less the forte of

British intellectuals teaching in India. One of the first notable Indian representatives of the academic aspect of philosophy and its concepts was K. C. Bhattacharya, who was followed in this task by his son Kalidas, his student R. V. Das and his admirers G. K. Malkani and T. R. V. Murti.

Subversion and Conformity

Though much of this early philosophic engagement was a subversion, directly or indirectly, of English hegemony, it is noteworthy that the basic act of condemnation also involved an act of conformity. For instance, European models of philosophic discourse were widely accepted and emulated. Ram Mohan Roy's particular hermeneutic system appeals to and reflects upon different traditions, simultaneously appropriating the alien while he asserts himself to be against the alien.

Though the terms 'Renaissance' and 'Reformation/Revival' have been commonly associated with the rise of Indian philosophic prose written in English, the term 'neo-Hinduism' is preferred in academic contexts. This brings to the fore the debate about suitable terminology and lexicographic problems which received much attention from thinkers such as Bankim Chandra Chatterjee. The Sanskrit exclusivism and the vernacular popularized by the Pali canon brought out ideas such as Buddhism being the fulfilment of Hinduism and the approach to ancient systems through the concept of practical Vedanta. Similarly the support of Hindu orthodoxy by people like Madan Mohan Malaviya resulted in the uplift of untouchables, who were then designated as 'harijans', the people of God.

Fluidity of Discursive Truth

Philosophy was no longer merely metaphysical speculation aimed at bringing out the intellectual brilliance of thinkers; instead it gained ethical and social currency. It acquired an imaginative and symbolic dimension, became more descriptive and contemplative. For instance, the literary masterpieces of Bankim Chandra underlined the philosophic ideal of anushilana (repeated practice); Rabindranath

Tagore, in his turn, advocated a personalistic absolutism and considered beauty and harmony of God's creative act as a fitting subject for both literature and philosophy.

The source of inspiration in the case of Devendranath Tagore was his own heart, in contradistinction to the privilege given to revelatory scriptures by other Brahmos. Here the fourth of Veeser's assumptions comes into play because both imaginative and archival discourse shows the alterable nature of truth. Keshab Chandra Sen borrowed from Christianity, while Vivekananda categorized the West as materialistic/pragmatic and the East as spiritual/impractical. Aurobindo attempted to establish the identity of Hinduism not by return to the past nor by asserting its timeless validity; for him it was the source of vitality and change, openness for question and experiment. Coomaraswamy spoke in defence of tradition in Hinduism through his criticism of Radhakrishnan, who, he felt, had failed in the task of actualizing and modernizing the tradition, as had several others. Krishnamurti did not show allegiance to any particular philosophic system or tradition and spoke of spiritual truths as lying deep within oneself, to be realized by one's own effort.

It was the unique privilege of Ramakrishna Paramahamsa and Ramana Maharshi to bring an experiential dimension to the expression of philosophic truths. The tolerance and universal dimension of Ramakrishna's spiritual message and the silence of Ramana, which is as eloquent as his words of wisdom, bring new levels of truth to philosophic discourse. But, of course, this was not the last word. It has been said that Vivekananda's use of the teachings of his guru Ramakrishna was styled in his own peculiar way to suit his purpose, for his ideas of mass-education and philanthropy were not directly mirrored in the teachings of Ramakrishna.

Discourse as Participation

Talking of the last of Veeser's assumptions, the long engagement of thinkers all over the world with Indian philosophy imparts it a market value not far to seek. The appearance of Vivekananda at the

Chicago Parliament of Religions in 1893 was the beginning of Indian thought's taking root in American soil. At the outset it was 'Vedanta and the West' but by the turn of the last century the juxtaposing conjunction 'and' had been replaced significantly by a preposition of involvement-'in'-so that now one speaks of 'Vedanta in the West'. Popular forms such as Transcendental Meditation, International Society for Krishna Consciousness (ISKCON), and personalities like Rajneesh, Mahesh Yogi, Swami Rama and others have captured the Western imagination.

Radhakrishnan, notwithstanding his alleged lack of originality, was one of the most successful spokespersons for neo-Hinduism in the West-as memorable as he was persuasive. His relentless crusade began with his objection to the European verdict of ethical deficiency in Hinduism in addition to its unsuitability to scientific progress. B N Seal went a step further and upheld the potential of Hinduism to bring about a European renaissance. Bhagavan Das articulated the opinion that philosophy should not be an end in itself as it was in Europe-a more or less intellectual engagement. He advocated the need for a practical philosophy helpful to man and society. P R Damle viewed the future of Indian philosophy as one of revival and constructive exposition of non-monistic and non-idealistic systems of thought. In all of these, the attempt is to make philosophy acquire a saleable value and the oft-repeated attempt to justify it in scientific terms of reference is just one more attempt in this direction.

Finally, it is significant that the terms darshana and tattvajnana, which are often used synonymously for philosophy in India, are pointers to the fact that philosophy has always been a mode of living, viewed as a perception that gives life its balance. Since philosophy is only one of the modes of presenting Indian thought to the world, it has to be seen in conjunction with literature, art and other areas of intellectual endeavour. As the New Historicist contention underlines, literary and non-literary texts circulate inseparably and therefore a complete picture is one which keeps all modes of presentation in view before any conclusive documentation is given shape.

Bibliography

Arabinda Poddar : *Tagore : The Political Personality*, Kolkata, Indiana, 2004.

Barua, B. P.: *Raja Rammohun Roy and the New Learning.* Hyderabad, 1988.

Carpenter, L.: *Review of the Labours, Opinions and Character of Rajah Rammohan Roy*, London, 1833.

Duttgupta, Bela : *Rabindranath Tagore and His World Windows : A Symphony in Poems*, Kolkata, The Asiatic Society, 2005.

Joshi, V.C.: *Rammohun Roy and the Process of Modernization in India*, Delhi, 1975.

K Nag & D Burman: *The English Works of Rammohun Roy*, Calcutta, 1945-48.

Karunamay Goswami: *Bangla Ganer Bibartan*, Bangla Academy, Dhaka, 1993.

Kopf, David: *The Brahmo Samaj and the Shaping of the Modern Indian Mind.* Princeton, 1979.

Nag, Jamuna: *Raja Rammohun Roy.* New Delhi, 1972.

Nagendranath Chattopadhyaya: *Mahatma Raja Rammohan Rayer Jiban Charit*, Calcutta, 1881.

Prasad, Lal Bahadur : *Indian Political System and Law*, New Delhi, Shree, 2005.

Rai Bhadur Lala Baij Nath : *The Adhyatma Ramayana*, Cosmo, New Delhi, 2005.

Sudhir Chakraborty: *Bangla Ganer Sandhane*, Aruna Prakashani, Calcutta, 1990.

Tagore, Saumyendranath : *Rabindranath Tagore : Philosophy of Life and Aesthetics*, Kolkata, Aparna Book, 2006.

Index

❑❑❑